PRAISE FOR DAN BOZUNG AND
PAJAMAS IN PUBLIC
and Other Crimes Against Humanity

"Finally! A book that enlightens the world on mulch, toilet seats, and Mexican hotel butlers. Humanity *needed* Dan to write this book, much like it needed him to swallow that entire jar of cocktail onions. Now *that* was something."

    —Greg Z., bartender, witness, scholar

"Wait . . . pajamas in public? That's the problem? I thought we all agreed it was China."

    —Overheard in the third-floor break room at US Strategic Command

"You know that's a toupee he's wearing, right?"

    —Kat D., former stylist who refused to get on board with Dan's retro nineties look

"Dan's command of language is rivaled only by his command of a crayon. This probably should've been a coloring book."

    —Frank P., the guy Dan beat out for the last spot on the 1995 JV cross country team

"This is great! It reads like David Sedaris . . . except when it doesn't, which is, like, the entire time. Actually, this is nothing like David Sedaris."

> —Rebecca Q., reviewer, furloughed barista, consumer of low-fat Pop-Tarts

"All right, I get it. Dan was in the Navy. So was that dude from Village People, but he didn't go around boring people with his stupid stories."

> —Andrew B., the guy Dan sat next to on that flight from Philadelphia to Frankfurt

*Pajamas in Public
and Other Crimes Against Humanity*

by Dan Bozung

© Copyright 2025 Dan Bozung

ISBN 979-8-88824-788-4

All rights reserved. No part of this publication may be reproduced, stored in a retrieval system, or transmitted in any form or by any means—electronic, mechanical, photocopy, recording, or any other—except for brief quotations in printed reviews, without the prior written permission of the author.

Published by

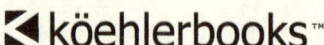

3705 Shore Drive
Virginia Beach, VA 23455
800–435–4811
www.koehlerbooks.com

PAJAMAS IN PUBLIC

and Other Crimes Against Humanity

DAN BOZUNG

VIRGINIA BEACH
CAPE CHARLES

The author (left) with Mike Petersen (right), admiring the cannon they'd constructed for a high school physics project—Greenville, Michigan, 1990.

For my buddy Pete.

It was awesome when you caught your face on fire that one time.
And I'm glad we didn't blow up Petersen Oil,
even though the cops were sure we had.
And I'm pretty sure Eva still thinks we stole that beer.
Man, that was close.
Yeah, we had some good times.
Really good times.

—Dan

Contents

Introduction 1

PEOPLE 5

   Pajamas in Public 7
   Mario's Catalina 12
   Valet Chaos 17
   Mind Your Manners 22
   Medal of Honor Misunderstanding 27
   Infrequent Fliers 32
   Asshole in the Rearview Mirror 37
   Be Happy Always 42
   Obsessive-Compulsive Superpower 47
   A Ref Goes Viral 52
   Breach of Commuter Etiquette 57
   Your Fine! 62
   Condo Outlaw 67
   Panera Bread Hell 72
   Fred Time 77
   Weirdos at the Y 81
   Starstruck by The Wiggles 85
   David Hasselhoff 89
   Catching Up with Mrs. Lawrence 93

WORK 99

- Doing It All Wrong, Part I 101
- Doing It All Wrong, Part II 106
- You're in Trouble, Mister! 111
- Phantom Dog Shitter 116
- Business Travel Adventures, Houston 121
- Cybercriminal 126
- Hotel Butler 132
- Easyrider Olympics 137
- The Kuwaitis Are Offended 142
- București Shakedown 148
- Hangin' with the General 153
- High School Spanish 159
- Lube Oil Delivery 163
- The 9/11 Commission 167
- Awkward in Zagreb 171
- High-Performance Takeoff 176
- Minor in Possession 179
- Ode to the G-1 Leather Flight Jacket 182

LIFE 187

- Nineties Hair 189
- Three Things Unsaid 194
- Keep Telling the Story 200
- Mason-Dixon Mea Culpa 206
- Getting Old, Part I 212
- Getting Old, Part II 217
- Don't Touch My Stuff 222
- The Story That Wasn't 227

In Trouble on Christmas (Again) ... 233
Six-Hundred-Dollar Oil Change ... 238
Early Riser ... 243
Pentwater, Revisited ... 248
Speed Limit Epiphany ... 253
The Balanced TV Diet ... 258
An Idiot Wears Contacts ... 263
Jury Duty ... 268
My Freakishly Hairy Forearms ... 274
To Hell with Mulch ... 280
The Best Damn Day-After-Christmas ... 284
Toilet Seat Scam ... 287
Antidote to the Life of Quiet Desperation ... 290
Pete's Garage ... 293
Pathetically Weak Hips ... 296
On the Yard ... 301
A Run Around Capitol Hill ... 306
Funny Car Fountain of Youth ... 312

Introduction

HOW DO YOU live with yourself? You do weird, stupid shit all the time. And you annoy the hell out of the people around you. I know you do. And so do I.

But you also do incredibly kind, generous, maybe even heroic things. Which your fellow humans may or may not notice.

But I notice. At least, I have for the last couple of years.

That's because I started writing and posting weekly essays not long after I'd caught up with a high school buddy.

They were about the kind of random stuff he and I used to talk about in his garage.

Pete's garage.

My buddy's name is Pete. Well, actually, it's Mike. But friends call him Pete, because his last name is Petersen.

He'd call me up, and I'd go slogging through the Michigan winter snow to drink beers with him in his garage.

We were teenagers.

Somehow, it was okay to drink in his garage, but not his house.

We didn't care. In fact, we preferred the garage.

He and I would cover a lot of ground in those conversations, much as we did when we reconnected some thirty years later.

I was back in our hometown, a large portion of which Pete had bought through the years. He'd taken over the family business, and he'd done quite well.

But he was the same old Pete.

As old friends do, we often revert to our high school selves when we catch up. It's fun to be seventeen again, at least for a while. We revel in all the stupid things we did as teenagers and take pride in the various acts that could have—should have—gotten us arrested, maimed, or killed.

And we talk about girls, of course. Most of whom have kids in college now. But anyway.

I'd toyed with the idea of writing some sort of column or blog for a while.

Two reasons.

One, I thought it might improve my writing. Like most others who write, I think everything I put on a page is brilliant. The truth is, most of it's shit. And I wanted to do something about that through regular, focused effort.

Second, I wanted a creative diversion.

I'd rather paint pictures and write books all day than endure corporate drudgery. So would anyone, probably. But a fella's gotta make a living, right?

If I could write something—anything—on a regular basis, perhaps it would make me feel like the artist I was meant to be—starving, or other.

So, then, what would I write?

Anything I damn well pleased. That was the deal I made with myself. I knew that if my weekly essays felt like work, I wouldn't stick with it, so I gave myself complete freedom.

Which was great. Sort of.

I soon discovered that when you're free to comment on whatever you want, it isn't immediately obvious what, exactly, is comment worthy.

And so anxiety would start to build as the week progressed, and I would approach my weekend deadline without having decided upon my topic. But once I settled on a topic, the writing usually took care of itself. Choosing my weekly subject thus became the central challenge.

After a few weeks of toiling, I started taking closer notice of things.

If I returned repeatedly in my mind to certain people or events,

I knew I had a potential essay topic. And so I paid attention to those things I found interesting, amusing, or annoying. And, I found, through the course of a typical week, there was much that interested, amused, or annoyed me.

Especially annoyed me.

That, in turn, caused me to reframe many of the mundane features and events of my life.

That high school kid who didn't wait his turn at the stop sign and cut in front of me during the morning commute? A punk, yes. But also a muse and a primer for a broader consideration of why parents don't put kids on school buses anymore and instead drive them everywhere or buy them cars.

No one bought me a car. My ass was on the bus.

And there you have it: a thousand-word essay on the virtues of school-bus-riding as both a rite of passage and a mechanism to keep dipshit kids off the road while I'm trying to get to goddamn work in the morning.

Committing to writing weekly essays made me pay greater attention to my own life. It helped me live in the moment. Which is supposed to be a good thing, right?

And it also caused me, on occasion, to reexamine past events.

There were some stories, especially from my Navy experience, that I just felt like telling. In other cases, how I reacted to certain people and events in real time had a lot to do with how I'd reacted to similar people and events in the past. Patterns emerged, which isn't terribly surprising.

But it did reveal just how petty and judgmental I can be.

That was good self-awareness.

I can't say it has or will change my behavior. Nor do I intend for such insights to change anyone else's. This isn't a self-help book, after all.

But it was nonetheless surprising, and highly gratifying, to have my stories resonate with my small but devoted audience.

As I continued to post my stories week after week, people started tuning in. And they stayed tuned in as I mused on topics ranging from mulch to toilet seats to Mexican hotel butlers.

People told me they could see themselves in the various situations I described. And that was reassuring, for them and for me.

We humans crave acceptance, after all.

So when I shared my desire to throat-punch the dude who mowed his yard in crooked rows—savage!—and readers approved, I felt good about myself. Which was nice.

So here we are.

What follows is a "best of" collection of stories from *Pete's Garage*.

That's what I named my blog. It seemed fitting, because this is the type of stuff Pete and I would discuss.

Yes, much of it is critical. But I endeavor not to swing below the belt.

And, for sure, the object of my criticism is often myself. I am by no means immune from doing stupid shit.

Even though I never have,

Nor will I ever,

Wear pajamas in public.

And neither should you. Or anyone.

Shall we begin?

PEOPLE

Pajamas in Public

BREAKFAST AT HAMPTON Inn. Not exactly a black-tie affair.

I was staying in one of the factory towns I frequent for work, and my go-to attire on such occasions is jeans and a pressed flannel shirt. The combination presents a put-together appearance without suggesting one's trying too hard.

I scooped some lukewarm oatmeal into a paper bowl and then took a seat at a small table in the hotel's dining area. Two tables over sat a guy and two women. All appeared to be in their forties. But they were dressed like nine-year-olds who'd just rolled out of bed to watch *SpongeBob*.

The guy, for example, wore patterned pajama pants, a T-shirt with a hole in the armpit, a worn trucker's hat, and a pair of camouflage Crocs. To complete the look, he still wore upon his face the pillow marks with which he'd awoken.

He had one of those make-it-yourself hotel waffles in front of him, piled high with whipped cream and sprinkles, which he dug into with a plastic fork.

The women also wore pajama pants and T-shirts. But, rather than Crocs, they'd instead opted for fuzzy slippers. Not casual shoes that resembled slippers, actual slippers.

They carried on as though they were at home, sitting around the kitchen table. And they apparently felt comfortable enough to dress for exactly such an occasion.

And then go walking around in public.

Which is certainly no crime. But, I have to be honest, it appalled me. And maybe I'm alone here.

Yes, we've become far more casual as a society. You don't need a suit to make your first billion. A hoodie will do just fine. That's who we are now.

And what's the harm?

Does it really matter how people look? How they dress? Perhaps not.

Maybe the pajama-pants-wearing, waffle-eating dude had recently rushed into a burning building to save a litter of golden retriever puppies. And maybe the women were the cofounders of a local charity that provided pomade to orphans with cowlicks.

Who was I to judge?

They could've been outstanding people in all respects. If breakfast for them was come-as-you-are, so be it.

But still . . .

It wasn't always this way.

During a recent walk through our local art museum, my wife and I stopped to consider a Manet. At least, I think it was a Manet.

The scene was that of an 1890s croquet match. Two questions came to mind as I studied it.

One, when was the last time I played croquet?

And two, how would I like to play anything in a stuffy wool suit?

The men in the painting all wore jackets, vests, and ties. The women had on enormous layered, poofy dresses and gigantic hats. It seemed the most impractical attire imaginable for any outdoor activity.

But that's the way it was back then. Ladies and gentlemen dressed properly for all occasions. There was morning wear. Afternoon wear. Evening wear.

And, apparently, croquet wear, which to me resembled... well, nothing by today's standards.

You can barely get a dude to put on a tie these days.

But, I have to say, the people in the painting looked fantastic. They were sophisticated, but in a relaxed sort of way. They exuded class. And money.

Lots and lots of money.

Now, I'm not suggesting we don our Brooks Brothers for another round of croquet. But I do believe in at least a minimum standard of decorum whereby one's dress and behavior are appropriate to the occasion.

Breakfast at the Hampton Inn does not call for white tie and tails—I recognize that. But neither should it give anyone license to wear goddamn pajamas in public.

No one serious, at least.

To be fair, there have been situations, some mildly traumatizing, in which I've found myself underdressed. There was that Harvard Business School Club of San Diego meeting.

It was held at a country club, with about fifty grads in attendance whose ages favored the retiree end of the spectrum. It being Southern California, I wore khakis and a polo. Which, I immediately discovered, was *not* the prescribed uniform for such meetings. Everyone else had on dress pants and blazers. I was already feeling like an idiot when a seventyish-looking guy pulled me aside.

"You know," he said, "only billionaires get to wear golf shirts to these things."

Chastened, yet defiant, I pulled off one of the few well-timed comebacks of my career.

How do you know I'm *not* a billionaire? I asked him.

He gave me a smirk and walked away.

Asshole.

But point taken.

Then there was the time I joined members of my team for a round of sales calls in Germany. I'd done business in the country before, where I'd always found an open collar and jacket acceptable attire. So I was surprised by my colleagues' horrified looks when I met them in the hotel lobby prior to our meetings wearing such an ensemble.

"No, no, no, no . . ." one of them said in accented English. "This won't do."

"We can just blame it on his being an American," the other said. "The clients will understand."

Apparently, the dress code for customer calls in that industry and that region was business formal. Suit and tie required.

Not wanting to be the ugly, ignorant American, I insisted my colleagues take me to a nearby store to buy a tie. The tie I purchased wasn't entirely suitable for the occasion, but it got me by.

I don't want to ever just get by, though. I'm not wired that way. And I wasn't raised that way.

I'd once ventured down the path of the Hampton Inn pajama guy but was resolutely knocked off it by my grandfather.

He and my grandmother had taken a buddy and me on a cruise as a high school graduation gift. The first morning underway, my friend and I wandered into the ship's main dining room to join my grandparents for breakfast. We both wore T-shirts and backward-facing ball caps. It was a look I'd been experimenting with throughout my senior year, but to which I hadn't yet committed.

Upon sitting down at the table, my grandfather, a kind but

serious man, looked at my buddy and me and said, sternly, "Boys, kindly remove your caps while you're in the dining room."

The words bit, and we couldn't get our hats off fast enough.

To this day, I wouldn't consider wearing anything on my head while seated at a table, or almost anywhere else indoors. Especially while eating.

My grandfather had done me a terrific service. He'd shown me the way. The proper way.

Back at the Hampton Inn, I finished my oatmeal and stood to exit the dining room. Before I did, I approached the table with the man and two women.

Excuse me, I said. You don't know me, but may I ask you a question?

"Sure," the guy said as the women nodded along.

Then I put on my best pirate accent. And I sang, "Whoooooooo… lives in a pineapple under the sea?"

Without hesitating, all three lit up and sang in reply, "Sponge-Bob-Square-Pants!"

Ah, yes, I said.

That's right.

I thanked them and turned and walked back to my room.

Satisfied.

Actually, none of that happened.

No way would I ever have the guts to do something like that.

But how sweet would that have been?

Right?

Mario's Catalina

Mario's Catalina

SUDDENLY, IT HIT ME:

Mario's!

Remember Mario? I asked my wife.

It was a couple of years ago. We were in Fort Lauderdale to get some warm weather between Christmas and New Year's, and I'd decided that a trip to South Florida required dinner at a Cuban restaurant.

So, I turned to the internet, which was rolling the dice, of course. The web is as likely to get it wrong as it is to get it right.

I did a quick search for Cuban restaurants. Many looked promising, but one stood out. It had pages and pages of gushing reviews. Which, again, could have all been bullshit. But, with no other source of intel, what was I going to do?

It was a Monday night, and most people were chilling out for the holidays. The restaurants in the immediate vicinity of our hotel were doing a steady business but were far from overwhelmed. The same was true of Mario's Cubano.

At first.

The restaurant sat two and a half miles inland from the beach on a road that paralleled the interstate. Frankly, it wasn't much to look at on the outside. The entire area was nothing but strip malls and ten-minute-oil-change shops. Mario's facade was equally unremarkable.

My wife, daughter, and I pulled into the mostly empty parking lot wondering if we—well, I—had made a bad call.

That all changed as soon as we walked in the door.

For starters, the place looked and felt as though you were walking into someone's home. Not in a creepy, intrusive sort of way. Rather, it gave you a comfortable, familiar sort of feeling. And that feeling was magnified as soon as Mario noticed you.

"Ah, yes!" he said. "There you are."

He'd been expecting us, he said. Which may or may not have been true. I explained that, yes, I'd called to make a reservation.

But a reservation, I quickly observed, was a loose concept for Mario. He'd find room for anyone who wanted to be there.

As we walked through the restaurant to the table Mario had saved especially for us—so he claimed—people called out to him from all directions.

"Mario! Hey, Mario . . ."

And he'd wave, blow them kisses, and say, "Be right there."

What in the hell is all this? I thought. Who is this guy?

He finally sat us at our table in the back part of the restaurant. We had our own little corner with views of the bar, which was all decked out in Christmas lights.

Even though Mario acted like he'd known us for years, he still took the time to get our entire story. Where were we from? How long were we in town? Where were we staying?

And then he disappeared.

I assumed he was grabbing us menus and a round of ice waters. Instead, he came back with drinks: mojitos, his signature cocktail, and a Shirley Temple for my daughter. We hadn't asked for any of it. Mario just brought it.

And kept bringing it for the remainder of the night.

We eventually received our menus, but only after Mario had delivered another round of mojitos and a plate of these incredible dried plantains, accompanied by pickled peppers and onions.

The place continued to fill up.

And, despite Mario's being pulled in a thousand different directions, he intuitively sensed the precise moments to arrive back at our table to answer a question or deliver another dish or drink. He appeared to do the same for all the other patrons, even when the place became completely full. The entire visit was unlike anything we'd ever experienced.

And it had everything to do with Mario.

We were old friends by the time my wife, my daughter, and I stood to leave.

He kissed the girls on their cheeks, gave me a hug, and then presented us with a bottle of wine and a gift card for a future visit. And, despite my having lost count of the number of rounds of mojitos he'd brought to our table, our bill revealed that he hadn't charged us for any of them. I mean . . . who does that?

Mario, that's who.

So, you can understand why I'd want to return to Mario's Cubano if I were anywhere within five hundred miles of the place.

As my wife and I were recently.

We'd headed to Boca Raton for spring break, and I'd carefully planned the week's activities, making dinner reservations at various restaurants. But I hadn't done so for the day of arrival. Once we got settled into our hotel room, we turned to the question of dinner.

What sounds good? I asked my wife.

"I dunno," she said. "What sounds good to you?"

We went back and forth like that for a while before I remembered Mario's. I gave him a call.

Hey, Mario! I said. You don't remember me, but I'd like to make a reservation.

"Wonderful!" he replied. "So, you've visited me before?"

Yes, I said. I explained that my family and I had thoroughly enjoyed the experience.

He then pointed out that he was in a new location under a different name: Mario's Catalina. But he assured me I would enjoy the experience just as I had before.

Oh, and about the reservation, I said. Is six o'clock okay?

"It doesn't matter," Mario replied. "Just come."

Ah, Mario . . .

My wife and I arrived an hour later. The new restaurant was in the same general location as the last. But, frankly, it was even less inviting looking on the outside. Which, as I'd learned before, didn't mean anything.

There appeared to be two entrances in front, and it wasn't entirely clear which we were supposed to use. My wife and I started in the direction of one of the doors, only to have Mario come running out of the other one and into the parking lot to usher us in.

"There you are!" he said once again.

And, again, he treated us as though he'd known us for decades. Even though I seriously doubted he remembered us.

The interior of the new restaurant resembled the former location but lacked the same homey feel. It seemed Mario was still breaking the place in, and that was fine.

Mario sat my wife and me at a linen-draped table in the front window. And, almost immediately, he began delivering drinks and dishes to our table.

There would be no menus this time.

Mojitos. Dried plantains. Empanadas. Tamal with pork. It just kept coming. The main course was plantain-encrusted snapper with rice and beans, and it was incredible. By the time it arrived, I'd already consumed three days' worth of calories.

But I didn't care.

I'm just going with it, I told my wife.

And, when I thought I couldn't manage another bite, Mario

brought us the most incredible tres leches cake I'd ever had. When I asked for a simple cup of coffee to go with it, I instead received an immaculate, barista-quality cappuccino. Mario was pulling out all the stops.

Nearly three hours after we'd walked in, I began to mull over the experience. It was extraordinary.

Just as I expected the check to be.

But, again, Mario charged us for only a fraction of what we'd consumed. I mean . . . why? Why us?

Mario walked us to the door as we prepared to leave. And, along the way, he kept kissing my wife on the cheek, saying, "I just love you." Which, strangely, didn't bother me one bit. It didn't bother my wife, either.

It was Mario, after all. One of the most incredible human beings I'd ever encountered.

It is just so damn refreshing—and life-affirming—to find someone in exactly the right place, doing exactly what they were put on this planet to do. I couldn't imagine Mario in any other setting.

And, I suspect, neither could he.

As I turned to shake Mario's hand one last time, he slid me another gift card. A very generous one.

"For next time," he said.

Yes, I will see you again, and you may or may not remember me.

But I know you'll treat me like family.

Or even better.

Because you're Mario.

And you wouldn't do it any other way.

Valet Chaos

THE DESCENT INTO CHAOS was accelerating.

No matter how hard the girl at the podium tried to restore order, the forces of randomness and entropy continually reasserted themselves, overwhelming her and her two twenty-something, black-polo-wearing colleagues.

It all started with the chow chows.

You know, those puffy, wrinkly-faced, ill-tempered Chinese dogs? Which, apparently, will rip your throat out when sufficiently provoked. So I've heard.

I'll get to them in a minute.

First, I thought I'd taken all the necessary steps to avoid such a scene. Upon checking into the hotel and handing my keys off to the valet, the dude at the stand asked for my phone number.

"I'll send you a text with a link," he explained. "And, when you need your car, just use the link to request it, and we'll have it waiting for you by the time you get downstairs."

Cool. I'm all about using technology to make life easier.

I hit the link, as instructed, the following day, about forty-five minutes before I needed my car. Better to give myself plenty of time, I reasoned.

When I got down to the valet stand, I saw my car sitting, by itself, in the outermost lane in front of the hotel entrance. There were no other cars in sight.

That's my car over there, I said to the two guys at the podium. I guess I didn't need to request it forty-five minutes in advance, huh?

"No," they said. "Ask for it right before you leave your room, and that will give us plenty of time to have it out in front by the time you get here."

Okay. Lesson learned.

And that's exactly what I did later that evening. I had dinner reservations but was running ahead of schedule. And that was fortunate.

When I arrived at the valet stand, I could immediately sense the rising tide of disorder. There were cars everywhere. Half belonged to people who were checking in, half to those seeking to leave.

Five people were arranged in a semicircle around the valet's podium, vying for the attention of the poor girl who was running the show. They all tried to speak at once.

"Sorry," she pleaded with them. "We're understaffed."

Of course you are, I thought. So's everyone these days.

And perhaps I would have been more sympathetic had the hotel not totally done this to itself. Despite having a large garage on the property, the only parking option was to valet. You couldn't park your car yourself. Maybe there were legitimate reasons for that.

Or maybe it was a ploy to extract additional fees from guests.

Don't know, don't care. All I wanted was my damn car.

I informed the beleaguered girl that I had requested my car via the app. Just as I was supposed to have done.

"And what's the name?" she asked me, checking her computer. "Right," she said when I responded. "Your car should be on its way." And then she repeated, "We're understaffed this evening . . ."

Yup.

I moved to the side of the valet stand to wait. And a very bizarre scene began to unfold.

A black minivan was parked immediately in front of the hotel entrance. Sounds of dogs barking emanated loudly from inside, and three grandparent-aged people stood behind the car, two women and a man.

One of the women, slouched, with thinning hair and a highly unfortunate red dye job, lifted open the van's rear door. Inside, I could see two chows occupying individual wire cages, one of these dogs doing all the barking.

"Quiet!" the woman demanded.

Upon hearing this, the other woman came to stand beside her to help calm the increasingly pissed-off dog.

"Uuughhhh!" she groaned. "Uuuuughhhh . . ."

It was a guttural, unnatural sound that an unhappy Neanderthal might have made to its mate, not a twenty-first century old lady to a chow.

The dog kept barking.

So, the two women continued, alternating.

"Quiet!" the one would say.

Then, "Uuughhhh!" from the other.

The man with them just stood there, not saying anything. Which seemed about right.

This went on for a couple minutes before the women finally gave up and started to unload the minivan. The man wheeled over a luggage cart, which the red-dyed-hair lady began to load. Eventually it was revealed that there were four dogs in the car, along with a bunch of dog gear and luggage.

It was a slow process, and it all but ground the car parking and retrieving process to a halt. One of the valets, noticing this, pitched in to help, and thus decreased the odds that I'd see my car any time soon. I continued to stand there, feeling both annoyed and amused.

Then came the dance girls.

A steady stream of nine-year-olds with moms, dads, and huge rolling trunks began to flow out from inside the hotel. The girls all looked the same from the neck up, with slicked-back, tightly pinned hair and heavy, heavy makeup. But the makeup was all black—lipstick, eyeliner . . . all of it. It gave them a creepy, goth kind of look.

Like Marilyn Manson.

Yes, that's right. They were Marilyn Mansons. Which no nine-year-old should ever be.

The moms' T-shirts helped me piece it all together. Each read *Dance Mom* in sparkly letters. And even one of the dads, built like the Rock, wore a shirt that read *Dance Dad*.

Guys like him can pull off such things. Guys like me cannot.

Anyway.

The dance troupe was apparently in a hurry to get to a competition. So, all the moms closed in around the podium to give the valet girl hell. But all she could do in return was plead. "Yes, I totally understand. We'll get the cars down as quickly as we can. But we're understaffed this evening . . ."

This, as one of her two colleagues continued to unload the chows and all their gear. The dance moms became progressively pissed. The dogs continued to bark. The dog grandmas continued to shout "Quiet!" and "Uuughhhh!" The dog grandpa just kept his head down and his mouth shut.

It was all a bit surreal.

Is this some kind of act? I wondered. Was it all being staged for my benefit? Would a clown on a unicycle eventually ride by? Would there be jugglers?

It was quite an odd slice of humanity assembled around the valet stand that evening. And I was grateful I had given myself a little extra time to take it all in.

But I still wanted my damn car.

It was about then that I shifted my gaze to the outer lane of the parking area. And there, once again, sitting all by itself, was my car. It looked like it had been there for a while. I maneuvered through the chows, chow gear, luggage, dance girls, dance moms, and dance dads to the front of the valet stand.

That's my car, I told the girl. May I have the keys?

She began sifting through the thirty or so sets that lay haphazardly in the top drawer of the podium. When she finally found them, she acted as though it was the first thing that had gone right for her the entire evening.

Poor kid.

"Ah! Here they are," she said. "Sorry about that." And then she reminded me, "We're understaffed this evening."

Yup. Got it.

And then I walked to my car, wondering if dinner would be even half as interesting,

But hoping it wouldn't.

Because I'd had enough of humanity

And chows

And dance girls

And valets

For one night.

Mind Your Manners

I COULDN'T UNDERSTAND what I was seeing. It was just . . . befuddling. I mean, where did he think he was? At a goddamned picnic? Or a tractor pull? Is that how people ate at tractor pulls? Are those still a thing?

I don't know. I've never been to one.

But the cliché seems appropriate here. This was a restaurant. Yes, a casual one. In small-town, rural Missouri. I certainly hadn't expected a Michelin-starred kind of experience.

But this . . .

I was in town for work, due to visit a factory the following morning. I had pretty low expectations for dinner as this was not an area known for fine dining. Or anything remotely healthy.

I'd scanned the menus of a half dozen restaurants online and found one that had at least a couple items that weren't deep-fried and covered in melted cheese, which were rarities in this part of the country. Even a salad there was so loaded down with bright-orange, straight-from-the-bag cheddar cheese, bacon bits, thick-asmayonnaise ranch dressing, and gumball-sized croutons a person risked bypass surgery even while confining himself to such "lighter" options.

The people in the restaurant seemed unconcerned.

The group at the table next to me ordered two rounds each of jalapeño poppers and onion rings before moving on to cheeseburgers and overloaded plates of alfredo. I was by myself, in my usual state of semiboredom, and took notice of these things.

A couple walked into the restaurant about ten minutes later and took the table right in front of mine. The gentleman appeared to be in his mid-sixties with closely cropped hair. He wore a pair of jeans and a quarter-zip sweater over a button-down oxford. The woman who accompanied him was petite, of Asian descent, and tastefully dressed. They chatted quietly until the waiter came over to take their order. I noticed the gentleman was seated a couple feet back from the table, legs and arms casually crossed.

A few minutes later, two salads and a basket of breadsticks arrived at their table. The woman started in on her salad, eating daintily, one lettuce leaf at a time.

And the guy . . .

He remained seated some distance from the table while he leaned forward and propped his phone up against his wallet a couple inches from the table's edge. He scrolled around until he found what appeared to be a live feed from ESPN. Then he picked up his salad plate, and, with his chair still pushed back and legs still crossed, leaned back, held the plate up to his mouth, and started shoveling in the salad. While he did so, he completely ignored his wife and focused intently on SportsCenter.

Which didn't seem to bother her in the least.

It was one of the most bizarre scenes I'd witnessed in any restaurant, ever. I figured it couldn't go on like that for long. I mean, the guy would eventually come to his senses, put his plate on the table, shut off his goddamned phone, and eat like a human fucking being, right?

Wrong.

He eventually gestured to his wife to pass him the basket of breadsticks. She did so, while he sat his empty salad plate on the table. And then he held the basket under his chin while he shoved down two breadsticks, still pushed back some distance from the table.

How could anyone with even an ounce of self-awareness eat like that? How does one come to have such colossally poor manners? Had he never learned? Or did he just not care? Had he experienced some form of trauma that had led him to regress to a Freudian, infantile state?

Shit, I'd seen toddlers in high chairs better able to comport themselves in public than this guy.

Whatever the case, I wanted to understand him. And then I wanted to punch him.

Why?

Because manners matter. They're an indicator as to whether a person should be taken seriously. Or as an idiot, like the guy in this restaurant.

Good manners should not be misunderstood as something reserved for stuffy elites. They're not about extending one's pinkie while lifting a teacup from a saucer. Employed correctly, good manners put people at ease. They evidence respect for one's surroundings, the occasion, and the company in which a person finds himself.

A practitioner of good etiquette has a certain "it factor." You can't always explain it. All you know is that when you're around that person, you want to be a better version of yourself.

I have a powerful memory from my formative years. As a young Navy petty officer, I was invited to a black-tie dinner on base. I hadn't the first clue as to how to behave at such an event, so I figured I'd take my cues from the officers in attendance.

I'd come to enjoy the officers in my squadron. They were all pilots, which I desperately wanted to be, and they treated me like a little brother.

The dinner kicked off with an open bar, of course. And, before long, in fine Naval aviation tradition, the officers from my squadron were discarding portions of their uniforms and flinging rolls at each other.

It went downhill from there.

In contrast, seated at the opposite end of the ballroom was the captain in charge of the base's Marine Corps detachment. Even as the night progressed and the scene at my squadron's table deteriorated, the captain remained a vision of composure.

I watched how he ate. How he conversed with others at his table. How he escorted his wife to and from the dance floor. How he presented himself to the base commanding officer. And how he graciously took leave the moment just before things got really out of hand.

He was pure class.

And I remember thinking how incredible it must be to work for that officer. Without even knowing him, I instinctively wanted to follow him. As a Navy guy, do you know how hard it is for me to say that about a marine? But it was the damn truth.

The captain's impeccable manners were his calling card. In a good way.

The converse can also be true.

I have a buddy who partnered with a guy he barely knew on what turned out to be a reasonably successful business venture. It probably could have been even more successful had the guy not turned out to be a complete sociopath.

My buddy recalled the dinner at which he first met him. The guy ordered a steak, which he proceeded to eat with his hands.

"That should have been a red flag," my friend had said.

A messy break between the two eventually ensued, complete with threats, temper tantrums, lawyers, and an untold amount of destroyed value.

The steak should have indeed been a red flag.

Speaking from my own experience, I know a guy who is a complete bully-narcissist, who thinks nothing of interrupting, belittling, and backstabbing—on a good day. And that should have come as no surprise following the dinner at which I sat next to him early in our acquaintance.

He, too, was fond of eating with his hands, as well as licking his fingers, slurping, belching, reaching, and speaking with his mouth full, even before others at the table had received their food and taken a single bite.

In a word, he's disgusting.

At the risk of sounding like Judge Smails at Bushwood, chastising Rodney Dangerfield's character and saying, "You! You! You're no gentleman!"—allow me to repeat myself.

Manners matter.

So, please, people.

Elbows off the table. Hands off the food. No speaking with your mouth full. Be thoughtful of others. And put your goddamned phone away.

Ann Landers and I will thank you.

Medal of Honor Misunderstanding

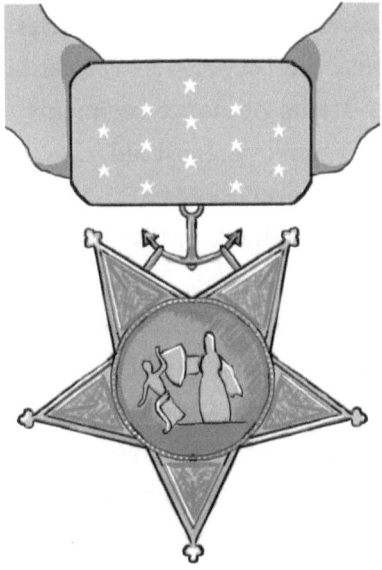

"**WHAT ARE YOU** talking about? You think I didn't know how to swim?"

He seemed irritated. Maybe even pissed.

"Listen, pal, you try swimming across a goddamned river with your arm half blown off and your back full of shrapnel. Let's see how well *you* do it."

Yup. He was pissed.

It was Medal of Honor recipient Sammy L. Davis, staff sergeant, US Army, retired.

And I'd just managed to insult him.

Insult him!

A person who, at that very moment, was wearing our nation's highest military decoration around his neck. The Congressional Medal of Honor. The Blue Max. Just to see one in real life gave me chills.

As long as I'd worn the uniform, I'd revered its recipients. These were people who'd done the unthinkable, the unimaginable, under the most desperate circumstances. Their stories, through history's great conflicts, varied. But they also shared certain similarities.

You often hear Medal of Honor recipients say things like, "It was all a blur. I wasn't thinking. I just did it."

Or "I didn't think I'd ever survive,"

Or "I did it for my buddies, because I know they'd have done it for me."

And, sadly, when speaking of their heroic deeds, you also hear them say, "Frankly, it was a day I'd rather forget."

Such comments make you wonder, what would I have done in such a situation? Would I have risen to the occasion? Would I have acquitted myself honorably? Or would I have shrunk in fear and indecision? Would I have fought or frozen?

These are important questions for military people, because only a fraction of servicemen and women see combat. Very few will ever be put into situations like those faced by Medal of Honor recipients. And so, you wonder.

Which makes people like Sammy L. Davis all the more special. Even though, at that very moment, he wanted to kick my ass. And, despite being my parents' age, I was pretty sure he could have.

That was a shame. I'd been looking forward to the event for weeks. Well, part of it. I was definitely excited to meet the Medal of Honor recipients. The rest I could have done without.

Somehow, I'd wound up as a spokesperson and media adviser for a large corporation. It was yet another in a long string of roles for which I was ill-suited, poorly qualified, and totally disinterested, representative of most of my civilian career.

I'd traveled to a midsize Midwestern city for the grand opening of a newly built wing of one of the company's many factories. The congressman for the district in which the plant resided was the event's guest of honor. The Medal of Honor recipients, who apparently traveled in groups and were often tapped to make appearances at such events, rounded out the VIP guest list.

I had coordinated the congressman's visit with his DC staff, and it was my job to lead him through the event. I would discretely instruct him to "stand here." Then there. To meet such and such. To smile for this camera. To pretend like he was interested in a certain piece of equipment. To ask this question during the plant tour . . .

You know, stuff like that.

There was a time when I would have relished such an opportunity. I was awed by the entire DC scene. But not anymore. Frankly, I couldn't be bothered with the congressman, but it was my job.

My plan was to get him in and out of the plant as smoothly and quickly as possible, which I did. He got his photo op and a short segment with the local news station, and then he was on his way, freeing me up to go meet Sammy L. Davis and his fellow recipients.

I'd brought with me a book I'd received when I was a US Naval Academy midshipman. It contained the citations for all Medals of Honor that had been awarded since its inception. I'd dog-eared the pages containing the write-ups for the recipients who'd be attending the event in the hopes they'd all sign their respective citations for me. That book was a real treasure, and it would be made priceless by those signatures.

I started with Colonel Leo Thorsness, the Air Force F-105 pilot who'd downed a North Vietnamese MiG while trying to protect his wingman who'd ejected from his aircraft. Later that same month—April 1967—Thorsness himself was shot down and would spend the next six years in the notorious Hanoi Hilton.

Incredible.

I then met the outgoing, vivacious Hershel "Woody" Williams, the marine who'd miraculously, single-handedly cut his way through a large swath of the hellscape that was Iwo Jima in February 1945. He was awarded the medal by President Truman.

And then I met Staff Sergeant Davis.

He'd been an Army artilleryman and one of forty-two soldiers who'd fended off an assault of more than fifteen hundred Viet Cong at a remote fire support base in the Mekong Delta in November 1967. Of the forty-two Americans at the base when the assault commenced at two o'clock in the morning, only eleven were left standing at sunrise.

Staff Sergeant Davis was one of them.

At one point during the assault, Davis spotted a group of wounded comrades on the other side of the river that separated the fire support base from the attacking Viet Cong. The staff sergeant immediately set out for their location, grabbing an air mattress to assist him across the river.

The other ten were convinced they'd only survived thanks to his actions that night and petitioned Army leadership to bestow upon him the nation's highest military honor. According to Davis's Medal of Honor citation, "Disregarding his extensive injuries and his inability to swim, Sergeant Davis picked up an air mattress and struck out across the deep river to rescue three wounded comrades on the far side."

Unbelievable. It was an act of extraordinary grit and heroism.

But therein lay my problem.

I'd interpreted that portion of the citation to mean Staff Sergeant Davis didn't know *how* to swim. As in, for whatever reason, he'd never learned. To me, it was like saying that I had an inability to speak Farsi. Or to make a passable crème brûlée. It wasn't that I was incapable of doing those things, I'd just never bothered learning.

I thought the same was true of Staff Sergeant Davis and swimming.

So, when I handed him my book of citations and asked him

to sign his page, I wisecracked to him, Gee, that must have been a tough time for you to have to learn how to swim.

It was a stupid, stupid thing to say.

Davis dropped his pen and looked up at me, glaring. He thought I was razzing him in front of his fellow recipients. Which, of course, I was not. But still, the damage was done, and I went into full retreat.

No . . . no, sir. I didn't mean it like that at all, I told him.

And, yes, I could appreciate how challenging it might be to swim across a backyard pool, let alone a moving river while under fire, with a back full of jagged pieces of medal.

I explained to Davis that I'd misinterpreted the language in his citation, that it was all just a big misunderstanding.

He wasn't convinced.

He thought I was just some corporate-suit-wiseass, which still haunts me to this very day.

I'm sorry, Staff Sergeant Davis.

I didn't mean to insult you.

And thanks again for signing my book

Instead of kicking my ass.

Even though I may have deserved it.

Infrequent Fliers

I SPEND A lot of time on the road. And that's the way I like it. I get antsy if I sit around the office for too long. And although she wouldn't admit it, I suspect my wife's happy to get rid of me for a few days.

I get that.

Air travel has never lost its novelty for me. Yes, there's such a thing as too much, particularly when you're crossing multiple time zones. But rare is the trip in which I don't get a spring in my step when I'm walking through the airport.

It's the grown-up version of cruising the mall. The whole vibe is so . . . chic. I mean, in some places, you can buy a Rolex, for Chrissake. Even though there exists no recorded case in which a person actually bought a Rolex at an airport.

But you could.

And I *love* those duty-free stores that reek of Dior perfume and have entire rows of Toblerone chocolates. I've never spent a dime in one, but I've lingered in several, in a variety of countries, to pass many a layover.

And what about those ubiquitous Hudson News stores? They're fantastic for getting caught up on the current bestseller list and to see which celebrities have new memoirs out. I've never bought nor read any of them, but I have bought the bags of mixed nuts displayed next to them, priced five times higher than those you'd find at your local grocery store. Throw in a bottle of Perrier, and you can pay the same price you would for a decent dinner out.

It's a very elevated experience. Totally worth it.

I wouldn't go so far as to travel in a suit, even though I do enjoy those ads from the old *Life* magazines that depict men and women sitting on planes in their Sunday best. My go-to travel uniform does include a deconstructed blazer, but mostly for practical reasons. I like all the pockets.

Most people dress for comfort these days. Like the dude I saw in the Dallas Fort Worth Airport a while back in sweatpants and cowboy boots. Doubtful he was jetting off to a board meeting, but I suppose I shouldn't assume.

Yes, I do enjoy the trappings of air travel. Mostly because I have my routine dialed in. I've figured out how to optimize every phase of the airport evolution to minimize inconvenience and pain.

I park in the garage right next to the terminal. And pay a slightly ridiculous price to do so.

I do *not* check a bag, enabling me to skip the ticket counter on departure and baggage claim on arrival.

I use TSA PreCheck to avoid the long line and cattle chute to which most travelers are subjected. And I get to keep my shoes on, my laptop in my bag, and my toiletries in my carry-on.

I maintain frequent-flier status on two airlines, putting me at the head of the line for boarding. Which means there will be plenty of overhead-bin space when I get on the plane. And I won't have to be one of those people at the very end of the boarding process, looking helplessly up and down the aisle for someplace, *any*place, to put their luggage.

I always sit in the aisle, which makes it easy to stretch my legs from time to time. And to get the hell out of my seat the very instant the seat belt sign switches off when the plane hits the gate.

More generally, I've learned to adopt the behaviors and to extend the small courtesies that keep the whole process moving along efficiently.

Let's face it, when you're packed together in close quarters with that many people, you have to be nice.

Mostly.

We are dealing with humans, after all. And humans, particularly those who don't travel frequently, will inevitably find a way to fuck it all up. Like those I recently observed during a weekend trip with my wife.

She likes to have plenty of clothing options when she travels, which requires a larger suitcase. And that suitcase must be checked. Which means we had to go to the ticket counter. And there, we encountered a guy who, by any reasonable standard, was a complete disaster. He had a bunch of kids running around him and about seven oversized suitcases arranged on a luggage cart. It was clear he was from out of town.

He held his phone in his hand, with which he was having a conversation with someone in his native language. It was on speaker, set to max volume, so anyone within a hundred feet could hear it blaring. The guy would yell into his phone, then confer with the ticket agent in English.

"So, I go to Newark first, yes?" he asked the agent.

That's correct, she said. You're connecting through Newark.

And then he'd shout into his phone again while his kids played an impromptu game of tag, colliding with other passengers in the check-in line. All of this at five o'clock in the morning.

As the disaster unfolded, the other ticket agents began to abandon their posts to help, forcing the rest of us to wait in line. It was infuriating.

By the time we finally got my wife's bag checked, I was cooked.

She had never gotten around to signing up for TSA PreCheck and would therefore have to stand in the long line, take off her shoes, and stand with her arms in the air stick-'em-up-style in that body scanner.

A more supportive spouse would have joined her in line with the rest of the schmucks. I was not such a spouse. I didn't have the patience for any of that and headed straight for TSA PreCheck.

See you on the other side, I told her.

We reconnected a while later and made the short walk to get twenty-dollar airport smoothies for breakfast. We then proceeded to the gate, where I sipped on my delicious peanut butter shake until boarding.

Without fail, there's always a handful of people who fail to grasp the concept of boarding groups and approach the gate as soon as preboarding is called. This time was no different. A little old lady made her way to the front of the line and presented her boarding pass to the gate agent. She was in for some bad news.

"Oh, no . . ." the agent said upon examining it. "You're actually on the Miami flight. This one's going to Atlanta."

And, unfortunately, the Miami flight had already finished boarding, and the gate had been closed. The little old lady was not getting on that plane. She looked at the agent, bewildered.

Poor thing.

Anyway.

In my one act of chivalry, I gave up my aisle seat for my wife and took the middle one. This would more easily facilitate her getting up to use the lavatory, which she typically does about nine times during a flight.

Both our outbound and return legs proceeded smoothly. I managed to keep my usual impatience with my fellow travelers in check.

Until we got home.

At the baggage claim, I observed an annoying phenomenon. People lose all sense of decorum the moment they spot their bag on the conveyor. They will mindlessly hip check and shove aside anyone in their way as they move to retrieve their goddamn suitcases. When I see such a thing happening, I stand my ground. If someone wants me to move, I expect them to ask.

"There it is, Jackson! Go get it!" the mom said to her kid.

She'd dispatched him, like a golden retriever, to fetch her suitcase. The kid, about twelve years old, made a beeline for it, brushing against me as he passed. And then he hauled it off the conveyor and swung it around right in front of me to carry it back to his doting mother.

As he did so, he gave me a look that said, *Aren't you going to move?*

And I, in turn, gave him a look back that said, *Sure, kid. All you have to do is say "Excuse me."*

Of course, he didn't. So I just stood there.

Then he came right at me, nearly taking out my right knee with Mommy's overweight suitcase in the process. The little shit.

I suppose I should say the democratization of air travel over the past few decades has been a good thing. More people are able to stay connected with friends and family across cities, countries, and continents.

Yeah, I should say that.

But I won't.

Because it's a lie.

A complete,

Boldface,

Capital L,

Fucking

Lie.

Asshole in the Rearview Mirror

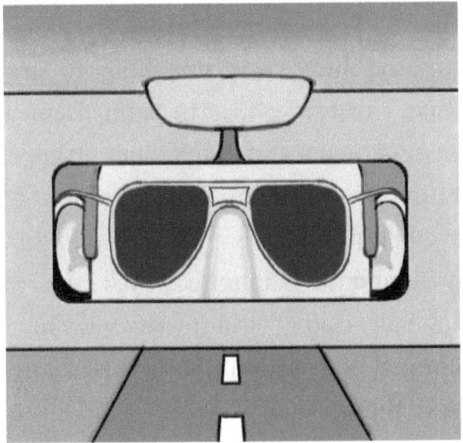

I HAD AN INTERESTING conversation with myself the other day. I was driving home from the airport, midafternoon, following my usual route.

When I exited the expressway, I noticed the two dudes in the car behind me as we stopped at a light.

I immediately disliked them.

Of course, I had no idea who they were, but they had all the characteristics of people I instinctively looked down upon. Their manner. Their dress. Their grooming and personal appearance. The way they interacted with and gestured to one another. The type of car they drove.

All these combined to paint a picture of two complete strangers whom I was certain I did not like. I was generalizing, dealing in stereotypes in the worst way. And when I caught myself doing so, I gave myself a rather stern lecture.

There you go again, I said.

These could be kind, generous people, with great families, on whom friends and neighbors rely in a pinch, who work hard and make honest livings. They could be all those things, and more, I reminded myself.

Yet I, in my snobbery, was unwilling to grant them that possibility, because I instead chose to paint them with the broad brush of my own experience and judge them on appearance alone.

What if they, in turn, were doing the same to me?

As they drove behind me, there were certain things they might deduce from my car and the manner in which I drove it. Maybe they would see my Ray Ban–clad eyes in my rearview mirror and decide I was the embodiment of a certain stereotype that invoked strongly negative feelings in them.

It cuts both ways.

And why is that? Is that really necessary? Why can't we judge people on their merits, not their appearance?

It's an age-old question that many have asked before. And the answer has to do with evolutionary biology. I'm no expert, but I've read a thing or two about it.

The gist of it is: Stereotyping arose out of a need among us animals to make snap decisions about other animals to survive. Primitives needed to determine, quickly, whether the thing with the big fangs was going to eat them, or if they could eat it.

And based upon our collective experience, handed down through the millennia, of either eating or being eaten, we developed instincts that enable us to make near-immediate judgments of people based upon a very small set of cues.

There are certain parts of the brain that govern all this, and it largely happens without any prompting or effort.

We see, we judge. It's that simple.

And those judgments are often accurate. But, sometimes, they are not. And that can have unfortunate consequences.

Like world wars.

Anyway.

I'm driving along, scolding myself, contemplating this innate feature of the human condition, convincing myself that I'd likely find the two dudes behind me agreeable, if only I got to know them.

And they, in turn, having thus been disarmed by my charm and wit, gained through an enlightened ability to overcome implicit biases, would find me to be a likable guy. And, I don't know, maybe we'd all have a good laugh over it and then go get a beer.

Hey, it could happen.

We eventually came upon a school zone, where one of those signs with the flashing yellow light told me to slow down to twenty-five miles per hour. There wasn't a kid or school bus in sight, but I abided.

Sort of.

I reduced my speed from forty to, like, twenty-nine, so any nearby cop would see that I was at least making an effort. And as I slowed down, my attention shifted to my windshield, for no particular reason, which I noticed was covered in dust. I'd parked in the airport parking garage in one of the outer rows, which was open to the elements. That likely explained the dust.

I switched on the wipers and gave the windshield a quick hit of washer fluid. Then, a moment later, still in the school zone, I noticed something blur past me on my left.

It was the car that had been behind me, whose occupants I'd been observing since exiting the expressway. The driver had gunned it and pulled around me, maneuvering directly in front of my car. Once there, he jammed on his brakes and slowed to a near crawl, forcing me to do the same.

And then he turned on his windshield washer, spraying down both his car and mine with washer fluid.

He was like a Chinese Sukhoi fighter pilot making an unsafe

intercept of a US patrol aircraft over the South China Sea.

Real mature, I thought.

The driver appeared to think I'd deliberately slowed down and washed my windshield as some form of harassment.

Which was ridiculous.

Once I'd safely averted rear-ending the guy, I stayed right on his ass, determined to show him his little temper tantrum had no effect on me.

Even as I started to develop a healthy case of road rage.

Ten seconds later, he flipped on his blinker and turned off into a neighborhood. And I continued on my way, asphyxiating the driver in my mind with a well-executed choke hold.

Fucking asshole.

I eventually snapped out of it and started coaching myself through a breathing exercise to help me calm down. And I lamented why I couldn't have had fifty-caliber machine guns pointing out of my headlights like James Bond.

Suffice it to say, I had an entirely different conversation with myself during the remainder of the drive home. Rather than lecture myself on giving in to stereotypes, I instead congratulated myself for having judged the occupants of the car behind me perfectly the first instant I'd noticed them.

Not only had the driver's behavior reinforced my existing notions of all people who shared his same characteristics, but it will also serve to perpetuate them indefinitely. Whenever I see another person who even slightly resembles that dude, I will instinctively assume the worst.

Which may or may not be fair.

But, frankly, who gives a shit? It's like this: We're hardwired to make quick generalizations about the people we encounter, based upon the observable qualities they present. And sometimes those generalizations are inaccurate, leading us to misjudge people.

While it's unlikely we'll ever stop stereotyping, it's useful to develop the discipline of routinely challenging one's preconceived notions of people.

Even while you leave open the possibility that your initial impressions are accurate.

And that's because no matter what stereotype a person fits, good or bad, assholes are everywhere. And, apparently, those assholes hate it when you wash your windshield while driving in front of them.

Which is exactly what I'll do
Every time
I see dudes like them
Driving behind me.

Be Happy Always

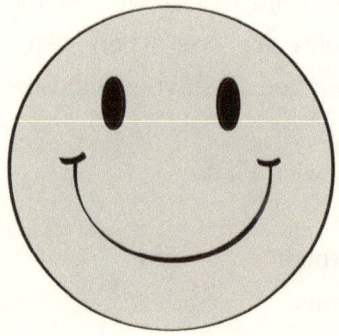

EXCESSIVELY HAPPY PEOPLE annoy the shit out of me. Especially at restaurants.

"Hi! My name is Meagan, and I'll be taking care of you."

Crap. Here we go.

"So, how's everyone doing today? Everyone doing great? Is this your first time here? Yes? Awesome! Well, welcome. We are soooo happy to have you!"

Meagan beams as though she's just found her new BFF.

"How about we get you started with some of our famous bacon-wrapped scallops? Soooo good. They're my personal favorite. That would be awesome, right?"

Sure, Meagan. That would be awesome.

It goes on like this. The entire time. And I can't get the hell out of there fast enough. Part of it's temperament; I just can't stomach that stuff. The other part is training.

During those portions of my Naval Academy summers—spent under the tutelage of a retired Navy captain determined to mold me into the quintessence of Navy officership—I received mandatory instruction in fine dining.

In addition to choking down rare steaks and dry martinis, I learned the important subtleties of good service while taking a tour of some of the nicest restaurants in Washington, DC.

Foremost, neither a host nor server ever shared his name or attempted to ingratiate himself to patrons through happy chitchat.

"I don't give a damn who you are or what your name is," the captain would say of the restaurant's staff. "I just expect you to do your job."

And that job entailed the staff's intuitively sensing a diner's tastes, based upon only a limited number of cues.

For example, at one of the captain's favorite places, the very moment he finished his first martini, the waiter quietly appeared with a second. The captain hadn't asked for it, but the waiter, having carefully observed him since arriving at the table, knew precisely how he operated when it came to cocktails.

And he was exactly right. *That* is good service.

A good waitstaff also knows how to manage the pace of a meal without requiring any direction. The best example is the removal of dishes from the table. At most US restaurants today, waiters and waitresses take away used plates the instant a diner drops his fork. This, even if other members of the party are still eating.

In the world of fine dining to which the captain exposed me, that would *never* have happened. That's because it is impolite to make anyone at the table feel rushed by clearing any portion of the table before everyone is finished.

All of this seems to be lost upon the Meagans of today's restaurant industry, at least below a certain price point. And, being the prick I am, no matter where I'm eating, it drives me mildly berserk when the restaurant staff departs from the captain's standard of proper service.

My standard.

Which brings me to Robert.

I was back in Michigan for the weekend to catch up with some buddies. Upon landing, I did a quick search online for a Mediterranean restaurant between the airport and my hometown for lunch. I was in a falafel kind of mood.

There was a place right along my route with glowing reviews, so I decided to check it out. As I approached the front door, I could see the restaurant was almost entirely full. That was promising. And as I stepped inside, I was met by the smell of fresh naan baking in an open brick oven.

Also good.

But then, as I stood there congratulating myself on my choice of restaurant, I was greeted—more like *accosted*—by the host.

Robert.

"Hello! Welcome! Good to see you! I am soooo glad you're here!"

He was shouting, enveloping me in a sudden, rapid-fire happiness ambush. He was Meagan on speed.

"My name is Robert! And it is my privilege to be your host today!"

Robert looked to be in his late fifties and of Middle Eastern descent. He was dressed in a burgundy shirt with a loud patterned tie and black pants. Around his neck, arranged over his tie, he wore some sort of gold medallion. It looked as though he'd won an Olympic medal for . . . I don't know, being annoying.

"Is this your first time with us?" Robert asked me.

I'd learned a long time ago to say no, no matter what, to dodge the question. Because if you say yes, people like Robert will want to know where you're from and your whole goddamned life story. And then they'll want to tell you theirs.

I have no patience for any of that.

I'd been there before, I told him.

"That's wonderful!" Robert said. "Well, welcome back. Let's get you situated, so you can enjoy some amazing food and wonderful service."

He then walked me to a table halfway between the front door and kitchen. From there, I was safely out of Robert's clutches, but still able to observe him as he ambushed other patrons while they entered the restaurant. A steady stream of people arrived, all greeted by a shouting Robert. Standing at the podium just inside the entrance, he was like Liberace at the piano . . . aggressively, flamboyantly happy.

When a young couple arrived, the two were met with, "Oh, my *gosh* . . . look at those smiles! Just look at those, would you? They light up the entire room! Fantastic . . ."

When he wasn't accosting arriving customers, Robert was either working the room or giving orders to the restaurant staff in a combination of French and Arabic. That made me think he was North African. As I sat and observed, two things became apparent.

First, Robert ran a tight ship.

The kitchen staff was in constant motion, as were the waiters, all of whom looked and sounded to be family members. The young guy who waited on me was courteous and efficient. It was obvious he'd been well trained. And the falafel was incredible, some of the best I'd ever had.

None of that happened by accident. Robert had high standards and held his people to them. I respected that.

Second, as much as Robert's over-the-top happiness made me want to vomit, I had to admit it seemed genuine.

He really was happy.

Maybe he'd come to the US as a refugee, fleeing some war. Or maybe he just felt life had dealt him a good hand, and he was grateful for it. Whatever the case, there was no part of his interaction with customers or staff that seemed forced or feigned.

That was just Robert.

I noticed he said the same thing to all patrons as they departed: "Be happy, always!"

Which, of course, is delusional. No one is *that* happy. Even happy people.

The next morning, I took off for a run on the trail that loops around my old hometown. It's incredible—exceptionally well constructed and maintained. And it was just past peak fall colors in Western Michigan. Ideal running conditions.

The full trail makes a six-mile loop, and you can add an optional two-mile loop if you circumnavigate an adjoining lake. I thought I'd start with six miles and see how I was feeling. Turned out I was feeling great.

Until, that is, about five miles in, when the trail suddenly ended on some back road out in the middle of nowhere. I must have zoned out and missed a turn.

Rather than backtrack, I decided to navigate my way back to town. And my six-mile run quickly turned into a half-marathon. But, instead of getting pissed about it, I found myself repeating, like a mantra, "Be happy, always . . . Be happy, always . . ."

Damn you, Robert!

And thank you, because, surprisingly, it helped.

To paraphrase the song by AJR, I wasn't happy about missing a turn and subjecting my shins to an additional hour of abuse.

But, I had to admit, I was way less sad.

Nonetheless, the question remains: What would my mentor, the captain, have thought about Robert, his restaurant, and his gushing, in-your-face happiness?

Probably not much.

Likely, he would have called the cops and had Robert arrested. Robert is not the captain's kind of guy. Nor is his restaurant the captain's kind of place. And that's fine.

Me?

I'd definitely go back.

Not for a dose of Robert's ridiculous happiness.

But for the falafel.

Definitely the falafel.

Obsessive-Compulsive Superpower

I WANTED TO choke the guy on the riding mower.

There he was, zigzagging across his lawn, creating asymmetric rows, oblivious to the chaos he was sowing in the universe.

He looked about sixty. Recently retired. The yard he was mowing sat across the street from my office's parking lot in a somewhat affluent area, and it surrounded an otherwise well-kept two-story house.

I'd walked out to the parking lot to retrieve something from my car. It was just after one o'clock on a perfect late-summer afternoon. The sun was shining. It was warm, but not excessively so.

Sitting as I do in an over-air-conditioned office most of the day,

I'd decided to take a few minutes to linger in the parking lot to soak it in. I don't spend nearly enough time outside, and the sound of the riding mower had caught my attention. I'd walked, for no particular reason, to the far side of the parking lot to check it out.

It's part of the male condition. We're instinctively drawn to the sound of heavy equipment, power tools, and mowers. Plus, mowing has always been my thing. It was the one household chore I consistently owned while growing up.

My dad had started me mowing in about the fifth or sixth grade. Once I got over the noise and bulk of the mower, I came to appreciate the transformative effect it produced not only on the lawn, but also the whole house. It made the entire property look better, if done correctly.

And by that, I mean straight, even rows; sharp edges; a clean-swept sidewalk and driveway. A well-cut lawn can elevate an entire neighborhood, no matter how modest, while a poorly mowed one can drag down even the swankiest.

Like this guy was doing with his thoughtless, half-assed, minimal effort.

Yes, I'm sensitive to these things. I used to yell at my siblings for walking on the grass.

My grass.

And it drove me crazy that our dog would shit all over the backyard, even though that was exactly what the dog was supposed to do. The yard was my canvas, and the precise, uniform rows I mowed into it was my art. The dog shit was a blight. Plus, it required that I take a shovel and a little bucket around the yard to pick it up before I mowed. And, of course, I'd always miss a pile, which I'd discover only after I'd run over it with the mower.

And then I'd have dog shit all mashed into the treads of the mower wheels. And I'd have to find a stick and try to scrape it out. And I'd never get all of it, which made the garage smell like dog shit for a week after I put the mower away.

But anyway.

I continued watching from the parking lot as the barbarian on the riding mower finished his lawn. He completed his last swerving row and then drove the mower straight into a little shed in his backyard.

A moment later, he was backing out of his driveway in a silver Lexus. He gave me a quick wave as he drove past, and I waved back, grudgingly, assuming he was off to sabotage a power grid or commit some other act that would further tip the world into a state of entropy.

I mean, just look at that lawn, for Chrissake!

It's been suggested that I'm a little uptight, and as I walked back to my office, thoroughly disgusted, I caught myself.

Maybe I care *too* much about straight rows. Or that books on a shelf be arranged in descending order of height from left to right. Or that belts and shoes match in precisely the same shade and color. Or that the bottom edges of a towel hang in perfect alignment on the rack.

I keep small handheld levels in both my upstairs desk drawer and in the cupboard at my downstairs bar. Why? Because in both places there are pictures hanging on the wall that inexplicably tip themselves crooked about once a week. I can feel it when it happens, and it drives me freaking crazy.

None of this happens by choice. I'm just wired this way.

Which poses an interesting question: Is my need for order a superpower or a curse? If, in fact, I choked the guy on the riding mower into submission, forcing him to mow only straight rows from now on, would I be doing the world a service? Or would I be presenting the world with evidence of my own mania?

I turned to the National Institutes of Health—the NIH—for insights.

Probably the most fitting descriptor of this condition is obsessive-compulsive disorder, or OCD. According to the NIH, OCD, as the name implies, combines an obsession and a corresponding compulsion in a manner that produces undesirable thoughts or behaviors in the person who possesses them.

Among the common obsessions giving rise to the disorder is a need to have things symmetrical or perfectly arranged.

Okay.

And one of the typical associated compulsions is a predisposition for precisely and meticulously arranging objects.

Uh-oh. That sounds a little too familiar.

Clearly, I have strong obsessive-compulsive tendencies. But nothing, I think, that rises to the level of disorder. Yes, I annoy the shit out of my family with my maniacal insistence on straightly hung towels, precisely level pictures, and a thousand other things. But I'm able to get out of bed in the morning, leave the house, and be a generally productive human being.

Maybe even an exceptional one.

See, the flip side to having a strong need for order and symmetry—when you're not busy annoying people, at least—is that you get put in charge of stuff. Like, all the time.

At seventeen, I was the youngest recruit in my Navy boot camp company. There were ninety of us, and the drill instructors were required to designate a recruit chief petty officer, the recruit who'd nominally be in charge whenever they weren't around.

My grandfather, a thirty-year Navy veteran, had advised me the best thing I could do to make it through basic training with the least amount of pain was to keep my head down and mouth shut. Fly under the radar, he'd said. Do not draw attention to yourself. Do exactly what you're told and nothing else.

Made sense. And that's exactly what I set out to do.

The problem was, given my obsessive-compulsive tendencies, I was a little too good at doing what I was told.

For starters, you had to make your bed with a ruler every morning. Every fold, crease, and corner had to meet a precise standard. Most guys found it infuriating. I found it liberating.

It all made perfect sense to me.

The same was true of putting on a uniform. From skivvies to boots, there was a prescribed, correct way of doing everything. And when those procedures were properly followed, the result was a clean, crisp, orderly appearance.

Brilliant!

Even with my shaved head, I looked fantastic. Which, of course, resulted in my being selected as the recruit chief petty officer. And it put in motion a series of events that continues to present day.

I've been tapped to lead everything from a Naval Academy regiment to a maintenance department; from reserve units of varying size to manufacturing businesses, juries, classrooms, and a myriad of other organizations and entities in between. You name it, and someone's probably tried to put me in charge of it.

Whether I was actually qualified to lead any of them is debatable, but that's beside the point. I always *looked* the part. A wonderful—and dangerous—thing.

So, superpower or curse?
I suppose that all depends
On whether you're the guy on the riding mower
Or the guy standing across the street
Wanting to choke him
Just to make the neighborhood
And the world
A better place.

A Ref Goes Viral

ALEX KEMP WENT VIRAL.

Normally a bad thing for an NFL referee, I assume. If a ref's performance is extraordinary enough to capture the web's imagination, it probably isn't for reasons that would make a fan want to buy him a beer.

Far better is for an official to be unremarkable.

Impartial, efficient, and professional? Yes. Memorable? No.

In a well-run game, we'll remember the long balls, the goal line stands, the runs that broke loose. And we'll completely ignore how quickly the ball was returned to the line of scrimmage between plays, the minor scuffles that were broken up, and the sideline conversations held with coaches to determine whether penalties would be accepted or declined.

The smooth management of the administrative matters necessary to keep the game moving—we'll take all that for granted. We won't attribute any positive outcome to the work of a referee. But we'll blame him for all sorts of negative outcomes, both real and imagined.

Mostly, we just want refs to get the hell out of the way and *let them play*. We don't care who they are or where they came from.

Referees have long dressed in the same black-and-white stripes and spoken in the same clipped monotone to remove any element of individuality. Sure, you get the occasional Ed Hochuli, whose massive biceps made him instantly recognizable. But the average ref is a nameless, faceless number. It's all very *1984*, which is exactly the way we fans want it.

And then there was Kemp.

Who turned an otherwise forgettable moment in a Sunday game between the Lions and Seahawks into one of the most talked-about sports highlights in recent memory.

The Seahawks quarterback, Geno Smith, had just overthrown receiver Tyler Lockett by a wide margin due to an apparent miscommunication. Whatever the reason, by rule, it was intentional grounding.

Referee Alex Kemp switched on his mic to make the call. "Intentional grounding," he began, moving his hands in a downward, diagonal chopping motion. "Offense, number seven. Ten-yard penalty..."

But, before he could finish, Smith stepped directly in front of him—quite rudely, by any decent person's standards—to argue the call.

In response, Kemp, unperturbed, and without switching off his mic, calmly informed Smith, "I'm talking to America here. Excuse me."

In other words, *Pipe down, son. The grown-ups are talking.*

Kemp then continued. "Ten-yard penalty and a loss of down. Second down."

As he finished rendering the verdict, the cameras cut to the

Seahawks' sideline, where Coach Pete Carroll was losing his fucking mind. The juxtaposition was striking—and made Kemp's unbothered comment all the more exquisite.

Commentator Greg Olsen immediately judged it "the best line I've ever heard out of an official."

And perhaps it was.

For those of us who've never spent time on an NFL field or sideline, all we know of an official's body of work in this area is what we've heard from the stands or on television. By that measure, Kemp's comment stands out, if only because it represents a very small sample size.

Refs don't usually say stuff like that. Not into a microphone, at least.

But I also think it was of sufficient enough quality to merit a place in the broader canon of all-time memorable comebacks.

We humans love a good zinger, after all. Mostly because so few of us can pull one off.

Like when George lamented to Jerry in *Seinfeld*'s "The Comeback" episode, saying he'd come up with the perfect retort—jerk store!—to a coworker who'd insulted him, but only after the moment of insult had long passed.

A missed opportunity. That's how it usually happens.

Rare indeed is the person who can conjure exactly the right words, at exactly the right moment, to put some asshole back in his or her place.

Winston Churchill was expert at it.

"Mr. Churchill, you are drunk!" lashed a female member of Parliament with whom he'd been arguing during a dinner party.

"And you, madam, are ugly," Churchill shot back. "But I shall be sober tomorrow."

Certainly, Churchill was a highly accomplished verbal jouster, given his long career as a politician and writer. That helped. But so, too, did his towering intellect.

Let's face it: IQ figures prominently in a person's ability to stick a good comeback. And it bears remembering that most NFL referees have day jobs. They're accomplished professionals in a variety of fields. Hochuli was an attorney and the founding partner of a law firm. Kemp is a business owner.

These are not intellectually bereft people. That may have explained, in part, Kemp's ability to meet the Geno Smith moment so perfectly.

But there's more to it.

A good comeback has to be spontaneous. Never contrived.

During a 1988 vice presidential debate between Dan Quayle and Lloyd Bentsen, Quayle, often criticized for his lack of experience, made the mistake of comparing his time in Congress to that of President John F. Kennedy. "I have as much experience in Congress as Jack Kennedy did when he sought the presidency," he said.

Bentsen, a longtime friend of the late president, pounced. "Senator, you're no Jack Kennedy," he countered, uttering words that still endure in today's political lexicon.

It was truly an epic zinger.

But also well rehearsed, it turned out. Bentsen had test-driven the line during mock debates, which, for me, totally diminishes the achievement.

Now, I don't know if Alex Kemp stood in front of his bathroom mirror the morning of the Lions-Seahawks game and repeated to himself, "I'm talking to America here . . . I'm talking to America here . . ." and then set out to manufacture some episode in which he could employ the line.

But I highly doubt it.

He was there to officiate, not seek favor with spectators by doing material. His comment, with Geno Smith yapping in his face, seemed genuine, completely in the moment.

And dammit! It was funny. That's another key ingredient in the truly memorable comeback.

Kemp's line was clever, for sure, but also delivered deadpan, with the skill and timing of a professional stand-up. It made you laugh, and that's what separates a comeback like Kemp's from the pedestrian, fuck-you variety.

The other thing I found brilliant about Kemp's "talking to America" remark was the way it aligned, albeit briefly, the referee with the viewing public. In that moment, he was talking to us. Not Pete Carroll. Not the guys in the booth. Not Roger Goodell or NFL officials back in New York.

Kemp was having a conversation directly with us fans.

That being the case, *Who the hell did Geno Smith think he was?* Asshole.

When Kemp shut him down, it seemed justice had been served, an immensely satisfying thing.

I hope that at some point after the Lions-Seahawks game Kemp took a moment to reflect upon his magnificent achievement, and to appreciate how, in a single moment, he had captured the kind of glory that so often eludes George Costanza and the rest of us.

He totally fucking zinged a guy—who deserved it—for the whole world to see.

And, in doing so, became the Winston Churchill of NFL referees.

If only for a Sunday.

Nicely done, Kempy. We're proud of you.

Breach of Commuter Etiquette

BACK-TO-SCHOOL TIME MEANS the days of my leisurely summertime commute are over.

The morning drive is once again crowded.

And annoying as shit.

The adults are bad enough. I mean, why do parents drive their kids to school? Make them ride the damn bus! Even though that's the last thing any kid wants to get caught doing after about the eighth grade.

I sure as hell didn't.

Still, I spent plenty of frigid Michigan mornings standing at the bus stop, my feathered hair frozen neatly into place because I refused to wear a hat. I'd rather risk hypothermia than have messed-up hair, thank you.

Even worse than the swollen ranks of parents on the road at seven thirty in the morning are the high school kids. For starters, who are these entitled punkasses whose parents bought them cars the second they turned sixteen? Probably the same ones who'd been driving them to school their entire lives so their asses never had to touch a puke-green vinyl bus seat.

God forbid.

I didn't get a car when I turned sixteen.

Yeah, my wife did.

And so did my daughter.

But that's beside the point.

So, you have all these kids driving themselves to school, who could, or maybe *should*, be riding the bus, which contributes to the traffic-volume problem. But that's only one side of the shitty-commute coin.

The other side is the behavior of said drivers and the resulting stress it imposes upon what, only days before, had been a mostly pleasant drive.

Allow me to offer an example.

Everyone knows about the Zipper, right? That's the maneuver by which two streams of traffic merge, either at an intersection or on-ramp, with cars in the merging streams proceeding in alternating sequence. One car from one stream goes, then one car from the other.

One car.

We have such an intersection in our little downtown area. It gets a lot of traffic because it feeds the main artery out of town, into the city, and to the suburbs beyond. It also sits on one of two main routes to the high school. So, from August until June, you find a mix of work and school commuters traversing the intersection. And it's a rather awkward one. It's triangular, with the bulk of traffic meeting at a T where the two main roads feeding the intersection combine.

Now, I don't know if the Zipper gets taught in driver's ed. It's been a few years. But it's intuitive, and not really something you need to be taught.

If, that is, you were raised in a society that values the rule of law, by parents that instilled in you the correct moral code and some decent fucking manners.

The high school kid I encountered at the intersection had not been so raised. How do I know?

Because this little prick totally thumbed his nose at the Zipper.

Everything was moving along just fine. There were probably thirty cars on each road approaching the intersection. One by one, each driver on either side patiently waited his turn, gave a momentary tap on the brakes at the stop sign, and then proceeded behind the car that had just exited the adjacent lane.

When it came my turn at the stop sign, the driver of the black MDX to my right shot a quick glance in my direction to double-check that I was yielding and then proceeded through the intersection. I hit the gas to fall in behind her, thereby forming another interlocking tooth in the Zipper.

At least, that's what was supposed to have happened.

But about the time I got my two front tires beyond the stop sign, I noticed the white Nissan Maxima behind the MDX right on its back bumper, having followed it through the intersection.

As I hit the brakes to avoid a collision, I saw the kid behind the wheel, who was all of sixteen with shaggy brown hair hanging in his face, leaning forward into the steering wheel, grinning.

Grinning! That sonofabitch. He knew exactly what he was doing. He knew about the Zipper, and he didn't give a shit.

So then there was one long, two-car tooth in the Zipper. Awkward.

But worse, one of the most important norms of decency that governs the safe and orderly flow of people from their homes to their offices each day had been flagrantly violated. That was unacceptable.

And I intended to do something about it.

I shot through the intersection after the kid, intent upon punishing him somehow. Ideal would have been to whip out one of those old-school Hawaii Five-O–style sirens and put it on my dashboard. I'd give the kid a menacing look and gesture for him to pull over. Of course, I have no idea what would have happened then, but ten bucks says the kid would have pissed himself.

Or something.

But, alas, no siren. So I did the next best thing I could think of: I got *right* on his ass. I mean right on his ass.

Now, I know what you're thinking. *Real mature, there, Dan.* And not particularly safe, either.

Fair point.

But hear me out. I'm a former Naval aviator, and I've been trained to manage such situations.

In formation flying, you learn all about relative motion. The pilot of the lead aircraft is charged with maintaining a steady platform, while the person flying wing is tasked with making whatever control inputs necessary to hold the same position relative to lead. And the way you do that when you're in the wing aircraft is to pick out a couple of reference points on the lead and hold them in exactly the same relative positions.

For example, as long as the top rivet connecting the wing to the fuselage stays on a direct line extending from the canopy handle above it, you'll be in the correct position.

So, as I'm driving behind the punk in the Maxima, I pick a spot on his trunk and line it up with the top of the raised piece of metal where my left windshield wiper arm meets the blade.

And it works beautifully.

I see the kid shooting nervous glances at me in his rearview mirror, his eyes darting back and forth.

That's right, asshole. I see you. I know what you did.

We go on like this for about a mile.

Of course, at any moment, the kid could decide he's had enough and jam on his brakes. I'd immediately rear-end him, and it would be entirely my fault. But this kid needed to learn a lesson.

We reach the point at which I have to turn right to get on the expressway. The high school is another half mile up the road in the same direction in which we'd been traveling. I move over into the turning lane and accelerate.

For a moment, I'm even with the kid. I look over to give him one final, menacing glare. And, as I look, I see the kid's mouth moving. He's laughing, waving his right hand around, having a raucous conversation with someone.

That's right, he's on the goddamn phone. And was likely oblivious to the punishment I'd been meting out over the course of the last mile.

He hadn't learned a damn thing.

So, I guess it will be up to you, fellow commuters, to teach this kid his lesson. Hopefully before he graduates and becomes the next Pharma Bro

Or Disgraced Crypto Financier

Or, worse:

Member of Congress.

Your Fine!

I'M WALKING DOWN a sidewalk in Omaha, Nebraska.

A guy passes me with a T-shirt that says, *Shut Up Liver Your Fine!* in big letters. The fine print suggests it came from a bar in Cabo San Lucas, Mexico.

That's awesome! is my first reaction.

I can picture myself parked on a stool in some crappy Mexican bar. I'm knocking back bottom-shelf Mexican tequila, having exactly that conversation with my own liver. I mean, who hasn't had that conversation at some point in his drinking career?

Whoever came up with this T-shirt is pretty genius, for sure.

But also grammatically inept.

My brain seizes on the wonderful humor and creativity captured in this T-shirt—for about two seconds. And then immediately goes to work correcting the grammatical errors.

Let's see . . . the first and most egregious mistake is the use of the word *your*.

What's required here is the contraction for *you are*, or *you're*, not the second-person possessive pronoun. That's a huge pet peeve of mine.

Okay. What else?

This is a declarative statement addressed to an animate object, the personified liver. As such, *liver* should be offset by commas, as in, "Shut up, *liver*, you're fine!"

But we aren't finished.

"Shut up," with an implied *you* as the subject, and "You're fine," could stand alone as distinct sentences.

And perhaps they should.

In my estimation, it would add greater emphasis to the message if written as two separate sentences.

"Shut up, liver. You're fine!"

See? I like that.

And what about the exclamation point? I agree that at least one is appropriate. But what about two?

I certainly don't subscribe to the overuse of exclamation points, or any form of punctuation. But would it be useful here?

"Shut up, liver! You're fine!"

I could imagine myself getting pretty animated in such a conversation with my liver. So, yes, I think I'd go for the second exclamation point. Feel free to disagree.

So, there you have it. I should be on a plane to Cabo to share the grammatically correct version of the expression with the bar owner, so he can make the necessary adjustments in his next run of T-shirts.

Am I right? Who's with me?

Of course, this raises an important question: What the fuck is the matter with me?

Why do I do this? I can't even help it. My brain just does it. Instinctively. Automatically. And for what purpose? To what end?

A few days later, I'm boarding a flight to Atlanta. There's a young family behind me. Dad, Mom, and two little kids. As we walk down the jetway, I pick up on their conversation. The mom is in teacher mode, explaining some newly discovered phenomenon to the kids.

"That's right," she says. "If you work for the airlines, you get to fly for free."

"Oooohhhh," the kids say.

Kids love freebies. Especially when it comes to domestic air travel, apparently.

"Yeah," Mom continues, "it's a French benefit."

Wait. What did she just say?

I know she meant *fringe* benefit. But it sounded like she said *French*. I'm sure I misheard her.

"Especially for pilots," Mom says. "They get all kinds of French benefits. Like sitting in first class."

I hadn't misheard her. She'd meant to say French. Wow.

What's my move here? I'm thinking. Report the mother to child protective services? Because the kids' brains are highly malleable. If they're taught to believe there's such a thing as French benefits, what long-term impact might that have on their cognitive development?

To me, it's tantamount to giving them a pack of Marlboro Reds and saying, "Light up, kids!"

What kind of life will these kids have? How will they turn out?

Likely, they'll end up like the porn shop owner just west of Columbia, Missouri. About twenty miles west of town, you start seeing signs for Passion's Adult Superstore.

That's right: *Passion's*.

You already see the problem, don't you?

Why use the possessive form?

Is Passion a person?

Did Joe-The-Investment-Banker quit Wall Street to set up shop in rural Missouri under the alias *Joe Passion*?

If so, *Passion's*, the possessive, makes sense.

But I'm afraid that's not the case.

Having driven this stretch of I-70 numerous times and studied Passion's half dozen billboards, I've come to a different conclusion. *Passion's*, with the apostrophe-s, is intended to be plural.

Plural!

Which is a crime against humanity.

Since when did it become acceptable to move from singular to plural via an apostrophe-s? All you need is the s, dammit! Isn't that what we were all taught in kindergarten?

But this apostrophe-s thing is everywhere. I saw it written in a news article not too long ago. *"There are too many car's on the road,"* the resident reported.

I mean ...

I mean ...

I don't know what I mean. Maybe it's just me.

And, in fairness, I've gotten my grammar and word usage wrong from time to time. I've been known to use words just because I like the sound of them, not because I fully understand their meaning. I did that once in a final exam I'd written for my western civilization class at the Naval Academy.

And was rightly crucified by the professor as a result.

And, certainly, if my eighth-grade English teacher were to grade this essay, or any other I've written in the past ten years, she'd likely give it a C-plus at best.

That's because I'm fond of sentence fragments and the occasional f-bomb. But I use such things knowingly and by design.

I *know* I'm breaking the rules.

Is the same true of the bar owner in Cabo? The mother boarding the flight in Atlanta? The proprietor of Passion's?

I don't know. And it probably doesn't matter.

I suppose we have more important things to worry about in this world. Even if our nation's weakening grasp of its own language causes me tremendous mental anguish.

I should just Shut Up.

So, hey . . .
If Your Fine,
Then I guess I should be fine, too.
(Even though I'm not fine.
Not fine at all.)

Condo Outlaw

I AM HIGHLY RITUALISTIC. Especially in the morning. And I wake up ridiculously early to protect my morning ritual, no matter what.

Even on vacation.

We go to the same place in Florida every year. After a quiet hour of coffee drinking and reading on the lanai, I go for a longish run.

And I don't wear a shirt when I run.

That's not what you do on vacation.

Now, I'm certainly not turning heads on the beach a la Daniel Craig in *Casino Royale*. But I don't think I'm embarrassing myself, either, running the streets of a South Florida beach town sans shirt.

And immediately after my run, I like to jump in the ocean.

There is no better way to cool down. I occasionally swim out to a buoy about three hundred yards offshore.

And try not to think about sharks.

During flight school, instructors would sometimes let you make a low pass over Pensacola Beach on the way back to home field.

To check out the talent, as they'd say.

And it wasn't uncommon to see a shiver of sand sharks mulling uncomfortably close to a group of unaware swimmers. The vision of sand sharks always creeps into my head at some point during my swim, and I wind up hauling ass all the way back to the beach.

But that's fine.

Then, after a quick open-air rinse-off, I head back to the room for more coffee and something to eat.

The complex where we stay has a loose no-shoes-no-shirt-no-problem policy, so I feel perfectly comfortable walking around in my shorts and flip-flops. That's the way it's supposed to be on a beach vacation, right?

I do enjoy my morning vacation ritual, but it required some tweaking this year.

Fort Myers Beach is our usual place. But, unfortunately, it was all but leveled by Hurricane Ian. So, we relocated to Clearwater.

We're staying in a high-rise condo building, set back from the beach about a quarter mile. Among the building's residents, those with an AARP card far outnumber those without. There are signs everywhere directing occupants to wear beach cover-ups and footwear in all common areas.

No shoes, no shirt, big problem, apparently. Senior Floridians' love of rules is well established, as Jerry Seinfeld observed of residents of Del Boca Vista in 1998.

Still, I assumed there had to be a loophole for early-morning runners not wanting to wear T-shirts. But, in case not, I exited the building the first morning, shirtless, via the stairwell.

No one ever uses the stairs in a place like this, I figured.

I got out of the building without encountering anyone and proceeded on my run. But, when I returned, I found the door to the stairwell locked from the inside, and I was unable to get in.

So I took the elevator. And, of course, I immediately encountered a retiree who wryly observed, "Looks like someone stole your shirt."

Okay, dude. Message received.

I don't want any trouble here.

Of course, my other problem was the distance between the condo and the beach. In Fort Myers, it's literally steps from our door. Here, it's a haul. And I have no interest in making that haul after a run in the subtropical humidity.

But the pool, on the other hand, is right out the back door. So the next day, I placed my towel and shirt on one of the poolside chairs before heading out for my run. It was about six thirty. When I returned an hour later, I showered off, jumped in the pool, and paddled around for half an hour. It was quite nice.

I did notice, on the list of rules covering the entire wall next to the pool, that it apparently didn't open until eight o'clock. Again, I thought there might be a loophole for early-morning runners.

So, the next morning, I once again walked through the little gate onto the pool deck and staged my towel and T-shirt. But, when I went to leave, I found the gate had locked upon my entrance. I couldn't get out now. Through the gate, at least.

My only option then was to jump the wall. And hope some overzealous senior-citizen resident didn't see me and call the cops.

I went on my run, hoping for the best. Then, when I returned, the security guard at the front entrance stopped me. "Was that you in the pool yesterday morning?" she asked me. "I could see someone in the pool on my camera, and it looked like you."

Whew. She didn't mention the wall jumping.

Yes, I told her. I was in the pool.

"You can't be in the pool until eight o'clock," she said, sternly. "That's the rule."

Well, I said, I didn't realize that until I was already in the pool.

And why not get in the pool? As Maverick explained to Viper in the original *Top Gun*, I had the opportunity, so I took it.

Made sense to me.

"How'd you even get in there in the first place?" she asked.

I walked right in, I said.

"Well, that gate's supposed to be locked," she said, displeased. "I'll have to talk to my night security manager about that."

Yes, you should do that.

And stop bothering me about it.

Now, in fairness to her, I'm sure the condo board president is all over her ass on a regular basis about enforcing these rules.

Peace be with you, security lady.

The next morning, I readied my towel and T-shirt as before, but without actually entering the pool area. I reached over the wall I'd jumped the previous morning and dropped them onto a chair on the pool deck below. And I timed my departure to return just after eight o'clock. That way, I could enjoy my post-run swim without breaking any rules.

I took off running and returned as planned.

This time, I encountered the security guard as she was walking away from the pool area toward the front gate.

Is the pool open for business? I asked her, trying to exude a no-hard-feelings-about-yesterday vibe.

"Yes," she said curtly. She was clearly still annoyed with me.

And then I noticed she was holding my towel and T-shirt.

"Are these yours?" she asked me.

I told her yes. Those are indeed mine.

"Well, how did they get into the pool area? I *told* you you couldn't be in there before eight o'clock," she said.

I wasn't in the pool area before eight, I explained. I dropped them over the wall.

She seemed confused.

"But you can't be in the pool area before *eight*," she said again, starting to get angry.

I *wasn't* in the pool area before eight, I repeated.

"Well, your *stuff* can't be in the pool area before eight, *either*," she said with finality.

Shit, lady. You're exhausting me.

Stepping back, I'm reminded of a couple things.

First, I'm really no different than the people on condo boards throughout Florida who set these ridiculous rules. I enjoy rituals. They bring order and comfort to my life. Rituals require rules, and I have plenty of my own, some of which others may find absurd.

Like my wife and daughter.

Second, I should be happy I'm still young enough to laugh at these crazy condo rules. That point was driven home when I read the last rule on the sign at the pool.

Incontinent persons without bladder or bowel control are not permitted in the pool.

Yikes.

At least I still have bladder and bowel control.

For now.

You win, security lady. You won't find me or my stuff

Or my bladder

Or my bowels

Anywhere near the pool before eight o'clock.

Ever again.

You're welcome.

Panera Bread Hell

"SORRY IF I'M talking funny, but I just got my tongue pierced."

The teenage girl behind the counter spoke as though she had a mouth full of cold oatmeal. And she apparently wanted me to understand why.

My brain struggled to process the comment. I'd been awake since two o'clock in the morning, so anything would have been a struggle.

But a pierced tongue?

I mean...

What do you even say to that?

It must have been obvious to the girl that I was struggling.

"Seriously," she said. "It was just, like, two hours ago."

Did she want me to be sympathetic? Impressed? I was mostly disgusted. And totally perplexed as to how I had crossed into this hellscape the moment I'd walked into the Panera Bread in Council Bluffs, Iowa.

The pierced-tongue girl was only part of it.

I had stood the early watch in the Global Operations Center at US Strategic Command, just down the road from Council Bluffs at Offutt Air Force Base. This was my Navy Reserve annual training.

Rather than jet off to Spain or Hawaii or Croatia, I'd instead driven through cornfields to Omaha, Nebraska. All the rooms on base had been occupied, so the Navy had put me up at a Holiday Inn in Council Bluffs, just across the Missouri River from downtown Omaha.

Tired as I was, I had zero ambition to do anything interesting for dinner. I saw the Panera off the expressway and decided it would do.

Two older couples had preceded me into the store. It appeared they were all together, and I'd guess they were in their early eighties. Upon entering, the group broke formation. One couple went to one register, and one went to the other. I stood in line between the two registers, figuring I'd follow whichever couple finished ordering first.

And from that vantage point, I was able to take in both conversations.

"Let's see," started the gentleman on the right. "I want the chicken sandwich, but only half. How much is that?"

The girl behind the register started to explain that half sandwiches were only an option when paired with soup or salad as a combo.

"Soup?" interrupted the gentleman. "I don't want any soup. Who said anything about soup?"

Over at the left register, the lady was trying to order a salad.

"Well, can you show me the different sizes?" she asked. "I don't want to pay for the big one if the small one is enough."

The girl behind the register then went somewhere in back and came out with two plastic bowls to show the lady.

"How much is this one?" the lady asked, holding the smaller of the two bowls.

Meanwhile, back at the right register, the gentleman was struggling with the choice of sides.

"Do you want a baguette, chips, or an apple as your side?" the girl asked him.

"Baguette?" he asked. "You mean bread?"

Yes, the girl replied. She meant bread.

"Is it toasted?" the gentleman asked. "I don't want anything toasted."

But before the girl could answer, the lady next to the gentleman chimed in. "He'll have the chips."

"Chips?" the guy replied, indignantly. "What *kind* of chips?"

And it kept going on like that at both registers. For a while.

Presented with too many choices, these octogenarians repeatedly took the teenagers down successive rabbit holes to thoroughly exhaust every possible menu combination and option before making a decision. At that rate, I figured I wouldn't get my turn to order for another half hour. When I finally did, I shot through my order in ten seconds with the pierced-tongue girl.

Now, I know what you're thinking.

Classy move there, Dan, taking a cheap shot at a group of budget-conscious senior citizens.

That's not it at all. I have three issues here.

The first two concern my long-standing Restaurant Rules.

One, know the menu options in advance and be 90 percent certain what to order before you show up.

Two, if you're not comfortable ordering the most expensive thing on the menu, don't go to that restaurant. Pick a less expensive one.

The third issue deals with one of my primary concerns with getting old: the complete breakdown of situational awareness.

There could have been a line out the door, and these seniors would have been oblivious. They would have kept asking their questions, not the least bit aware of how much of other people's time they were wasting.

I suspect one's concept of time changes in one's later, post-career years. When every day's Saturday, what's the hurry? I get that. What I don't get is the discourtesy of it all.

You, Mister Retiree, may not be in a hurry. But I sure as shit am.

So, can we keep the line moving here, please?

I finally made it to the front of the line, suffered through the conversation with the pierced-tongue girl, and got my Baja Bowl. Then I found a seat in an out-of-the-way corner of the restaurant. After the ordeal at the register, I was in no mood to have any further interaction with anyone. I got about two bites in when the lady a few tables over started shouting into her phone. She was probably ten years younger than the people I'd stood behind at the counter.

Again, I was witnessing a total senior-citizen breakdown of situational awareness. The lady had no idea how loud she was speaking. Nor, likely, did she care.

"Yes!" she said. "Seventy-three dollars."

She'd apparently received a PetSmart gift card from someone and was detailing what she intended to do with the remaining funds on it.

"What?" she semi-shouted. "No, no . . . they're dead! They're all *dead*!"

What the hell is this all about? I thought. It wasn't exactly what you'd expect to hear in a conversation about pet supplies. Not that I wanted to hear any of this, mind you.

She continued. "It was Turtle. I know it was him. He killed them all!"

Excuse me? What was she talking about, some kind of gang-related hit?

Shit was getting *real* in Council Bluffs.

I eventually pieced together that both Turtle and his victims were goldfish. And, under certain circumstances, some goldfish, like Turtle, apparently eat others. This, according to the PetSmart gift card lady. She hadn't found out until it was too late. So, a portion of her remaining gift card funds would go toward replacing her eaten goldfish.

And getting Turtle a separate tank.

The lady continued to shout into her phone, nonstop, the entire time I was there, which wasn't long. I had to get the hell out of there—I was completely wrung out.

Shit.

I don't know which depresses me more, the inevitability of aging and decline, or the thought of spending another week in Council Bluffs, Iowa. Which I'm sure is a lovely town, full of lovely, self-aware people.

Who do *not* hang out

At Panera Bread

At five o'clock

On a Tuesday.

Fred Time

"**MIGHT BE TOUGH** getting around to it this week," he said. "You know... now that we finally got decent golf weather."

Fred, the contractor, was noncommittal.

"And then, of course, I go to Canada for my fishing trip next week."

Maybe he'd get around to resurfacing my deck, and maybe he wouldn't. Fred wasn't about to be pinned down by me. Or anyone.

"Maybe sometime after Father's Day, closer to the end of the month," he offered. "Might be able to get to it then."

It was maddening.

"Of course," he continued, "if you got somebody else ready to do the work, then go right ahead. Won't hurt my feelings."

This wasn't some negotiating ploy on Fred's part. He was totally serious. He'd be just fine if someone else did the work. Fred works on Fred's time—no one else's.

Take it or leave it.

Why, you may wonder, do I put up with this? Three reasons:

One, Fred does excellent work.

Two, he charges very reasonable prices for his excellent work.

And three, do you know how hard it is to find a contractor who does good work at a good price and doesn't totally screw you in the process?

Take your time, Fred.

Of course, I'd love it if you kept a regular schedule. I'd really appreciate it if you'd commit to starting a project on a certain date and then kept that commitment. And it would be great if I didn't have to call you every other day to find out if you still had any intention of doing my project at all.

Yes, that would be very helpful. But I get it: Fred Time.

Even though it frustrates the hell out of me.

See, guys as mechanically inept as I are at the mercy of the Freds of the world. Contractors, mechanics, plumbers . . . whoever. I have to accept that.

All the more reason I tolerate Fred. Or, more accurately, I try to give Fred ample reason to tolerate me. And, if you're Fred, you couldn't be in a better position, could you?

Think about it.

He works by referral only. All his clients come prescreened. No assholes allowed.

How did I make the cut? I know a guy who hired Fred to build his house. He's a Fred A-lister. When I asked him last summer to recommend a contractor for a variety of projects on my house, he immediately suggested Fred.

"He's a little quirky," my friend had said. "But he's the best out there."

A few weeks later, after Fred had played in a couple of golf tournaments and taken a vacation, he showed up at my house, unannounced. I had no idea he was coming.

I went out to the backyard where he and one of his guys were repouring the footings for one of my decks.

"Who are you?" he asked me, visibly perturbed by the interruption.

Um . . . I'm Dan, I said. This is my house.

It was like I was apologizing.

"Oh, well . . . okay," Fred replied, as though my being there was an irritant he'd simply have to accept. I got the message and left him alone.

And I'm glad I did. He did a fantastic job.

In addition to working with only a select number of prescreened clients, Fred only does the projects he wants. After I got to know him a little, I cautiously shared my list of other items with which I wanted his help.

"Nope," he said. "I'm not doing any of that. But check this out..." He pulled his phone out of his pocket and showed me a picture of a huge, fifty-foot-long retaining wall he'd built for what had to be a five- or six-million-dollar house.

It was gorgeous.

"See that?" he asked me. "That's the stuff I'm working on."

In other words, *Don't waste my time with your piddly shit.*

Okay. Sorry, Fred.

And while I have no idea what Fred made on the retaining wall, my friend's house, or any other project, I assume he did well. Besides all the golf and vacations, he drives a newish F-150. You know, one of *those* trucks. One that looks like a simple, working man's truck, but costs twice as much as my corporate-dude Lexus.

Yes, I assume Fred does quite well.

So, to summarize:

Fred works only *when* he wants.

He works only *with whom* he wants.

He works only on *what* he wants.

And he gets paid well to do it.

Game, set, and match.

Me? I can't claim any of those things. I work for The Man.

I work when *he* wants.

With whom *he* wants.

On what *he* wants.

And get paid what *he* decides.

There's nothing I do that is so valuable as to work like Fred.

And that's a little concerning.

Without some sort of differentiated offering, I'm just a commodity.

Well, you say, if you don't like it, do something about it. It's all within your power. Just reinvent yourself. So say the self-help books. And celebrities, like Madonna and J. Lo.

The trouble is, I'm not sure you can just flip a switch and *poof!* become a Fred. That's because Fred himself didn't become a Fred overnight. My guess is he's spent decades mastering his craft, getting progressively better, gathering insights with each new project on what works and what doesn't.

He's figured out, over the course of years, which jobs play best to his core skills and allow his work to stand out. And he's learned, sometimes the hard way, that certain types of clients should be avoided, no matter what they're willing to pay.

That's how Fred became Fred.

So, what's that mean for the rest of us? The non-Freds? I suppose the best any of us can do is find a way to add value.

Whatever the hell that means.

Rock on, Fred. You impress me. And, yes, you infuriate me.

Now, about my deck.

Call me?

Please?

Weirdos at the Y

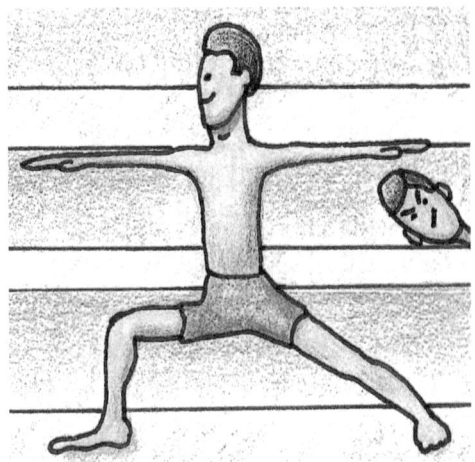

I OPENED THE DOOR to the sauna and squinted through the steam. This was phase five of my Sunday-morning routine.

Coffee. Paper. More coffee. Swim workout at the YMCA. Sauna.

I do enjoy my Sunday mornings.

Except for the weirdos.

We'll get to them in a minute.

The sauna is a relatively new addition to my ritual. I'd been aware of the benefits of immersing oneself in steam for some time. Improved circulation. Lower blood pressure. Healthier skin. What's not to like? But I couldn't figure out where to fit it into my schedule.

Then it hit me one day after an hour in the pool:

I'm already wet. I have a towel. And flip-flops. And the sauna is right on the way to the locker room.

Thus, the sauna became an addendum to my pool routine. And

Sundays are ideal, because I can take my time. I don't like to rush the sauna.

It took me weeks to build the necessary tolerance to really enjoy it. The first time I tried it, my heart rate went through the roof in less than five minutes. I staggered out, panting, unable to catch my breath.

You have to respect the sauna.

Or it will hurt you.

The Korean lady with the dolphin-print aqua socks understands that. I see her in there every time.

She sits perfectly still, legs crossed in the lotus position, eyes closed. It's impressive. She's there when I walk in, and she's still there when I leave. It's like she's been soaking in saunas her entire life.

Perhaps I'm generalizing, but it does seem the Asian cultures are far more advanced when it comes to sauna-going than the West, a trait suggested by my time in Japan, which is a great sauna country. Lots of steam-soaked history there. And while I was there, the Japanese were staunch adherents to proper sauna etiquette.

Americans? Less so.

And that's a problem, because the steam room at my local Y is about the size of a walk-in closet. I stepped into the sauna a couple months ago and took a seat next to a normal-looking guy. I gave him a polite nod as I sat down, which I consider the full extent of acceptable sauna discourse.

You aren't there to chitchat. You're there to think. To contemplate. To breathe. And to sit. Just sit.

Not this guy.

After a couple minutes, he gets up, stands right in front of me, and launches into this full yoga routine. He's warrior-posing. Downward-dogging. Forward-folding. Child-posing.

The whole act.

About six inches in front of me.

And I didn't appreciate that, because you can't bend at the waist more than about fifteen degrees in the sauna without sticking your ass in someone's face.

My face.

Now, I'm no expert, but I have heard of yoga being practiced in high-temperature rooms. It's a thing: Bikram yoga. Maybe that's what this dude was after. But, the whole time I'm thinking, how is this not awkward for this guy? How could he possibly think this was okay?

I eventually managed a curt "excuse me," but it didn't even phase him.

He kept right on downward-dogging.

Thankfully, about the time I was ready to tell him to get the hell away from me, he finished his final pose and left.

I try not to let stuff like that bother me, but it does.

I know, I know. I need to be more like the lady in the aqua socks.

That was especially true this past Sunday morning.

Like I said, I opened the door to the sauna and checked out the seating situation through the fog. It's theater-style in the sauna, with two levels, and it was a full house, except for a single seat in the corner of the bottom row.

On the row above the seat, there was a guy lying flat on his back, knees bent. He was about five eight but, in that position, taking up way more than his fair share of sauna real estate.

So, I took my seat in the row beneath him and started slowly inhaling the steam. I intended to enjoy the experience, as I did every Sunday morning. But suddenly, my quasi-meditative state was broken by the sound of grunting.

Grunting?

I turned around, following the sound. It was the guy behind me, furiously doing crunches. Well, attempting crunches. The guy looked serious. And sounded serious, what with the grunting.

Which strongly suggested, serious or not, that he rarely does crunches.

Maybe he was thinking, I'll have a large pizza and a two-liter

Mountain Dew every night for dinner, but then I'll do crunches in the sauna on Sunday morning. So, you know, it'll all even out. And if it doesn't, it will at least be amusing.

That's conjecture on my part.

But what isn't conjecture is how uncomfortable it is to be in close proximity to anyone farting out a set of crunches. Especially in a sauna. Trust me.

The guy kept at it for a good five minutes, grunting the entire time. When he was finally finished, he lay there, chest heaving, thoroughly exhausted. I turned back around, trying to remember the proper ratio of breaths to chest compressions for CPR. I was convinced a heart attack was a very real possibility for this guy.

He sat up after a couple minutes and looked around at the rest of us. His expression suggested he sought our approval for his noble effort. I, in turn, gave him a look that said, *You're an idiot.*

And then he stood up and walked out.

Now, I make it a habit *not* to comment on our current state of incivility and all that. You know this by now, surely.

But come on, 'Merica!

Yoga in the sauna? Crunches? Some things are simply unacceptable, and we need to do better. Much, much better.

So, thank you in advance, prospective sauna-goers,

For keeping your ass out of my face.

And please do the same for the dolphin-socks lady.

Even though she doesn't seem to mind.

Starstruck by The Wiggles

THE WIGGLES WERE HUGE in my house.

And if you had a preschool-aged kid in the mid-2000s, they were huge in your house, too.

Every day I'd come home and my daughter would be singing along with Anthony, Jeff, Greg, and Murray to one of the group's megahits. Like "Fruit Salad."

Frickin' genius. You had to love these guys.

They were four Aussies who'd gotten together in the early nineties to promote the educational songs they'd written while studying to be preschool teachers. At least, that was the story according to Anthony Field, one of the cofounders.

You may recognize him from his time with The Cockroaches, the Australian pop band.

Or not.

Doesn't matter. What does matter is that The Wiggles created songs and characters that kept kids in a hypnotic trance for thirty minutes every day. So you could get a little peace and quiet.

Unless you were singing along with them, as I usually was.

Those damn songs . . . they stuck. They were like fly paper on your brain. Taylor Swift had nothing on these guys when it came to creating a catchy hook.

That was especially true of "Big Red Car."

The guys would cruise around the Australian countryside in this giant toy car. It was clearly being hauled around on the back of a flatbed, given the way Greg would flail his arms and *not* check his mirrors while he was *supposed* to be driving.

But whatever.

The car made an appearance nearly every episode. It was a Wiggles go-to, so it was no surprise my wife used that particular song to pitch seeing The Wiggles live in concert with our daughter. We were living in Boston, and the group was playing in nearby Worcester.

"Just think, you could see their Big Red Car . . . *in person*," she said.

I wasn't persuaded.

While I enjoyed singing along with the guys on TV, I had zero interest in driving to sit in an arena full of little kids on a Saturday afternoon. Not until I had a kid of my own did I come to understand how much I loathed doing kid stuff.

Like going to a *Wiggles* concert.

"Come on," my wife said. "They'll probably have beer."

Okay. If they have beer.

So, we loaded up our daughter and a bunch of kid gear and snacks the following Saturday and made the drive to the Worcester exhibition hall. As hoped, there was beer. And, as feared, a bunch of screaming preschoolers who couldn't sit still for the freaking life of them.

Many were wearing stuffed dinosaur tails belted around their waists. It was a nod to Dorothy the Dinosaur, one of the more popular Wiggles TV characters. The tails were available for purchase at various kiosks outside the concert hall for the low, low price of fifty bucks or something absurd like that.

My daughter was wearing one, of course.

The kid was ready to party: dinosaur tail on her ass, juice box in one hand, and a squeezy applesauce snack pack in the other.

I noticed there were a handful of other dads in the crowd, some nursing overpriced beers like I was. We were all wearing a look that said, *Let's just get this damn thing over with*. The moms were loosely corralling the kids and getting them pumped up for The Wiggles' impending entrance.

Finally, the lights went down, and the announcer said, "And here they are... from the Land Down Under... Anthony, Greg, Jeff, and Murray... boys and girls... The Wiggles!"

Little-kid screams engulfed the hall.

Yeah, yeah, yeah, I'm thinking. Get it going already.

The far-left corner of the darkened stage was lit up with a spotlight, just as singing started from backstage.

Toot-toot!

Chugga-chugga!

Big Red Car...

Totally predictable. Of course they'd lead with "Big Red Car."

Then, into the spotlight and onto the stage drove Anthony, Greg, Jeff, and Murray.

The Wiggles. In the *actual* Big Red Car.

I paused for a moment to take it all in. The car. The guys. The singing. And, as I did, something weird happened to me.

I felt... delighted. And, strangely, a little starstruck.

How could this be? I thought.

I had no inner child. And I absolutely did not like this kid stuff.

Sure, I believe I'd fairly judged The Wiggles on their creative merits. I respected their work, and I'd given them credit where it was due. But none of that explained the odd feeling of joy that had overcome me.

I spent the rest of the concert belting out every word of every song, right along with the screaming preschoolers. It was a surprisingly good time. And totally unexpected.

It was nearly a week before my daughter and I came down from our Wiggles high. Which may explain, I suppose, how The Wiggles grossed, like, fifty million dollars a year.

Fine with me.

They earned every nickel.

Especially that Saturday afternoon in Worcester.

Thank you, Anthony, Greg, Jeff, and Murray.

Rock on, mates,

Wherever you are.

David Hasselhoff

"**NOPE. NO WAY.** Can't be done."

The group of us gathered in Jeff's room was highly skeptical.

"Bullshit!" Jeff shot back. "Yes, it can. I can totally get him to say it."

The gauntlet had thus been thrown down. Jeff was going to somehow dupe our Naval Academy company officer into saying "David Hasselhoff."

Publicly. With witnesses present.

"You'll see," Jeff said. "Just watch me."

It was a tremendous challenge.

Company officers at the Academy ranged from den mothers to prison wardens. Ours, The Lieutenant, was, shall we say, a bit uptight. He was far more interested in the minutiae of Academy regulations than he was in anything relating to popular culture, like *Baywatch*.

Hasselhoff was an object of fascination for those of us in Fifth Company. We considered him both a legend *and* a buffoon.

I mean, *Knight Rider* . . . come on. You couldn't deny that.

Or all that running around in swim trunks with Pamela Anderson? And that chest hair?

Fantastic.

But, then, there was that song. Hasselhoff's "Looking for Freedom" had somehow become the anthem of Communism's demise in Eastern Europe.

It was awful. And embarrassing.

Or glorious, if you were a German. Why did they take him so seriously over there?

Anyway.

I don't remember how the idea of The Lieutenant's saying "David Hasselhoff" had originated. But there was wide agreement that anyone capable of managing such a feat would have achieved something truly epic.

And if anyone could pull it off, it was Jeff. He was hypersmart with a complete inability to take anyone in a position of authority seriously.

Lieutenant Tom Keefer's observation in Herman Wouk's novel *The Caine Mutiny* came to mind when one thought of Jeff. Those who designed the Navy system were geniuses. Those who worked within it were idiots.

I was one of the idiots. And I was okay with that.

Jeff, to the extent he even gave a shit, qualified as one of the geniuses. So when he said he could pull it off, you at least had to consider the possibility.

A few weeks went by, and the matter was forgotten. At least, we thought it was.

Then, one day, after lunch, all of us Fifth Company sophomores—Midshipmen Third Class—were directed to report to the company wardroom. The wardroom was a shared space for upperclassmen with theater-style seating. You went there to attend training lectures during the day and to watch *Seinfeld* and *Friends* at night.

We were mulling around when a loud "Attention on deck!" announced The Lieutenant's arrival. He strode to the front of the room and told us to take our seats. There was some new regulation to be announced. Again.

The Academy was still recovering from the scandal surrounding the theft of an electrical engineering exam and the subsequent cheating perpetrated by numerous midshipmen. The superintendent had been fired, and one of the Academy's previous superintendents, then a four-star admiral, had been brought back to clean up the place.

And we midshipmen had watched our freedom steadily erode as a result.

This new regulation had something to do with civilian clothes. Whereas sophomores were previously allowed to wear civvies out in town on weekends, the new regulation stipulated that Midshipmen Third Class would only be permitted to be out of uniform on certain weekends and outside city limits.

It was bullshit, as were most things at the Academy.

The Lieutenant delighted in such things. He read the regulation verbatim and then took his time to explain the various penalties associated with violating it. "Any questions?" he asked when he'd finished.

Jeff's hand shot up.

"Well, sir, let's just say, hypothetically . . ." he began.

Come on, Jeff, we all thought. Don't drag this out. We just want to get the hell out of here.

"Let's just say," he went on, "that Midshipman Third Class . . . I don't know, let's call him . . ." He threw his arms up at his sides and looked around the room, as if searching for the right name. "Let's call him Midshipman Third Class David Hasselhoff. Let's say his sponsors live in town, and he's just hanging out at their house for the weekend. Would Midshipman Hasselhoff get in trouble for wearing civvies then?"

Sponsor families were those that volunteered to host midshipmen on weekends to give them a respite from the Academy. At first, we thought Jeff was just being a pain in the ass, trying to exploit a gray area in the regulation. Then it dawned on us.

He was going for it.

He had just baited The Lieutenant.

We all shot sideways glances at each other, careful not to betray Jeff's incredible stunt. And then we waited. And waited.

Finally, The Lieutenant replied. "Well, if he'd read and understood the regulation, Midshipman Third Class David Hasselhoff would already know the answer: No, he cannot be in civvies anywhere within city limits. That includes his sponsors' house."

"Oh, okay," Jeff replied. "Understood, sir."

It took a second to sink in.

We sat there, stunned.

Ho. Lee. Shit. By God, he'd done it.

We all struggled to keep straight faces.

"Any more questions?" The Lieutenant asked.

Nope.

"Have a nice weekend," he said. "Dismissed."

Outside the wardroom, it was chaos. Guys were trying to lift Jeff into the air, like Notre Dame football players hoisting Rudy on their shoulders to parade him off the field under the approving gaze of Touchdown Jesus.

The US Naval Academy is a special place. A place of high achievement.

And through all the years I've been associated with it, no other achievement stands higher.

Well done, Jeff.

David Hasselhoff would be proud.

I know I sure as hell am.

Catching Up with Mrs. Lawrence

"**BILL LAWRENCE IS** in the bathtub." Mrs. Lawrence said it matter-of-factly as she watched a passing ski boat.

Admiral Lawrence disliked bathing. Not as a matter of hygiene, but as a matter of pride.

He'd fought his way back from a stroke that would have killed most people. But he still needed help getting in and out of the shower.

Which he didn't like at all.

And who could blame him? The man had been on the short list for NASA's Project Mercury. He'd been the first Naval aviator to fly twice the speed of sound. And he'd survived six years of torture and isolation in the Hanoi Hilton.

Six years.

So, no, the admiral didn't appreciate the fact he couldn't take a goddamn shower by himself. But that was the hand he'd been dealt. He was stoic about it, as you'd expect.

As was Mrs. Lawrence.

I'd caught up with her at the end of the long dock that extended from their backyard into the Severn River. She was relaxing in an Adirondack chair and invited me to join her. I always enjoyed speaking with Mrs. Lawrence. She was so . . . poised. Pure class.

And tough as shit.

I'd been brought on, ostensibly, to help the admiral finish his memoirs.

But really, I was part of his therapeutic regimen.

"Just keep him talking," Mrs. Lawrence had said. "Bill Lawrence has the most incredible stories. Make him tell you. It's good for him."

She always referred to her husband as "Bill Lawrence." I found it amusing.

I'd come over every Sunday morning, and the admiral would settle into his leather recliner and start talking. And I'd start typing.

Alan Shepard was a favorite topic.

Yes, that Alan Shepard. First American in space. There was a signed photograph of Shepard hitting a golf ball on the moon hanging in the admiral's study.

For Billy Lawrence, it was inscribed.

He and Shepard had been squadron mates in Korea and test pilots together at Pax River. The two of them may or may not have flown under a couple bridges in the area during that time.

The admiral's daughter, astronaut Wendy Lawrence, had told me to ask him about it.

"*Under* a bridge, you say?" the admiral demurred. "Well, of course, that would have been against regulations."

And he left it at that.

I told Mrs. Lawrence.

"Well, that's Bill Lawrence for you," she replied. She continued to stare out at the river. "We've had some good times," she offered. She talked about how they'd met.

In 1973, Mrs. Lawrence had been running a thriving physical therapy practice. One of her patients, a recently returned Vietnam POW, had the idea to set her up with a friend.

"You two would really hit it off," he'd said.

Mrs. Lawrence wasn't interested in meeting anyone at the time, but the patient persisted.

The patient was John McCain. The friend was Admiral Lawrence.

Apparently, the future senator held the admiral in high regard and very much wanted him to meet someone. It had to do with a recent turn of events.

There was an image of then-Captain Lawrence that had circulated in the newspapers in March 1973. He was standing, still emaciated looking, in front of a bank of microphones in his service-dress khakis. A plane had just deposited him on a tarmac in his home state of Tennessee, one of his first stops in the US after having been released by the North Vietnamese and repatriated.

It was the homecoming for which every POW had dreamt.

But, for Admiral Lawrence, the home to which he returned was very different from the one he'd left. Only days before standing on that tarmac, he'd learned that his wife of twenty years had divorced him and remarried while he was in captivity. He'd had no idea.

Can you imagine?

John McCain intended to do something about it. And he did.

Admiral Lawrence and Diane Wilcox Raugh, McCain's physical therapist, were married in August 1974.

"When I picked him up to move into our new house, everything he owned fit into one box," Mrs. Lawrence said. "I nearly wept."

The admiral never spoke of his former wife, and I certainly never asked him about her.

He once commented, however, that "she was just as much a casualty of war as I was."

Incredible.

Mrs. Lawrence and I chatted out on the dock for half an hour.

"Well," she eventually said, "we'd better see about Bill."

I followed her into the house. She started up the stairs to the second floor while I waited in the kitchen. Halfway up, she stopped.

"Come on," she called down. "I'm going to need your help."

I headed upstairs, not entirely sure why. This really wasn't my department. Someone from the admiral's medical staff usually helped with the bathing.

Mrs. Lawrence stood in the bathroom doorway and motioned me in. There, I found the admiral. Lying in the bathtub, just as Mrs. Lawrence had said. He was fully clothed and staring at the ceiling.

"Bill," Mrs. Lawrence called to him, "Dan is here."

"Oh," the admiral said, snapping out of his trance. "Hello there."

I immediately jolted for the bathtub and helped the admiral to his feet. He was deadweight.

"I couldn't pick him up," Mrs. Lawrence said. "But I knew you were coming."

Later that day, Mrs. Lawrence gave me the full story.

The admiral had apparently become obsessed with getting his weight down to what it had been when he'd played football at the Naval Academy. As a result, he weighed himself on the bathroom scale several times a day.

The scale was right next to the bathtub.

That morning, the admiral had apparently been weighing himself, lost his balance, and fell into the bathtub. Mrs. Lawrence had heard the thud, went in to check on him, and found him lying there.

Her trained eye had told her the admiral wasn't hurt, but she didn't have the strength to get him out. So, she'd gone outside to wait until I'd arrived. And when I had, she'd decided that we should first catch up before going upstairs to deal with the admiral.

What's the hurry? she figured.

We got the admiral put back together and settled into his chair.

"Where were we?" he asked me. "Oh, yes," he said, and launched into another story, resuming our conversation exactly where we'd left it the week before.

The admiral didn't seem the least bit bothered he'd spent much of the morning in a bathtub.

He'd endured far worse.

Vice Admiral William P. Lawrence died later that year. A division of Super Hornets flew the missing man formation over the Naval Academy Cemetery during his funeral.

Just as Admiral Lawrence had flown an F-4 Phantom over Arlington National Cemetery during JFK's internment in 1963.

It was a fitting tribute to an extraordinary man, and an extraordinary life.

Of which I got to be a part, for the briefest of moments.

For which I'll always be grateful.

And thank you, Mrs. Lawrence.

I'm glad we had the chance

To catch up.

WORK

Doing It All Wrong, Part 1

I'M DOING IT all wrong.

Whereas the woman in front of me was consumed with activity the entire flight, I was completely idle.

It was a two-hour leg from Kansas City to Houston, during which I'd usually nap. That's what I do on most flights. As soon as I feel the plane push back from the gate, I'm out. And I remain so until the aircraft is established at cruising altitude. Then I usually wake up and find something to read, or I watch a couple of episodes of *Beavis and Butt-Head* or *Curb Your Enthusiasm*. They're my airplane go-tos.

This time, I decided to depart from my usual routine. I was fascinated with this woman sitting across the aisle to my front left. From the moment she'd sat down, she had continuously cycled between her phone, iPad, and laptop, furiously scrolling and pushing buttons. I had a clear view of everything she was doing.

Not that I was snooping.

Well, yes, I was snooping, because I was indeed curious. I could not understand how someone could be *that* busy. She opened numerous spreadsheets, added information to various cells, re-sorted columns and rows, and color-coded everything. Then she'd switch to one of the twenty emails she had open.

The woman would cut and paste a portion of one of her spreadsheets into the open message and type a couple of densely worded paragraphs to accompany it. Then she would start a new email, insert other portions of other spreadsheets into it, and, again, pound out more commentary at about eighty words per minute.

This went on the entire time the plane was above ten thousand feet.

And then, upon our descent into Houston, after she'd put away her computer, she pulled out her phone and powered through three different crossword puzzles on some app. I mean, it was incredible. She was completely absorbed. The time must have flown by for her, and honestly, I was jealous. I've long struggled with boredom.

But it wasn't always that way.

Early in my Navy career, my time was consumed by myriad demands. There was always something to do, and I often felt there wasn't enough time to do it all. That was largely thanks to the fact that I spent up to ten hours per day flying, getting ready to fly, or filling out paperwork after I'd flown.

Everything else had to be crammed into the remaining hours of the day, along with working out, lingering in the wardroom after dinner to bullshit with friends, and, of course, catching at least one movie.

The days were full, and boredom was a foreign concept. This continued through successive assignments. As a result, I developed various productivity hacks to limit my activities to the Critical Few. And I completely ignored everything else.

This did not go unnoticed.

Some, who thought they had license to foist their agendas upon me, protested. But I quickly learned that both the protestors and the ignored activities which invited their protests were of absolutely no consequence. I thus did myself, and my work, a great service by disregarding both. It was liberating, and I took this approach with me to the private sector.

Where it promptly failed me.

And that's because I repeatedly landed in a Bullshit Job.

In such a role, aptly dubbed by anthropologist David Graeber in his book, you guessed it, *Bullshit Jobs*[1], all the inconsequential stuff I'd taught myself to ignore *was* the job. By setting aside all the superfluous, unimportant, non-value-adding activities, I had nothing left to do.

I mean, nothing. And that came at a bad time:

The Great Recession.

I was in a large corporation, where butts-in-seats were of prime importance. And so, to protect your livelihood, you put your butt in that seat and looked as busy as you could. It didn't really matter what you did, as long as you did *something*.

Like Bullshit.

Lots and lots of Bullshit.

Which caused me great emotional distress—and still does.

I possess the skills and experience necessary to set my own priorities and optimize my own workflow. I am loath to waste my time and that of others. But, as a survivor of the Great Recession, I have a need to be perceived as a person who spends adequate time with his butt in a seat looking busy.

If one is so wired, how does one resolve the cognitive dissonance to which the modern workplace gives rise? What do you do? I don't know. But I can tell you what *not* to do.

And that is to have an honest conversation with your boss about it.

---

1 David Graeber, *Bullshit Jobs: A Theory* (Simon & Schuster, 2018).

That is absolutely the last thing you want to do.

See, you think you're doing the organization a favor by suggesting to your superiors that perhaps your efforts could be channeled into more productive pursuits. But what you're actually doing is branding yourself as a self-absorbed malcontent who thinks he's too good to do the work required of the role.

And then your name moves to the top of the boss's People To Be Gotten Rid Of list.

So, no, you don't want to attempt an honest conversation with your boss. About anything, really.

But anyway.

The way to get ahead in a Bullshit Job is through prodigious amounts of activity, regardless of whether it accomplishes anything.

Now, it's entirely possible the woman on the plane was doing real work. Maybe she was on the cusp of curing the world of excessive foot odor, and all those spreadsheets and emails were critical to that effort.

But I doubt it.

Judging by her behavior, I assumed the woman on the plane to have a Bullshit Job. And I certainly didn't begrudge her for it. Quite the contrary.

I applauded her for it.

She'd clearly cracked the code. I mean, look at her! I thought to myself. She's nailing it. Sure, if I were to receive one of her ridiculous emails, I'd delete it without opening it.

But that's just me.

I'm not out there striving. I learned the folly of that a long time ago. This woman would, no doubt, ascend to a higher wrung on the corporate ladder than I. And I think we'd both be cool with that. Unless, that is, she were to become my boss and expect that I create the same sort of meaningless, time-wasting churn that facilitated her own ascent.

Then we'd have problems.

In the meantime, we can happily coexist. She can remain ferociously engaged, far beyond boredom's grip. And I can observe her and be both impressed and entertained.

Yeah, maybe I'm doing it all wrong. I should really do a better job of playing the game. Like the lady on the plane. I mean, why fight it? Who do I think I am?

I'll reflect on that.

And in the meantime,

What do you suppose Beavis and Butt-Head are up to today?

I should probably find out.

Doing It All Wrong, Part II

"IT'S EASIER TO get a smart person to do something hard than to get them to do something easy that doesn't matter." So says author and podcaster Shane Parrish in his popular blog *Farnam Street*.

I think he's exactly right.

Hard inspires people of ability to rise to the occasion. *Doesn't matter* disillusions and embitters them. Unfortunately, the latter better describes my work experience than the former. I've spent far more time bitter than I have inspired.

And why is that?

Two things would have to be true. First, that I'm smart, and second, that I can rightly judge what does and does not matter.

Neither should go unchallenged.

Looking back over my life, I can find ample evidence to disprove both. I've made numerous choices that can only be described as stupid. And, on too many occasions, I've completely ignored what really matters, even while it was staring me right in the face.

That's the stuff of regret, of which I carry my fair share.

Still, I've had plenty of demands made of me—or attempted to be made—at which any reasonable person would balk. And I usually slow-rolled the people making the demands in the hopes they would simply forget. Or I flatly refused to do whatever it was they were demanding of me.

Often, I would slow-roll them for a while and then refuse.

Which had consequences.

To which I would usually say "fuck it."

Even my beloved Navy would occasionally put me in such a position. I once worked for a captain who'd allowed himself to become embroiled in a petty, personal dispute with another captain on the other side of the planet. He somehow reported to this officer through a dotted-line, matrixed relationship.

I neither understood it nor cared to.

But I did care when the captain to whom I reported would try to drag me into conference calls with the guy. Some at four o'clock in the morning. The calls were apparently scheduled at times of the other guy's convenience, not ours. And the only reason I would ever attend one, according to my captain, would be to provide support.

Whatever the hell that meant.

I actively avoided them, but that didn't stop the captain from trying to task me with various things that came out of such meetings.

The group to which we belonged sent out a half dozen daily reports that provided updates on various activities. No one ever read them, but we still did them. There was just no getting around it. I was responsible for a couple of these reports, which I knocked out in the first thirty minutes of every workday.

One morning, the captain decided that I should do an extensive analysis of a year's worth of reports to identify certain trends. I judged the task would consume several hours over the course of a week. And, when complete, I further judged that no one would likely give a shit about the results.

Just as no one gave a shit about the reports themselves.

Worse, we didn't have any sort of specialized software with which to conduct the analysis. It was all spreadsheets and word-processing documents. The analysis would be manual and incredibly tedious. Not hard, but annoying.

When I shared all this with the captain, he brushed it aside. And then he revealed the purpose of the analysis: to provide him with some bit of trivia with which to zing the other captain in one of their meetings.

His antagonist was apparently convinced some occurrence-I-can't-recall was happening, based upon anecdotes and assumptions. The captain disagreed but lacked the data to prove it. And, being slow-witted, he was often bested by the other guy during debates on the topic.

No doubt, the other captain was a complete asshole. I'd observed that myself. And I was 100 percent on board with zinging the guy. But no fucking way was I going to waste a second of my time on some worthless analysis to do so.

When I told the captain that, he was taken aback. He assumed the other captain was our common enemy and that taking him down in some stupid meeting was our common cause. I assured him he was wrong on both counts.

I didn't give a shit about the other guy and neither should he, I told him. Not only should I not waste my time on his analysis, but neither should anyone else. The captain should instead put on his big-boy pants and have an adult conversation with the other captain to reset the relationship.

"So let me make sure I understand what you're saying," said the captain. "You are unwilling to do what I'm asking you. Is that correct?"

I think what you're asking me to do is a gross misuse of time and resources, I replied, and you shouldn't ask me—or anyone else—to do it.

That ended the discussion.

And changed the nature of the relationship between the captain and me. He didn't seem to think much of me after that. But so what? He wrote me a damn-with-faint-praise fitness report upon my departure, which seemed harmless enough in the broader context of my career.

Still, there are certainly no stars in my future.

I can't say whether the captain hurt my future, but he certainly didn't help. And that's one of the consequences of thinking you're smarter than your boss and making your own decisions about what you will and won't do.

I do have to give the captain credit for being honest about his intent, though. He at least told me, truthfully, why he wanted the analysis. I've had other bosses attempt to task me with things equally as worthless, but without any explanation. Or, worse, some made-up, bullshit reason that any mildly competent person could see right through.

Now, I know how this all sounds. And you're exactly right.

I can be an incredibly shitty employee.

I don't dispute that.

But I do love to work—on stuff that actually matters. And I've learned the pursuit of meaningful work is one of life's most important endeavors.

Also one of the toughest.

I've also failed at times to recognize what truly matters when it's disguised as something trivial. Like when my daughter asked me to chase her. Kids love to be chased.

"Chase me, Daddy!" she'd once said.

The trouble was, we'd just finished brunch, and I had on my nice shoes, and I didn't want to mess up the shine . . .

And it was getting warm outside, and I didn't want to sweat . . .

And why couldn't she just get one of the other kids to chase her?

Or just run around on her own?

Why did I have to do it?

Maybe later, I told her, having no intention whatsoever of ever chasing her.

This was totally the wrong call. I missed an opportunity to do something that mattered—really, truly mattered—that I would never get back. And I regret that.

Telling the captain to piss off?

No regrets.

Passing up an opportunity to share a moment of joy with my young daughter?

Profound regrets.

So, the moral of the story:

If you think you're smart enough to know what's important and bold enough to stand up to those who would distract you from it, do it. Take that stand. But understand there may be consequences.

And the next time a kid says, "Chase me!" don't hesitate.

Whether she's five or thirty-five,

Chase the fucking kid.

And listen to her shriek with delight as you do.

That is what matters,

What really, truly matters,

Smart guy.

You're in Trouble, Mister!

WHAT DO A MISCREANT grade schooler, a Naval Academy plebe, and a corporate dude have in common?

They walk around feeling like they're in trouble.

All the time.

I should know; I've been all three. And I'm beginning to think that feeling is a permanent feature of the human experience.

It started when I threw a rock at a car.

I was in first or second grade, sitting on the curb in front of my house. A giant Buick went creeping by, as though it were casing the joint. I had a piece of gravel in my hand, a normal thing for me at that age. I never walked past a gravel driveway without picking up a handful of the stuff to inspect it for pieces of gold.

Because, hey, you never knew.

So the car's going by, super slow, and I'm turning the piece of gravel over in my hand. I'd already inspected it for gold and hadn't found any. And, for no particular reason, I thought, why not throw it at the car? I figured it was a good use for a non-gold-containing, otherwise worthless rock.

So I did. I threw it at the car. And when it hit the trunk, it gave off a very satisfying tink sound. I had a pretty good arm for my age. I was a regular on the Little League travel team. As I sat there, congratulating myself for the direct hit, I noticed the car abruptly stop, right in the middle of the road.

And then out came this little old lady.

She walked around to the back of the car and started feeling around on the door of the trunk. Her hand stopped on what looked like a chalk mark, and then she started looking up and down the street until she found me sitting on the curb.

"You!" she said. "You did this!"

She was pointing a crooked, arthritic finger directly at me. But that didn't stop me from hoping that maybe she was talking to someone else.

Who? Me? I asked, pointing at myself.

"Yes, you! Do you see anyone else around?" she asked, sarcastically.

I did not.

"Why did you throw a rock at my car?" she continued.

Well, there was my thing with gravel and my quest to find gold and buy a mansion with it, and then you drove by, and I had the rock in my hand, and . . .

Of course, I didn't share any of that with her. I just continued to sit on the curb in frightened silence.

"Well, let's just see what your mother has to say about this," she said, ominously.

And then she walked to my front door and knocked on it. My mother answered, got the whole story from the old lady, apologized profusely, and promised that I'd be severely punished.

As soon as my father got home.

"Daniel!" my mother shouted. "Get in here . . . *now!*"

I was ordered to my room, where I was to remain.

Until my father got home.

"Just wait . . ." my mother said.

Now, my father was not a harsh person.

He rarely raised his voice, played a decent game of tennis, and was fond of smoking a pipe at the end of our driveway most nights after dinner.

But, when the occasion warranted, he was pretty handy with a belt. And for that reason, I sat in my room that afternoon with a sense of dread. I was indeed in trouble. Interestingly, I don't remember exactly what happened when my dad got home. But I vividly remember the anticipation. That sense of dread.

The same sense I'd have in Annapolis nearly two decades later.

I'd just returned to my room from my plebe, or freshman, English class. It was approaching three o'clock in the afternoon, and I needed to quickly change before heading out to track practice. But as soon as I crossed the threshold to my room, I was struck with horror. There, sitting on my desk, in plain view, was my coffee maker.

Shit!

I usually kept it hidden in the cabinet under my sink behind a stack of towels. Small appliances of any variety were illegal in the Naval Academy's giant dorm, Bancroft Hall. That was because the place had been wired way back in the days of sail, or close to it, and the use of such devices risked burning the place down.

At least, that's what we'd been told.

I gathered that my coffee maker had been found during an unannounced room inspection. Those were regular occurrences in the life of a plebe. The trouble was, I didn't know who'd done the inspection and found my contraband coffee maker. Had it been an upperclassman? That would have been less concerning to me—most of the upperclassmen in my company were pretty chill.

The same was not true of my company officer. He was the commissioned officer in charge of the hundred or so midshipmen in my company and was an absolute stickler for the rules. Plus, he could mete out punishments that carried real consequences.

As in, those that affected one's class rank and could jeopardize one's ability to capture a pilot-training slot upon graduation.

Which I desperately wanted.

What should I do here? I thought. Whoever had found my coffee maker had left no identifying information. No angry note directing me to report immediately to him or her.

So, I went out to practice. A very long and shitty practice, given the sense of dread I carried with me. Dinner came and went. Then study hour. Nothing. Not a word from anyone.

Finally, the next morning, I got the story.

It came during my Friday come-around with my Firstie, the Midshipman First Class, or senior, to whom I reported. I arrived outside his room at 0630 to stand at attention and be quizzed on a variety of topics. Like the weapons, forward to aft, on a Ticonderoga class cruiser. That was a come-around. They were a daily occurrence and a prominent feature of the plebe-harassment package.

My Firstie, Mister Newell, began, "So, Bozung, about that coffee maker..."

Oh, shit, I thought. Here it comes.

"The Lieutenant found it," he said.

Yikes! Our company officer. That was the worst of all possible outcomes.

"And he told me to deal with it," he continued, gravely. "The trouble is... well, see..." Mister Newell looked up and down the passageway and then leaned in closer to me and lowered his voice. "The trouble is, I have a coffee maker, too. So, it's kinda hard for me to get on your case about yours."

Really? I thought. That's awesome!

"Just make it go away, all right? Get it out of the hall, and we'll forget the whole thing," he concluded.

Can do, sir.

I wouldn't have my morning coffee, but I wouldn't be marching tours, either. That was fair. And my sense of dread was relieved. For the moment, at least.

Fast-forward another couple decades, and I'm walking into a meeting with the CEO. I have that same damn feeling—that I'm in trouble. It's constant. And pervasive.

I've found that in any corporation, you're always underperforming. Always failing to meet expectations. That's because, as the saying goes, if the business ain't growing, it's dying. And growth often depends upon forces beyond one's control. Some years you get lucky. Most years you don't. So, you spend your days feeling like you're walking around at your own funeral.

"Are you going to hit your numbers this quarter?" the conversation begins.

And then you give an answer along the lines of, "Well, it'll be a challenge. As you know, the Chinese have entered this market in force, dragging down prices. And, since we're dealing in commodities, without any meaningful opportunity to differentiate, customers are defecting to low-cost providers . . ."

Blah, blah, blah.

Bullshit, bullshit, bullshit.

Translation: I don't have a friggin' clue as to whether I'll meet my budget.

Likely, I won't, because those numbers are totally unrealistic and always have been. But I'll do this little tap dance every month to make the boss feel as though he's holding me accountable.

It makes me feel like a kid again, waiting in my room for my father to get home.

Or a Naval Academy plebe, reporting for a come-around.

It never ends.

You're in trouble, mister!

Yup.

Aren't we all?

Phantom Dog Shitter

YOU SMELL IT FIRST.

That ripe, someone-forgot-to-flush-the-toilet smell. That's how you know it's there. That dog shit stuck to the bottom of your shoe.

We'll get back to that in a minute.

First, there was snow in the forecast, the first of the season. And I still had a thick layer of leaves covering my yard.

Once it snowed, my ambition for dealing with the leaves would be zilch, so I figured I'd better get out and do something about them. Luckily, the snow was due to hit early Sunday morning, so that gave me Saturday afternoon to clean things up.

I generally don't mind yard work. It doesn't require any skill, and it provides fresh air and exercise. Plus, in the late fall, it allows me to gear up like I just stepped out of the pages of an L.L.Bean catalog. You can't do serious yard work without a hearty flannel and Maine Hunting Shoes, right?

Well, I should say, that used to be the case. My yard is so treacherously steep that I've had to adapt my yard-work uniform to better meet the task. Lately, I've been dressing for lawn mowing and leaf raking as though they were CrossFit workouts. I wear a fleece pullover, running shorts, and a pair of baseball cleats I picked up on sale at the Fort Leavenworth Exchange.

Sounds ridiculous, I know. But the cleats are essential. Without them, I don't know how many times I might have gone careening into the woods behind my house.

So, once I was properly attired, the question was whether to rake or mulch. Is it better to rake the leaves into piles for disposal? Or run them over with the lawn mower and mash them into the grass? The articles I'd read online clearly favored the latter. The mashed-up leaves apparently act like lawn food.

So, it was decided. Mulch, baby, mulch!

I fired up the mower and, for the next hour, enjoyed the satisfying crunch of leaves being chewed up and spit back out all over the yard. And, when I was finished, I have to say, the place looked pretty damn good.

I put the mower away and tidied up the garage a bit. And then it hit me. The smell.

Oh, no, I thought.

No, no, no, no . . .

One at a time, I picked up my feet to examine the bottom of my cleats. And, sure enough, jammed into the crevices of the underside of my right shoe was a gooey brown mess.

Dog shit.

This was absolutely infuriating, since I don't have a dog.

So, who was to blame? Most neighbors are good about cleaning up after their pets. If someone's out walking his dog, and that dog makes a stop in your yard to do his business, that person, almost without fail, will break out a little plastic baggie and pick up after the dog. It's what you do when you live in a civilized society.

However, from time to time, one of the neighbors' dogs will liberate itself from its leash or the invisible fence surrounding its yard and make a break for it. And, when that happens, the dog will take great pleasure in sniffing around and shitting in your yard. I guess it's about the freedom . . . the novelty.

Dogs like that stuff, too.

It reminds me of the tradition of the Phantom Shitter on board a US Navy vessel. About halfway through a deployment, when things really start to drag, a pile of human feces will be discovered in a conspicuous place on the ship. The quarterdeck, or the ceremonial area on the ship's main deck, is a favorite spot.

Then begins the intrigue, which consumes the entire crew. *Who is the Phantom Shitter, and where will he strike again?*

After the quarterdeck, another favorite spot is the main passageway in officers' country. That's where the ship's officers live. Or, better, if the ship has accommodations for an admiral and his or her staff, flag country, as it's called, is another favorite target of a Phantom Shitter.

Now, I know what you're thinking. The most powerful, technologically advanced navy in the history of the world is populated by people who defecate in places other than toilets?

That's a fair question.

But, unless you've done one, it's hard to appreciate how monotonous and boring a deployment can be. Anything that spices things up—I mean, *anything*—is a welcome reprieve.

Halfway through my second deployment, a Phantom Shitter struck my ship, the *USS Fletcher*.

We'd been operating in the North Arabian Gulf for a couple months, hitting port about once every thirty days. It was *Groundhog Day*. The same damn thing over and over again.

And then the Shitter struck, electrifying the ship.

I even had the privilege to discover some of the Shitter's earliest handiwork. There it was, a pile in the center of the passageway connecting the hangar and the combat information center. It was about two o'clock in the morning, and I was on my way to combat to brief a flight. I carefully maneuvered around the pile, hugging the bulkhead as I passed it as though it were radioactive.

When I got to combat, I found the tactical action officer, the senior watch stander. Someone had left him a present in the passageway, I told him. He immediately sent one of the junior sailors to clean it up.

Poor bastard.

The ship's second-in-command, the executive officer, or "XO," is typically charged with rooting out a Phantom Shitter, as they're the ship's principal enforcer of good order and discipline.

I've observed XOs take two approaches to managing Phantom Shitters. The first, what I'd call the enlightened approach, has the XO taking the high road. "Okay, Phantom Shitter, whoever you are, you got us," he'll tell the crew. "But do you really want your buddies to have to keep cleaning up your mess? Not cool." And then the Phantom Shitter phenomenon typically dies out.

The other, more heavy-handed approach, like that taken by *Fletcher*'s XO, has the second-in-command going full Commander Queeg, like in *The Caine Mutiny*. He'll make it an inquisition, and then the Shitter phenomenon will persist, with the crew rooting him on every step of the way.

Myself included.

Fletcher's Phantom Shitter was never identified. Which still brings me a good deal of satisfaction.

So, you see, I'm not necessarily anti-Shitter. A well-placed, well-timed pile of shit can provide a huge boost to morale.

This can include dog shit.

Random piles will show up in my yard from time to time

throughout the summer, and I typically don't mind. I can spot them from a distance and take evasive action. And I don't believe my neighbors are secretly dispatching their dogs to leave piles of shit in my yard in the middle of the night just to torment me, Phantom Shitter–style. That seems highly unlikely.

But kudos to both the dog and owner if they are. I can't exclude the possibility that my neighborhood has a canine Phantom Shitter.

I guess my problem is when, while mulching a leaf-covered yard, the dog shit goes undetected. Fine, until you step in it. With your cleats on.

And then what?

I guess I'll be off to Fort Leavenworth to buy another pair.

Because that stuff's not coming out.

Bravo, Phantom Dog Shitter.

Whoever you are.

Bravo.

Business Travel Adventures, Houston

IF YOUR TRAVELS take you to places that require steel toes and a hard hat, your hotel options can be limited. That's because such places tend not to reside in the ritzier parts of town.

Foundries, factories, rail yards . . . these places don't coexist with country clubs and Michelin three-star restaurants.

And that's okay.

These are businesses where proud, honest people do unglamorous, often dirty work to drive communities and economies forward. They've survived through the years with a steadfastness that deserves our respect.

Even as we drive through the shittiest parts of town to visit their facilities.

As John Mellencamp once observed, ain't that America?

Indeed, it is.

Baby.

See, Mellencamp's America doesn't come with a wine list and high-thread-count sheets. But it does often come with a bunch of fucking weirdos. Like the ones I encountered the other week.

I'll get to them in a minute.

First, I was visiting a steel-fabrication business on the east side of Houston. It was in one of the many industrial areas bordering the Port of Houston, where, according to my host, Howard Hughes had produced bomber components during World War II. Several of the buildings nearby retained the appearance of aircraft hangars.

I thought this was pretty damn cool.

Following a quick tour of a foundry housed within one of the old hangars, we headed for lunch. There was a Mexican restaurant on the edge of the port where my host and his team were regulars.

"The best," was all he'd say to describe it. "Just... the best." That was high praise considering the town had more Tex-Mex per capita than almost any other in the country.

As we were driving to the restaurant, we noticed a half dozen police cars speeding by in the opposite direction, lights flashing and sirens wailing. Something must be up, we thought.

We got to the restaurant in a modest, generally well-kept neighborhood. The parking lot was completely full, always a good sign. And the food was, indeed, fantastic.

We finished lunch and headed back to the office, following the same route we'd taken to get to the restaurant. As we did, we passed by one of those payday check-cashing places. The parking lot was empty, with yellow police tape running its entire perimeter. There were police cars parked at various intervals, completely surrounding it.

"I wonder if those are the same cars we passed on the way to lunch," my host said.

A moment later, a colleague riding with us looked out at the parking lot and asked, "Is that . . . a body?"

The rest of us turned to see a white sheet in the middle of the concrete, a red splotch in the center and two feet sticking out from the bottom edge.

Yup. It was a body. Just like you'd see on some cop drama on TV.

We continued on in stunned silence. Finally, my colleague offered, "Well, you don't see that every day." A true statement. I'd been to countless business lunches, and none ever ended like that.

News of the event traveled fast.

Five minutes after arriving back at the office, someone had found the story online, the events leading up to the guy's demise spelled out.

He was apparently one of three criminals who had followed the owner of the check-cashing place to the local bank. There, the owner had made a large cash withdrawal before heading back to his store. Once back at the check-cashing place, two of the three guys following him jumped the owner as he walked through the front door.

He was armed, it turned out, and came up shooting, killing one of the would-be robbers. Then, upon hearing the commotion, an employee inside the building also came out shooting. He killed the other guy, the one lying with his feet sticking out from under the sheet in the parking lot. The third person, the getaway driver, disappeared. A city-wide manhunt ensued, and the cops eventually found him.

Another day in Houston.

The hotel in which I was staying was just under ten miles from the check-cashing place, just off I-10. It belonged to a reputable chain and was only a year or two old. So, I safely—and correctly, as it happened—assumed there wouldn't be any white sheets with feet sticking out from under them in the parking lot when I returned to the hotel that evening.

The next morning, I went down to the hotel gym. It was about six o'clock, and I usually have the gym to myself at that time of day.

In that area, most patrons are already in their F-350s and on the way to the refinery by then.

This time, there was one other guy in the gym. He had music blaring from headphones and was sweating and grunting his way through some kind of high-intensity interval workout. This wouldn't have bothered me, except the dude was doing all the sweating and grunting without a shirt on.

It seemed totally out of place.

This was a hotel gym, about the size of a two-car garage. Not the open-air Muscle Beach of Venice, California, circa 1970. When you're in a confined space, you wear a frickin' shirt. It's common courtesy.

And he wasn't exactly Arnold Schwarzenegger. I didn't know why he was so eager to show off his physique to begin with.

I was annoyed at first, but then amused. The shirtless dude finished his workout ten minutes after I arrived, and then I had the place to myself.

And all was once again right with the world.

I walked out of the gym around seven and took the stairs back up to the second floor, where my room was located halfway down the main hallway. As I opened the door from the stairwell, I immediately heard shouting. It was coming from a room a few doors down from mine.

"Say it! Say it!" a woman's voice screamed. "You the bitch! You the bitch! Say it!"

The occupants' morning was apparently off to an unpleasant start.

Intrigued, I paused at the door to my room to listen in.

"Nah, nah... don't even give that *bull*shit," the woman continued. "*You're* the bitch!"

Between the woman's outbursts, I could hear the muffled voice of a male in the room. I assumed him to be the bitch in question. His verbal assailant seemed to have him on the proverbial ropes.

"What? What!" asked the lady. "You gonna steal from your work again? Is that what you're gonna do?"

Another muffled response from the male followed.

Then the woman shot back, "Bullshit, *bitch*! Does your momma know you steal from your work? Does she? Well, maybe I'll just tell her then..."

Clearly, there were layers to this conflict. It was complicated, apparently involving possible workplace theft and the prospect of an adult perpetrator's misdeeds being reported to his mother.

And then there was the woman's insistence, through it all, that the alleged thief accept the label *bitch*, which he was seemingly reluctant to do.

That's a tough one.

I stepped into my room, showered up, and packed up my things. As I did, I reflected upon the previous twenty-four hours. Flight to Houston. Foundry visit. Top-notch Tex-Mex for lunch. Dead dude in a parking lot. Sweaty, shirtless dude in the hotel gym. Shouting lady in the room down the hall.

Business travel at its finest.

I made my way down to the lobby to meet my colleague for a quick breakfast. What did he think of the hotel and the events of the previous day? I asked.

"This place is great," he said. "Check it out: They have banana chips for the oatmeal!"

It was the finest selection of oatmeal toppings he'd ever encountered.

"I'll totally be staying here again, for sure," he concluded.

You know.

For the banana chips.

Cybercriminal

OUR MILITARY IS an all-volunteer force, an aspect I consider one of its greatest strengths.

But I do sometimes wonder...

Why do *I* continue to volunteer for this shit?

Take a recent weekend, for example. On Friday afternoon, I drove straight from the airport to US Strategic Command, or STRATCOM.

I wasn't officially on duty until Saturday, but I wanted to check in at the Global Operations Center to ensure my accounts were in order. On my previous two Navy Reserve duty weekends, they had not been. My unclassified, secret, and top-secret accounts had all been disabled.

Why? Because the Air Force doesn't talk to the Navy, the reserves don't talk to the active component, and no one, apparently, talks to STRATCOM.

You have to take this stupid, painful cybersecurity-training course every year. And if the training expires, or if you can't produce a current certificate of completion, you can't access any of the systems.

But that's only part of the problem.

In the Navy, the requirement is based on the fiscal year. And you complete the training via Navy Knowledge Online, or NKO, the Navy's online training portal. But at STRATCOM, the requirement is based on your check-in date.

So, even if you've already completed the training for the year, if you don't retake the course within a few weeks of checking in, you're considered delinquent, and your account is disabled. Which is what happened to me on previous weekends.

Luckily, I was able to produce my completion certificate from NKO, so the dude at the IT help desk re-enabled my accounts. But, of course, I wasn't going to assume I was home free. Problems like this in the military don't get completely fixed on the first, second, or seventh attempt. You have to keep at it, even after ten people have told you the issue has been resolved. I've learned this.

So, I rolled into the operations center fresh from the airport and sat down to log into my account, all of which were disabled. Again.

The comms guy in the operations center called the help desk on my behalf. And, again, I sent off my completed cybersecurity-training certificate. It took nearly two hours to re-enable my accounts. By then, it was after seven o'clock in the evening, and I was anxious to get the hell out of there.

Not wanting to have any additional surprises the following morning, I asked the comms guy what else might go wrong.

On a whim, he asked, "Where'd you do your cybersecurity training?"

At NKO, I told him.

"Ah," he said. "That's the problem. If you don't do it at JKO, the system will automatically disable your accounts."

JKO is Joint Knowledge Online. It serves the same purpose as NKO but is used by members of all branches at joint commands. And the JKO cybersecurity course is the *exact same fucking thing* as the NKO course.

Are you shitting me? I asked the comms guy.

"Sorry, I'm afraid that's just how it is," he said.

So, in order *not* to have my accounts disabled overnight, I sat there for an additional hour and completed the course at JKO.

When I finally got to the hotel, I had about four hours of sleep to look forward to. I was working the early shift Saturday, and I intended to give myself plenty of extra time to resolve any remaining issues with my accounts before clocking in.

The first dose of fall weather had arrived overnight, and my room was freezing when I woke up. I switched the thermostat from air-conditioning to heat. And, almost immediately, I noticed a burning smell. Not unusual, I figured. The furnace always smells funny the first time you kick the heat on.

After sixty seconds, however, it started to smell as though someone had lit up a Lucky Strike in my room. Something was no-shit burning. And then the smoke alarm started going off.

It was just after three o'clock in the morning, and I couldn't see any smoke, but the smell continued to get worse. I turned off the heater as the alarm continued to blare, then I grabbed my iPad and started waving it furiously to try to dissipate the smell.

If I didn't get that goddamned alarm to shut off, I assumed I'd wake up the entire hotel. And what if I set off the sprinklers?

Shit.

I noticed the alarm had a test button on its underside. I pressed it, and, thankfully, the alarm shut off. But my room continued to smell like someone was chain-smoking in it. I took a shower, hoping I wouldn't be the reason the hotel burned down.

Half an hour later, I rolled into STRATCOM. Thankfully, I was able to get into all my accounts. It was a little busy at the start of the shift, but otherwise a quiet day. And when I returned to the hotel, I saw that it was still standing. And my room no longer smelled like stale Lucky Strikes.

Things were looking up.

I hit my favorite restaurant for dinner and turned in early, assuming the weekend's drama was safely behind me.

Sunday morning got off to a good start. I didn't touch the heater, of course. And by the time I got packed up and out of the hotel, I was a few minutes ahead of schedule.

When I pulled into the STRATCOM parking lot, there was a base security vehicle with its lights on sitting behind a parked car. Maybe someone had locked their keys in it.

I maneuvered around the security vehicle and found a parking spot. Then I walked into the building, through four different security checkpoints, and eventually into the Global Operations Center. About thirty minutes later, having successfully logged into all my accounts, I stood up and casually crossed my arms.

As I did so, I felt an unfamiliar object in my flight suit's right chest pocket.

That's strange, I thought. What the hell is that?

It was my cell phone.

Ho. Lee. Shit.

I'd brought a cellular device into a top-secret space.

And kept it there for half an hour.

A *huge* security violation.

I immediately turned to the battle watch captain standing behind me and told him I needed to step out for a few minutes. I then hauled ass to the nearest security checkpoint and turned myself in.

"Wait here," the guard said. "Someone will come escort you to the security office."

Five minutes later, a kid in full battle rattle with an M4 machine gun slung across his chest appeared.

"Come with me, sir," he said, ominously.

We walked up two floors to the security office and a small interrogation room where I sat for the next forty-five minutes. Another dude came in and "interrogated" me, taking notes the entire time. I then had to sign a sworn statement and fill out an evidence tag for my then-confiscated phone.

When will I get it back? I asked the guy who'd escorted me in.

"I dunno," he said. "Usually takes a couple weeks."

The phone had to be thoroughly examined to ensure it hadn't recorded or transmitted anything while in the building.

Just. Fucking. Great.

Now, the irony is, I am not a person who cannot be without a phone. In fact, most of the time, I'd rather be without one. I use my phone for work. Not to doomscroll or watch cat videos.

So why, then, did I have it with me that particular morning, despite having developed an elaborate routine to ensure I did *not* take the damn thing into STRATCOM?

Because I had departed from that routine.

The cop car in the parking lot prevented me from parking in my usual place, which then threw me off just enough to make me forget to frisk myself for electronic devices. And I'd crammed a few extra things into my flight-suit pockets that morning, forcing me to switch my phone from my left to right pocket. So, even had I remembered to frisk myself, there's a chance I would have missed my phone, because it was in the wrong pocket.

In aviation, we say that mishaps like this one conform to the Swiss Cheese Model. No single hole in the block of cheese causes these incidents. But, when a sufficient number of holes align, bad things happen.

Like that morning at STRATCOM.

I do love the military, and if you stick around long enough, weekends like this happen.

But I'm not sure how much longer I can tolerate having them happen to *me*.

And mark my words:

Now that I'm a cybercriminal in the eyes of US Strategic Command,

Someone's gonna tell me,

That as punishment,

I have to take that goddamned cybersecurity course.

Again.

I guarantee it.

Hotel Butler

YOU LIVE, YOU learn. And I hope I live long enough to learn how to properly manage a hotel butler.

I'll get to that in a minute.

The place where we usually stayed in Mexico City sucked. There's really no other way to put it.

It was undergoing extensive renovations, and the portion of the hotel that remained open had gone to shit. Why bother keeping up the place if it's all going to get ripped out and replaced? I get that.

But it didn't excuse the used tissues my boss found on his bathroom floor. I mean, come on, guys. Let's make a *little* effort here.

The only reason we bothered with the place was because it was right around the corner from the US embassy in what was considered a safe part of town. And, in the not-so-distant past, it once had the reputation for being a pretty swanky place. That was probably why it had been recommended to us.

But the tissues were the last straw.

"That's it!" the boss had said. "I am *not* staying here anymore."

So, it fell to his executive assistant to find us a new place for our next trip. The CFO and I were hanging out at her desk.

"This looks nice," she said, looking at her computer. "How about the St. Regis?"

I'd been to dinners at St. Regis hotels in a couple of cities, but I'd never stayed in one. But, from what I'd seen, they did, in fact, appear quite nice.

"How much does it cost?" asked the CFO. That's what CFOs are supposed to ask.

"Let's see . . ." the boss's assistant responded. "Here," she said, flipping around her monitor for the CFO to see.

"What!" he exclaimed. "Nope. No way. We're not paying that."

This was a bummer, but not unexpected.

"Hang on," he said after a minute. "Was that in dollars or pesos?"

It was pesos.

He pulled out his phone, looked up the exchange rate, and did a quick conversion calculation.

"Oh," he said upon seeing the number. "That isn't *that* bad."

It wasn't cheap, but it wasn't exorbitant, either.

"Let's do it," the CFO decided.

A few minutes later, everything was set. We were staying at the St. Regis.

A couple weeks later, the driver delivered me to the hotel entrance, facing the famous Diana the Huntress fountain at Paseo de la Reforma. A porter greeted me the moment I opened my door. He wore a Secret Service–style earpiece and a little microphone clipped to his lapel.

"Welcome to the St. Regis, señor," he said in accented English. "May I have your name, please?"

I gave it to him, which he then found on a neatly folded piece of paper he'd taken from his jacket pocket.

"Ah, yes," he said upon finding my name. "I see you're with us for one night."

That's correct, I told him.

He then moved his lapel mic in the direction of his mouth and said, "Señor Bozung, llegando."

It was like getting gonged on board a warship. Tradition holds that when a senior officer walks aboard, he or she is formally announced by rank or title to the crew.

"Commander. Arriving."

And I loved the way he pronounced my name.

In the US, most people pronounce it Boh-ZUNGH. In Mexico, and most other places outside the States, people say Boo-ZOON. I find this amusing.

Hey, I'm the first to admit: It's a weird frickin' name.

The porter handed me off to a bellboy, who handed me off to the front-desk attendant, who then handed me off to another bellboy. At every step, and in encountering other random staff members, I received the same greeting. "Buenas tardes, Señor Boo-zoon."

It was a nice touch.

The bellboy led me through the lobby to the elevators. The atmosphere was calming. Pleasing. Soft jazz music played lightly in the background, and the entire place smelled like fresh-cut lilacs. Various water features emitted the sounds of bubbling brooks.

Very feng shui.

It made you think, *This must be how the Rockefellers did it.*

I'm sure there's an entire science behind hotel-atmosphere-setting. Places like the St. Regis employ the science to great effect.

The bellboy made polite small talk during the elevator ride to the fourteenth floor, where he then deposited my bags just inside the door of my room.

This was quite nice.

I immediately set out exploring to discover its various wonders. Five minutes later, there was a knock at my door. Probably another bellboy or assistant manager checking in to ensure I'd found the room satisfactory, I assumed.

What I found instead upon opening the door was a rather distinguished-looking gentleman in white tie and tails—it was after six o'clock, after all—holding a silver tray with a glass of champagne. Clipped to his lapel was a shiny brass name tag that read, *Andres*.

"Welcome to the St. Regis, Señor Boo-zoon," he intoned, formally. "My name is Andres, and I will be your butler for the duration of your stay."

My what?

Uh . . . okay, I stammered in response.

"May I come in?" he asked.

Sure, I said.

Upon stepping into the entryway, he extended the silver tray in my direction.

"A light refreshment," he offered.

When I politely declined, explaining—apologizing—that I unfortunately couldn't drink, Andres seemed disappointed. Ever the professional, he quickly recovered.

"I certainly understand, sir," he replied. "May I show you the features of your room?"

Again, I politely declined, because I was anxious to get settled in and on my way to dinner. And, through my earlier exploration, I had already found a variety of goodies.

The terry cloth robe and slippers. The shoeshine kit and felt-lined bag for sending shoes out for a quick resoling, if necessary. The espresso maker, identical to those found in the nicer European hotels. The fully stocked bar and neat jars of macadamia nuts. The sixty-dollars-a-bottle hand soap and lotion.

I felt like I knew my way around.

Again, a disappointment to Andres.

"Very well, sir," he said. "If you should need anything during your stay, simply press the button on the display above your nightstand, and I will be happy to assist you."

I thanked Andres and sent him on his way, feeling as though I'd failed both of us.

Now, in my defense, I didn't grow up in Downton Abbey. I've never had a valet or a footman. I don't know what to do with such people. I like to think I have good manners and a modicum of class, but the whole point of good manners—and of being a gentleman—is to put people at ease.

I didn't put Andres at ease. In fact, I think I may have insulted him.

Later that night, my room phone rang. It was Andres.

"May I bring you anything, sir? Perhaps a sparkling water or cup of tea?"

No, thank you, I told him. I'm quite fine.

And, again, he sounded dejected.

"Very well, sir. Please call if you need anything."

I'm sorry I failed you, Andres. I've never had a hotel butler.

Next time I'll do better. I'll bring shoes that need shining, clothes that need ironing, and a blazer specked with lint that you can brush clean for me. I'll have you fetch me extra towels that I have no intention of using. I'll complain about things that are wrong with my room, even though they aren't. And then I'll expect you to apologize for them and get the hotel management involved to "fix" them.

I'll say things like, "It's disappointing to see how precipitously the standards have declined here."

How will that be?

I'll be fussy, high maintenance, and a touch condescending.

Because I owe that to you.

And to your colleagues at the glorious, lilac-smelling St. Regis.

Yes, I'll do better next time.

I promise.

Easyrider Olympics

"**ARE WE REALLY** doing this?"

Booger, my squadron mate, was incredulous. We all were. He was just the first to verbalize it.

We usually went surfing on Friday mornings. But instead, all of us officers were instead standing in a gaggle—hardly a formation, by military standards—in the road in front of the hangar.

We all wore squadron T-shirts, as the skipper had directed, along with shorts and running shoes. It appeared the Old Man intended for us to go running around the base in formation.

Something Naval aviators avoided like nonalcoholic beer.

The scene was nonetheless picturesque. The sun was rising behind us, painting Oahu's Ko'olau mountains yellow-green. And the mountains, in turn, were reflected, mirrorlike, in Kaneohe Bay in the foreground.

The trade winds were blowing.

Palm trees were swaying.

Another perfect morning in paradise.

It was about 7:45 a.m. Friday, September 14, 2001. It had been a hell of a week.

For the entire country.

The phone had rung that Tuesday morning, just before four o'clock. It was my mother-in-law, back in Illinois, telling my wife and me to turn on the television. We did, just as the second plane hit.

Naively, my first thought was that there wasn't a cloud in the sky. How did that pilot not avoid hitting the building? It was all so unbelievable.

I decided to go for a run. It was still dark, so I strapped on the stupid reflective belt the Marines made you wear during non-daylight hours.

Clearly, the news was out. Lights were on in every house. And the Marines had definitely gotten word of the attacks, evidenced by all the Humvees and armored personnel carriers that rumbled down Marine Corps Base Hawaii's main drag.

It was surreal.

As I crested the hill near the officers' club, I was stopped by a foot patrol of marines in full battle gear.

"What are you doing out here, sir?" asked the corporal.

What the fuck does it look like I'm doing? I thought.

Just out for a run, I told him.

"Probably not a good idea this morning," he said.

Not one to argue with dudes with loaded weapons, I didn't disagree. I took the most direct route back to my house, showered up, put on a set of khakis, and headed into the squadron. I was the duty officer that day.

The commanding officer, who also lived on base, arrived shortly after I did. It was still early, so not many others were around. Soon, the phone in the duty office started ringing. Squadron members who lived out in town wanted to know whether they should come in. The base was in full lockdown mode, and access was limited. A long line of cars had formed at the front gate. I found the skipper in his office and asked what he wanted me to tell people.

"I don't care if it takes all goddamned day," he said. "Tell them to get their asses in here."

As the morning progressed, the situation remained unclear.

Were we grounded or supposed to go flying?

And to do what?

At one point, we were told to arm up a couple of helicopters with Hellfire missiles and head for Pearl Harbor. Someone thought the bad guys were on inbound merchant ships, looking to take out the fleet. That got the place spun up. But only for a short while.

Stand down, we were later told. But be ready.

The remainder of the day, and most of the week, played out much the same way.

Go! Stop. Get ready! Stand down.

There was talk of moving deployment schedules up to support a surge of multibattle groups to the Middle East. And then we heard deployment schedules would likely remain as is. All the back-and-forth made people anxious. We were on edge.

And then the skipper decided to form us up for a run around base.

Are you frickin' kidding me? I thought.

We were a nation at war. And this was the *Navy*, dammit. We were the HSL-37 "Easyriders." We prided ourselves on *not* doing ridiculous, yut-yut shit like that.

We stood there, out in the road, hoping it was all a joke. But it wasn't.

The skipper yelled, "At a double time...forward...*maaahhhch!*"

We all started shuffling, completely out of step. It was comical.

Seeing this, the skipper ordered, "Somebody call cadence, for Chrissake!"

Eventually, one of the new guys, who'd apparently been tapped for such duty in Officer Candidate School, started in with, "Left... left... lefty-right-a-lay-*uhhffft*."

It wasn't great. But it was passable.

So, we were running through the base, feeling as stupid as we looked. That was confirmed by the smirks on the marines' faces as we passed.

We made our way to the base athletic fields, about a half mile from the hangar. It was a large, open area with a ball diamond and connecting football and soccer fields. There, the skipper halted the formation and told us to gather around.

What now? we were thinking. He wasn't going to make us do push-ups, was he?

"Welcome to the Easyrider Olympics," the skipper announced.

The what? we asked.

The executive officer then appeared next to him, clipboard in hand.

"Okay," the XO began, "these are the teams."

We'd all been arranged into groups and assigned a series of competitions, including softball, flag football, volleyball, and various track and field events. Teams would rotate through each, with winners crowned at a beach barbecue later that evening.

Okay. Not a terrible idea.

Oh, and there was beer. So, *so* much beer.

At every venue, there were coolers filled with cases of it. The suds started flowing at about 8:30 a.m. And they didn't stop until well after midnight.

I don't remember much about any particular event.

Except for how our flight surgeon, Dave, who'd been a starting quarterback at Colorado State, pretty much single-handedly beat the entire squadron in flag football. *After* he'd had about six beers. The rest is pretty fuzzy. But it doesn't matter.

It was one of the most fun days of my life. And most instructive.

I don't recall any passage in my Naval Academy leadership textbook that would have suggested a commander organize a beer-soaked field day following the deadliest attack on US soil since Pearl Harbor.

But you know what?

It was fucking brilliant. The Old Man knew exactly what he was doing.

We emerged from the fog of our hangovers a tighter, more focused, more determined group. Yes, the future was uncertain. But we'd deal with it.

Together.

Thanks, Skipper.

I've never forgotten the example you set that day.

And I don't intend to.

Ever.

The Kuwaitis Are Offended

WE'RE ALL NATURALLY inclined to certain things.

The oversized, gregarious kid plays left tackle and eventually sells cars. The skinny, cerebral kid runs cross country and becomes a neurosurgeon. The student council president pledges Sigma Chi and goes on to a career in government, law, or white-collar crime.

And the uptight, reasonably well-spoken kid who hates to have his hair messed up is made a Navy protocol officer.

Never fails. At least, it's never failed for me.

I've never asked for it, but I've lost count of how many times I've been made the protocol officer. I'm like C-3PO, apparently. The protocol droid, whether I want to be or not.

And I certainly didn't want to be this time. Hell, I didn't even want to be in Kuwait in the first place. That's not to say I objected to being deployed. Quite the contrary.

It beat the shit out of being a corporate guy.

But, when I found out I was going to some weirdo maritime security unit to be a full-time watch officer, I figured there had to be a better use of my time. And there was.

I'd reached out to a SEAL officer with whom I'd worked at the Naval Academy. He'd been the commander of Naval Special Warfare Group Two in a previous tour, based in Little Creek, Virginia. He introduced me to the then-current commander of Group Two and let him know I had orders to the Middle East.

"Maybe you could use him," my former colleague suggested.

The current commander, a SEAL captain, invited me to a meeting at his office in the Group Two compound. It was brief.

"I'll put you on a plane tomorrow," he said. "We can always use air-ops guys."

Undisclosed location, of course. I wouldn't be kicking down doors, but I'd be directly supporting the guys who did.

Sweet! I thought. Not a bad way to earn a living.

I went straight to the commanding officer, or CO, of the maritime security unit to which I'd been assigned.

The SpecWar guys said they could use me, I told him. And all I needed was his permission to have my orders rewritten for Special Warfare Command.

"Listen," he said. "That sounds totally badass. But I have no idea what we'll be up against when we get to Kuwait."

Uh-oh. I saw where this was going.

"So, why would I surrender a resource if I didn't have to?" he asked.

I was the resource. And, I admit, I appreciated the CO's logic. I also appreciated that I would be bored out of my skull in the ensuing ten months, manning the watch in some shitty, over-air-conditioned trailer at Kuwait Naval Base.

And, indeed, I was.

Seven days a week, I woke up, worked out, killed about a dozen cockroaches on the floor of the bathroom I shared with an adjoining room, took a shower, had the chicken cordon bleu at the dining facility, and then went on watch.

And, on the way to watch, I passed the same pockmarked stone wall at the far end of the courtyard, around which officers' quarters was arranged. There was a line of starburst-shaped indentations in the wall, about shoulder high, that ran its entire length.

What's that? I asked one of our Kuwaiti liaison officers one day.

He said it was where Saddam's forces had lined up captured Kuwaiti Naval officers on August 2, 1990, and executed them. The Kuwaitis had left the wall unrepaired as something of a memorial.

A touch macabre, I thought. But a useful reminder of why we were there.

I'll tell you why I *wasn't* there.

To be a goddamned protocol officer.

But, of course, that's exactly what happened.

About halfway through our tour, the CO was scheduled to have his change-of-command ceremony. It's an elaborate, tradition-laden affair in which the mantle of command is passed from one officer to another.

Changes of command are a big deal in the military, and rightfully so. Command carries enormous responsibility. So I had no objection whatsoever to the CO's having a proper ceremony. I'm a sucker for tradition, after all.

But I had no desire to be the event planner, master of ceremonies, and general cat-herder charged with organizing and executing the event.

Which is what a protocol officer does.

I gently suggested to the CO that perhaps another officer was better equipped to accept the tremendous honor of serving as his protocol officer. But thanks for thinking of me, I said.

He wasn't having it.

"Nope," he said. "I don't trust anyone else to get this right."

The C-3PO thing was screwing me. Again.

The CO had the admin officer draw up a formal designation letter, whereby I was officially dubbed the protocol officer.

Fantastic.

So, I went to work putting this damn ceremony together. Luckily, given the long history and various regulations surrounding such an event, it was a pretty straightforward task.

Until I got to the invitations.

Can't we just email them? I asked the CO.

Nope. This was likely the only change-of-command ceremony he'd get in his career, and he wanted to do it right. That meant old-school, glossy-print cardstock invitations.

And how in the hell was I supposed to get those in the middle of the desert?

I eventually found someone back in Norfolk willing to airmail us invitations, provided we designed them. Again, this was a pretty straightforward task.

Service Etiquette, the protocol officer's Bible, dictated the format and content of change-of-command invitations. Nonetheless, I decided to add my own personal flourish to dress them up a bit.

The ceremony was to be held at Camp Patriot, a joint command that resided within the confines of the Mohammed Al-Ahmad Kuwait Naval Base. Both American and Kuwaiti officers were to be invited. So, beneath the base's English spelling, I had the name printed in Arabic.

I got the idea from the flight-suit name tags every aviator bought when he went to the Middle East. Someone figured it would be cool to have his name written in Arabic beneath the wings on his name tag. And so everyone did it. Including me.

Of course, the Arabic could have said, "This guy's a jackass," but no one knew. And no one cared. Because it looked cool.

Anyway.

I got the invitations and showed them to the CO. He thought they looked great. So then I worked with the US Naval attaché to get them addressed and delivered to all the right Kuwaiti officers. Everything was going great.

Then, a few days later, the attaché burst into the CO's office, distraught. "Your change-of-command invitations . . . You've offended the Kuwaitis!" he exclaimed.

Offended the Kuwaitis?

Apparently, the name of the base wasn't spelled correctly in Arabic, and the Kuwaitis had taken it as a slight. Google hadn't gotten the Arabic translation entirely correct.

Shocking.

But it wasn't *that* bad, I thought. The error was tantamount to referring to someone named *James* as the less formal, more familiar *Jim*.

No big deal, right?

Well, there was more to it than that, the attaché explained.

There's a thin line between peoples' perceptions of liberators and occupiers. While the Kuwaitis remained grateful for what we'd done for them back in 1991, some felt we had overstayed our welcome. And this whole change-of-command snafu apparently served to feed that fire.

"You need to get new invitations out—*now*," the attaché concluded.

So, I jumped through my ass and spent an obscene amount of taxpayer money to have new invitations overnighted to the base.

The change-of-command ceremony otherwise went off without a hitch. The Kuwaitis took their seats in the front row. They ate plenty of cake and drank plenty of tea. And they reminded us how generous they were for hosting us on their base.

Crisis averted.

Sorry I almost caused an international incident there, CO.

Of course, you could have avoided the whole thing had you let me deploy with the SEALs.

And you sure as shit didn't have to make me your stupid protocol officer.

Even though I do hate it

When my hair gets messed up.

București Shakedown

I COULDN'T TELL exactly where the conversation was going. But one thing was becoming increasingly clear:

A Romanian prison cell was likely in my future, and it was entirely the guys in Naples' fault.

At least, that's how I saw it.

"Just rent a car," they'd said. "It's an easy drive."

This, from a couple dudes who'd spent the previous five years traveling all over Eastern Europe. They were fully accustomed to the region's maniac drivers—I was not so accustomed.

But I'm getting ahead of myself.

I should first mention that I'd volunteered for this, the Eurasia Partnership Dive Exercise. It was a NATO thing, cosponsored by the US Sixth Fleet and Romanian Navy. Sixth Fleet headquarters was in Naples, Italy, where sat the two lieutenant commanders charged with planning the exercise. Both were aviators. My kind of guys.

But while they owned the planning, the responsibility for

execution fell to their reserve counterparts. A bunch of weekend warriors hanging out two days a month at Naval Station Great Lakes, Illinois.

I was one of those weekend warriors.

And when the call went out for an officer in charge, I took one look around my cubicle and decided a month in Romania was preferable to the corporate drudgery.

Even though I knew nothing about diving.

"Doesn't matter," the guys in Naples said. "Your job is to herd the cats. Our guys on *Grasp* will take care of the rest."

Grasp was a US rescue and salvage ship in the Black Sea. There was an entire Navy dive team on board. The cats consisted of Explosive Ordnance Disposal, or EOD, divers from Romania, Bulgaria, Hungary, Ukraine, Georgia, and Azerbaijan. It was a pretty high-profile thing, given the importance of our relationships with Black and Caspian Sea countries.

It didn't matter that the EOD guys were thugs. Professionals, but thugs.

Why did anybody think it was a good idea to put a reservist in charge?

And why diving? That, it turned out, was easier to explain.

While most, but not all, of the exercise participants shared Russian as a common language, *everyone* spoke the same language underwater. The sign language of diving is apparently universal, and everyone communicated just fine with each other in the water.

So, the plan was for all participants to converge upon the Mihail Kogălniceanu Air Base just inland from Constanța, Romania, on the Black Sea. It was where the Romanian Air Force used to keep its MiG-29s.

The EOD guys were all flying or driving directly to the base via military transport. I, on the other hand, would be flying commercially to Bucharest, then driving the two and a half hours to the coast.

The very thought of the drive stressed me out.

Have you ever driven around lost in a foreign country? I have, and it sucks. And there was high potential to get lost in Bucharest.

Humans have lived there since the Paleolithic era. Some of the roads are centuries-old, paved-over oxcart paths laid out with no discernible rhyme or reason.

I intended to take my Garmin GPS, but who knew if it would work in Romania? So, I fell back on my aviation training and conducted an exhaustive map study of the various routes from the Bucharest airport, through the city, and then on to Constanța. It wasn't perfect, but it would have to do.

The flight across the Atlantic was uneventful, and I made my connection in Munich with plenty of time. I arrived in Bucharest sleep deprived, but not miserably so.

I hit an ATM and grabbed a hundred bucks' worth of Romanian lei. Then I found the rental car place, checked out my crappy Dacia, and hit the road. It was about two o'clock on a Friday afternoon, and luckily my GPS was working.

I made it into the city, having navigated multiple six-lanes-deep roundabouts. So far, so good. Then I hit a stretch of mostly open road connecting two residential areas. I was driving along, beginning to relax.

Then, all of a sudden, this girl walks out into the intersection right in front of me. I had a green light, so I hadn't even thought to slow down. I swerved hard into the next lane to avoid the girl, thankful there was no oncoming traffic. As I did so, she literally leapt back onto the sidewalk behind her and began waving her arms and cursing at me.

I assume she was cursing, that is.

I maneuvered back into my lane, breathing hard, trying to get my heart rate back under control. A moment later, there were flashing lights behind me, along with that *weee-awww weee-awww* sound of European sirens.

The cops.

What the hell? I thought. I had a green light!

Of course, there was no place to pull over. I was on one of those ancient paved-over oxcart paths with no shoulder. So, I slowed down, put on my hazards, and began leading the Romanian police on a low-speed chase, looking for a place to get off the road.

When I finally found one, I hadn't even come to a complete stop before the two cops were out of their car and on either side of mine.

And they were *piiiiissed*.

They started yelling at me in Romanian simultaneously.

English? I asked.

Español? they answered.

When I replied no, one of them suddenly knew passable English.

"Papers!" he said, just like in the movies.

I handed him my passport, which he waved off, getting even more pissed.

"Papers!" he said again.

You mean, like, license and registration? I thought.

"It's a rental," I offered as I reached across the front seat into the glove compartment.

I handed him every scrap of paper I could find in there, and he took it all, nodding to his partner on the other side of my car. Then they walked back to their squad car and stood in front of it.

I could see them talking in my rearview mirror. And they were clearly still agitated.

And I wasn't entirely sure why.

I thought I'd done a pretty heroic job of not running over that girl back at the intersection.

They clearly thought otherwise.

For the next half hour, they continued to walk back and forth between their car and mine, stopping at my window each pass to yell at me in Romanian and ask for more papers.

Sensing things were going south, I finally said, "I don't

understand exactly what I've done. But if you intend to detain me any further, I need you to inform my embassy that you're holding a US Naval officer." And then I handed the cop closest to me my military ID card.

He took it, turning it over in his hand a few times and examining both sides. Then he said a few things to his partner in Romanian before handing it back to me.

"Get out of here," he said.

And I did. As quickly as possible. Thankfully, the remaining drive to Constanța was uneventful.

When I finally got to the base, I made a beeline for the Navy senior chief who was serving as the exercise's assistant officer in charge.

"Senior!" I said. "You're not gonna frickin' believe what happened to me."

The senior chief, also a reservist, was a Russian linguist and somewhat renowned Sovietologist who worked for the State Department when he wasn't playing weekend warrior. He'd spent loads of time in Russia and Eastern Europe.

When I finished telling him my story, he said, matter-of-factly, "You know, twenty bucks would have made that whole thing go away."

Huh?

"They were shaking you down," he said. "They just wanted your money."

Are you kidding me?

Rat bastards!

"Next time," he continued, "just tell 'em you're sorry and suggest that you pay a small fine. Twenty bucks usually does the trick."

Well, shit, I thought.

Welcome to Romania.

And thanks again to my friends in Naples.

Yeah, that was some easy drive.

You friggin' jerks.

Hangin' with the General

"THE GENERAL WONDERS if you'd like to join him up front." The major had an air of authority that was equal parts impressive and intimidating.

She'd made the short walk to the back of the plane where two of my fellow Naval Academy midshipmen and I were seated. While she'd presented the general's offer as a suggestion, it was anything but.

Put another way, the major's message was, *Get your asses to the front of the plane, pronto.*

Aye, aye, ma'am.

And why exactly did an Air Force lieutenant general want to see three lowly midshipmen?

"I dunno," my buddy whispered. "Probably something you did."

Thanks, jackass.

Not inclined to argue with a commissioned officer, particularly one whose boss wore three stars, we obediently followed her to the front.

The general came into view after a few steps. He was seated in the frontmost seat, facing aft, thumbing through a briefing binder. He wore reading glasses on the end of his nose and an Ike jacket with his name and three silver stars embroidered on the left breast. It was the same type of jacket you saw the president wear on Air Force One.

Frickin' Air Force, I thought. They have the nicest swag.

I was first in line behind the major as we made our way up the aisle. Upon closing within five steps of the general's seat, he looked up from his binder.

Shit! His general-ness hit me full force the moment his gaze rested upon me. The major nodded my way, a clear directive to present myself to her boss.

"Midshipman Fourth Class Bozung, sir. I understand you want to see us, General?"

A come-around with an Air Force three star was exactly the last thing any of us wanted. My buddies and I had really hoped to leave all this yes-sir-no-sir stuff behind for a while. It was spring break after all, a respite from the Dark Ages of our Academy plebe year.

We'd left Annapolis that afternoon with a destination, but no real plan. Puerto Rico. That's all we knew. How we'd get there, where we'd stay, or how we'd get back, well . . . those details would have to sort themselves out.

We considered it a low-risk operation. We weren't storming the beaches of Normandy, after all. And we had the resources of the US government at our disposal.

Space Available travel, or Space-A, is a wonderful benefit for active-duty members and retirees alike. On any given day, the military has planes flying all over the world. And unless the plane is on a bombing run, any open seat can be made available to Space-A travelers.

And it's free! Well, mostly free. Maybe you pay for a box lunch, but that's about it.

The tricky thing is, flight schedules can be fluid, and anyone in a higher priority category can take your seat.

Say I'm a retiree heading to Naval Air Station Key West to go fishing and stock up on tax-free liquor. Any active-duty member traveling on orders to participate in an exercise can take my seat. So, you need some flexibility in your schedule. But, if you have that, only the GI Bill eclipses Space-A travel as the ultimate military benefit.

Of course, the tax-free liquor is up there, too.

But anyway.

My buddies and I had caught a ride to Andrews Air Force Base outside Washington, DC. From there, we planned to leapfrog our way to the Caribbean, hopefully landing at US Naval Station Roosevelt Roads, Puerto Rico, before the end of the weekend.

Upon checking in at the Space-A counter at Andrews, we learned there were no direct flights available to Puerto Rico. No worries, we thought. We'll just catch anything going south.

"This is interesting," the airman managing the counter told us. "I have three seats available on an executive jet going to Maxwell."

It was an Air Force Gulfstream, taking some general to Maxwell Air Force Base in Montgomery, Alabama.

"You don't see those seats available for Space-A very often," the airman said.

Whatever. If it was going south, we'd take it.

An hour later, my buddies and I walked out to the far side of the tarmac to the glistening Gulfstream. The crew was walking around the exterior of the aircraft doing a preflight inspection. We were ushered up the steps into the cabin by another airman and directed to seats in the back. The Gulfstream had a very unmilitary look to it. We felt more like bankers than midshipmen.

A few minutes later, a black Suburban trailing a police car with flashing lights pulled right up to the steps of the aircraft. Black Suburbans were ubiquitous in DC. They were meant to be low profile, but instead screamed, "VIP!"

The driver, an Air Force guy in a beret, stepped out from the front seat and opened the back door. Out strode a silver-haired, athletic-looking guy with a regal bearing, followed by an entourage of aides.

The general.

He bound up the steps and said a quick hello to the guys in the cockpit.

Unsure of the proper military protocol surrounding a general officer's boarding of a Gulfstream, my buddies and I half stood from our seats and came to an awkward form of attention. The general, noticing us, gave us a quick wave as he sat down. He was then surrounded by his aides and went back to work on whatever he'd been doing at his desk at the Pentagon.

The pilots spun up the engines, and we were airborne in minutes. About the time the plane reached cruising altitude, the major had come back to summon my buddies and me to the front.

Upon presenting myself, the general's countenance completely changed.

He beamed.

"Hey, guys!" he said. "How's it going? Come on, have a seat."

O . . . kay.

"So," he continued, "what's going on at the Academy?"

Didn't see that coming.

We soon learned the general was an Air Force Academy graduate from the late sixties and had a son there a year ahead of us. He told us about all the crazy shit they had done at the Academy in his day. We, in turn, told him what level of punishment such stunts would likely merit at today's Academy.

"I'm pretty sure you'd get kicked out for that stuff today, General," my buddy offered.

The general loved that.

We then talked aviation. The general had significant combat experience in some of the greatest tactical aircraft of all time, including the venerable F-4 Phantom. Each of us midshipmen was an aspiring aviator, so we ate it up.

The conversation continued uninterrupted for the remainder of the flight. The general, it turned out, was positively delightful. We laughed. A lot. All of us. And we hardly noticed when the plane landed and taxied to stop at Maxwell.

"Well, this is where I get off," the general said. He seemed almost disappointed. "One more thing, guys. I know it sounds strange, but try to enjoy your time at the Academy. It goes fast."

It was a nostalgic moment for him. Perhaps it did people like the general some good to set aside the crushing weight of responsibility to relive their cadet days every once in a while.

A member of the flight crew had already lowered the stairs of the aircraft down to the tarmac. Not wanting to overstay our welcome, we bid the general farewell and headed for the exit.

Once again, I was in the lead.

As I stepped out of the cabin, I noticed a crowd of blue uniforms arranged in perfect rows beside the aircraft. There was a long red carpet extending from the bottom of the steps out to the formation, with saluting airmen standing on either side.

What the hell is all this?

And then a band struck up the opening chords of the Air Force anthem.

I took two steps down the stairs and stopped, my buddies colliding behind me as I did. It hit me: This must be the general's welcoming party. They sure as shit don't roll out the band for three pissant midshipmen.

What should we do? Should we go back into the plane?

As I stood there, equivocating, the guy leading the band shot a quizzical look at the colonel standing at the end of the red carpet. I assumed it was the base commander. The colonel, in turn, shot me a look that said, "Get. Out. Of. Here. *Now!*"

About that time, my buddy shoved me in the back. We hightailed it off the stairs to the rear of the plane and then sprinted the rest of the way off the tarmac.

Sorry if we spoiled your welcome party, General.

But what a great conversation! And what a privilege to have shared that flight with such a great man.

As for the rest of spring break:

We made it to Puerto Rico.

And had an epic, Bacardi-soaked week.
And got kicked out of officers' quarters.
And slept on the floor of a future three star's apartment.
And almost got lost in a rainforest.
But, alas, that will have to be a story
For another day.

High School Spanish

"PISO . . . CUATRO."

It was the third time the dude at the security desk had said that. He was trying to be patient with me.

Trying.

"Si. Comprendo. Pero . . ." I was struggling, hard. The words I needed were totally eluding me. "Uh . . . como se llama? Uh . . ."

Damn you, high school Spanish! You failed me. And at a totally inopportune time.

The CEO, standing behind me, looked mildly amused. The CFO, standing to my right, had his phone out and was thumbing through Google Translate, trying to rescue me from what was fast becoming an awkward situation.

If I'd learned anything through the years about working with and around senior people, it's that you avoid awkwardness. Always.

And I typically do.

Whenever I travel internationally, I like to keep a few simple phrases of the native language in my back pocket. Hello. Goodbye. Please. Thank you.

I've found these to be invaluable while navigating a variety of circumstances overseas. And when those don't work, some combination of pointing, gesturing, and charades usually does.

And cash. Always cash.

Of course, English is so widely spoken one rarely has to resort to such measures. But then sometimes one does. As I was then in Mexico City.

We were there for a meeting with a competing company's CEO and various members of his executive team to discuss a possible deal. An important deal.

As such, I'd personally managed all the logistics. Planes, cars, hotels, meeting agendas—everything had fallen neatly into place. Until we got to the office building where the meeting was to be held and encountered the guy at the security desk.

Who didn't speak a lick of English.

Ordinarily, it wouldn't have bothered me. In fact, I would have welcomed the opportunity to habla a little español. While I have no proficiency in any foreign language, I feel I could almost get by with Spanish.

Like most people I know, I took it in high school. And maybe because my brain was still in its formative stages, some of it stuck. Plus, I got to use it a fair amount when I was stationed in Puerto Rico.

It was my first official Navy duty station. I was eighteen. There were several native Puerto Ricans in my squadron who spoke Spanish almost exclusively, unless there were officers around. The leading petty officer of my division—my boss—was among the natives. His parents and extended family lived on the island. Some weekends, he'd take me to hang out with them in his hometown. It was great fun, even though I couldn't understand most of what they were saying.

But then, eventually, without even realizing it, I started to pick it up. I owed a lot of that to Vilmary. She was my boss's cousin.

When the Navy Ball rolled around later that year, I was informed I would be cutting the cake with the base commanding officer. It was a tradition. He was the oldest active service member on the base, and I was the youngest. So, together, we had to cut the cake.

Given the prominent role I'd be playing, I didn't want to seem a loser and go stag. So, my boss offered to set me up with Vilmary, who didn't speak a word of English. I accepted his offer, but doubted she would.

I was wrong.

My status as an official cake-cutter apparently convinced her of my merits as a date. And, I have to say, she played the part of date-of-cake-cutter brilliantly.

At one point, I got to introduce her to my squadron commanding officer. Not wanting to be rude to Vilmary, who was vastly outnumbered by English-only speakers, I made the introduction in Spanish. It was an improved version of my high school Spanish. I had to up my game as an official cake-cutter, after all.

Upon hearing me converse with Vilmary en español, my commanding officer looked over at the executive officer, standing nearby, and said, "Hey, XO, get this: He speaks Spanish, too!"

Which, of course, I didn't.

But I wasn't going to stop the skipper from thinking I was some kind of boy genius.

Anyway.

Back at the security desk in Mexico City, I was still flailing. The whole problem started when I had to fill out the building's guest registry. Most of the column headings in the registry were familiar.

Nombre. Yup.

Fecha. Got it.

Para ver, or "to see." Okay.

But then I got stuck on the fourth column, labeled *Piso*.

I couldn't for the life of me remember what that word meant. I told the security guy in my *very* rusty high school Spanish the name of the company we were there to visit and that I didn't know exactly where in the building it resided.

"Piso cuatro," he replied.

Yes, I know, I had to write down the *piso* in the *fourth* column of the registry. But I still didn't know what the hell a piso was.

"Piso cuatro," he said again.

Okay, now this guy's just being a wiseass, I thought.

I repeated, in my still-shitty Spanish, that I didn't know where in the building we were supposed to go or what the hell a piso was.

So now here we are, the attendant speaking up a third time. "Piso . . . *cuatro.*"

I was getting nowhere.

Finally, our CFO chimed in. "Piso means floor. He's telling you the office is on the fourth floor."

Oh. Okay.

I smiled awkwardly at the security guy and managed a meek, defeated, "Gracias," and made my way to the elevator.

We sat down at the meeting with the CEO and others. I pulled the manila folder out of my briefcase that contained all the details of the various topics on our agenda. As I did so, a portion of an email I had printed caught my eye.

When you get to the building, check in with the security guard and then head up to the fourth floor. Our offices are there.

Shit. There it was.

Piso cuatro.

Sorry, security dude.

And damn you, high school Spanish!

Lube Oil Delivery

"**WELL, I JUST** got hollered at by the guy at the tool and die."

Pete's dad, president of Petersen Oil, had just taken a call from a pissed-off customer.

"He says you just dropped that barrel of oil in the middle of a field."

That was only partially correct. Yes, I had left the barrel in the field adjacent to the maintenance shop. But I hadn't *dropped* it there. I'd *placed* it there, after having made numerous inquiries as to where it should be delivered.

"Did you take it to the north side of the building like I said?" Pete's dad asked.

He was funny like that. He had an innate sense of direction, like a carrier pigeon. Whenever he gave Pete and me something to do, it always came with cardinal points.

"Make sure you trim the weeds on the south side of the road," he'd say, or, "Paint all the curbs near the east entrance."

I never had the slightest clue what he was talking about. Put me in some random parking lot, and I wouldn't know north from south or east from west. Pete always knew. He'd inherited his dad's sense of direction. But that was worthless to me back at the tool and die.

Pete was at the beach for spring break. He'd gone with Arntz and Sloke and the other guys. At that moment, he was probably sucking down Busch Lights from a funnel.

Lucky bastard.

Of course, my parents said I couldn't go. They assumed I'd get arrested or kidnapped or something. Pete's dad wasn't concerned about any of that. So, Pete went to the beach, and I stayed in Michigan to enjoy the dirty, melting snowdrifts and solid-gray overcast.

Pete's dad said I could work at the station if I wanted. I figured if I couldn't be at the beach, I might as well make a little money. So, I showed up every day to shovel, sweep, mop, scrub, and paint, just like I did with Pete during the summer.

It was all going fine until Pete's dad told me to deliver a barrel of lube oil to the tool and die shop across town. I'd never made such a delivery by myself. I'd only done it with Pete.

He was always the guy in charge. And for good reason.

First, you had to manhandle the four-hundred-pound, fifty-five-gallon drum into the back of the pickup truck. That was tricky, because you had to use the tailgate as a sort of lever and get the barrel at just the right angle and then lift and pivot at just the right time.

Pete understood how to do this intuitively, which I assumed he'd inherited from his dad, like his sense of direction.

Then, once it was in the back of the pickup, blocked and wedged into place, you had to drive to wherever it was being delivered and unload it where the customer wanted it.

And the unloading was dicier than the loading.

You put the tailgate down, then stacked three old truck tires on the ground just behind and beneath it. After that, you rolled the barrel all the way to the end of the tailgate. Once it was there, you stood behind the tires, facing the tailgate, with both hands on the barrel. Then you slowly rolled it toward you until it fell off the tailgate and onto the stack of tires. The barrel would bounce off the stack, and, as it did, you'd have to steer it in midair to one side so it landed upright on the ground next to it.

It was a total finesse move. And not exactly OSHA approved.

I wasn't great at it. But I didn't want to let Pete's dad down, either, so I'd gone straight to the maintenance shop at the tool and die.

"I've got your barrel of SAE 30," I told the guy sitting at the desk near the back. "Where do you want it?"

He didn't even look up.

"I dunno," he said. "Ask somebody else."

Somebody else? Who? I asked

The guy didn't even respond.

I'd encountered his type plenty of times while working the register at Petersen Oil. He'd roll into the parking lot in his crummy pickup truck, totally ignore the designated parking spaces, and park at a forty-five-degree angle to the front door, so close you could barely open the damn thing. Then, once inside the station, he'd look right past me to the cigarette case behind the register.

"Pack of Reds," he'd say, as in Marlboro Reds.

Hard or soft? I'd ask.

That was an important question. Guys like this would lose their shit if you gave them a soft pack when they wanted a hard pack. I'd learned that the hard way.

I'd slide the pack across the counter, whereupon he would pull out a wad of dirty bills and hand it to me, expecting me to count out the correct amount. I'd give him his change, and, if I was feeling friendly, tell him to "have a good one."

"Same," he'd reply, shorthand for "Same to you."

Then he'd go back to his truck and drive off until it was time to come back for another pack of Reds. I can't say this was my kind of guy. But I'd at least learned how to communicate with such people.

Or so I thought.

I found three other guys outside the maintenance shop, all of whom either ignored me or told me to bother someone else. Eventually, I saw a barrel of oil sitting on a couple pallets by itself in the small field next to the maintenance shop.

That must be where the lube oil goes, I thought.

So, in plain view, with at least a couple guys watching, I drove the pickup out to the field by the barrel of oil and unloaded the new one. No one said a word or tried to stop me.

I explained all this to Pete's dad. He wasn't mad. But he wasn't happy, either.

"Next time, just give me a call," he said.

Fair enough.

"And don't worry too much about it," he added. "Those guys just like to holler sometimes."

That was generous. And I appreciated it.

Thus ended my career as a lube oil delivery man.

Pete's dad never asked me to deliver another barrel again.

Can't say I blame him.

Hope you enjoyed the beach, Pete.

Spring break in Michigan sucks.

The 9/11 Commission

"**UNLESS SOMEONE MORE SENIOR** than I am tells you to leave, *stay.*"

I appreciated the boss's vote of confidence. But one glance around the room suggested the odds of my staying were probably low.

The boss and I were the only officers not wearing stars on our shoulders. And given the sensitive nature of the discussion, it seemed likely one of those admirals or generals would tell me, the lowly lieutenant, to skedaddle.

The boss was definitely staying. He'd been called, by name, to testify before the commission. The 9/11 Commission.

He'd been the senior watch officer in the National Military Command Center the morning of September 11, 2001. Once it was clear the planes had struck the Twin Towers intentionally, the boss had helped direct the nation's military response to the attack.

So, yes, he was staying.

We'd spent much of the previous week driving back and forth between the Academy and the Pentagon. There'd been prep meetings to attend. Lawyers to consult. I hadn't been involved in any of that. My job was simply to deliver the boss. After that, I'd go find a cup of coffee or bullshit with a buddy until it was time to leave.

I assumed I'd play a similar role here.

We'd navigated our way to the hotel in Crystal City, not far from the Pentagon. The main floor housed the ballroom where the hearing was to be held, presided over by Thomas Kean, former governor of New Jersey.

The ballroom was set up like one of those Senate hearing rooms you see on the news. A row of chairs was arranged behind a long table for the witnesses, facing a raised dais for the committee members. Reporters were scurrying around, claiming little patches of floor in the area beneath the dais. Behind the witness chairs were parallel rows of seats where guys like me were supposed to sit.

And keep their damn mouths shut.

Having surveyed the ballroom, the boss and I made our way to the private conference room several floors up. There was to be a final prep meeting before my boss and other witnesses made their appearances before the commission. Upon entering the room, I noticed faces whose pictures I'd seen in newspapers and on television. The boss started working his way around the room, presenting himself to each, while I moved to the most out-of-the-way corner I could find.

There, I stood, at semi-attention, having no idea what to do next.

After a few minutes, a voice called out, "Gentlemen . . . the chairman."

And then in walked General Richard B. Myers, US Air Force. The chairman of the Joint Chiefs of Staff. The most senior officer in the entire US military.

Instinctively, I shifted from semi-attention to rigid, eyes-locked-forward, *Full Metal Jacket*–style attention. And I stayed like that until the chairman worked his way around the room to me.

When the boss noticed General Myers approaching, he deftly maneuvered to my side and said, "General, I'd like you to meet my EA, Dan Bozung."

EA. Executive assistant. Complete nobody, compared to the heavyweights in the room.

"Nice to meet you, Dan," said the chairman. "Glad to have you here."

He extended his hand. I shook it.

"It's a pleasure to meet you, General," I managed.

After the chairman finished working his way around the room, he took his seat at the head of the table. As the others were taking their chairs, General Myers asked, politely, "Could all the JAGs please excuse us?"

Judge Advocates General. Lawyers.

The chairman was kicking them all out.

Some of them were full colonels, holding a rank three times greater than mine.

Should I leave, too? I wondered. I mean, if the colonels have to go, would it make sense for the lieutenant to stay?

Then I remembered my boss's instructions. No one more senior than he had told me to leave. And I was not a JAG. So, I stayed put, fully expecting to get booted at any moment.

But I didn't.

As soon as the JAGs cleared the room, General Myers launched into a summary of the various military activities that had taken place the morning of 9/11, the rationale behind each, and the questions he anticipated from committee members. It was fascinating. And historic. This was like George Marshall briefing his service chiefs on the Pearl Harbor attack.

And there I was. The lowly lieutenant.

The chairman concluded by issuing a directive to those of us who would be observing from the audience.

"Do *not* react, in any way, to anything that is said during testimony," he said. "The last thing we need is a camera catching one of you rolling your eyes or smirking."

Makes sense.

Later that night, my wife and I watched excerpts of the hearing on CSPAN. And when the camera turned to my boss, there I was, sitting right behind him.

And it was clear I had taken the chairman's words to heart.

I was completely frozen the entire time I was in the frame. My face registered no expression whatsoever. Except, unfortunately, for my eyes.

"You look like one of those lizards," my wife said.

Even though my entire body was immobilized, my eyes were darting around the room, seemingly independent of one another.

Shit. She was right.

"I'm sure no one noticed," she said.

The next morning, my boss told me he and his wife had also watched the hearing. And, like my wife, his had apparently cracked up at my weirdo eye movements.

"She said you looked a little uptight," he said, laughing.

Funny coincidence, I said, and told him about the lizard comment.

"Well, whatever," he continued. "At least the chairman let you stay."

Yes, the chairman had let me stay.

And in so doing,

Allowed me to witness history.

I did exactly what you told me, boss.

And I'll always be grateful I did.

Awkward in Zagreb

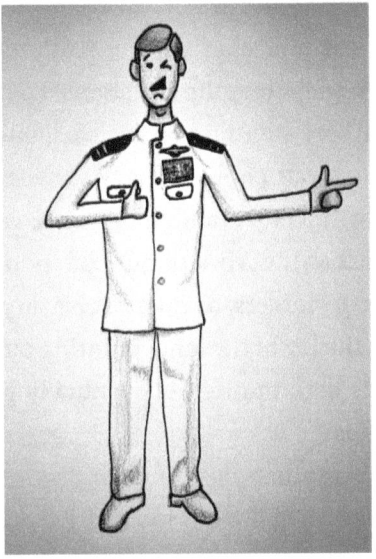

"**THE CHINESE GUY** is gonna want to talk to you," Rob says.

Okay.

"No big deal," he continues. "Just be polite and keep it vague."

US embassy, Zagreb, Croatia.

Rob's the Naval attaché. Former F-14 Tomcat pilot. He's one part diplomat, one part spook. I'm not sure which version of him is talking. Probably the spook.

It's a Fourth of July party, hosted by the US ambassador. As with so many of my Navy experiences, I have absolutely no business being here.

My buddy Ryan thought it would be a terrific idea. He's a Naval Academy classmate and in my reserve unit.

"You're gonna be in Romania doing that exercise, right?" he asks.

Yes.

"Just come to Croatia when you're finished," he says. "It'll be fun."

You know, just pop on over.

Typical Ryan.

He's both fearless and charismatic. Nothing scares him, and everyone loves him. Including the Croatians, apparently.

Rob, Ryan, and I are standing on the back lawn of the embassy, sipping champagne in our chokers. Navy service dress whites. The high-collared uniform Iceman and Slider wore while accepting the Top Gun trophy next to the Miramar O-club pool.

I look fantastic in chokers, as do most Naval aviators.

Rob's giving us the lay of the land, pointing out who's who in the Croatian diplomatic community. He eventually peels off to "work." Whatever that means.

Ryan and I grab another glass of champagne and start working our way through the crowd. It's our job to drive positive engagement with our international partners.

One glass of bubbly at a time.

Sure enough, the Chinese guy finds us. "Haven't seen you guys at one of these things before," he says in perfect English. "What brings you to Croatia?"

"A short-term training assignment," I answer. "It's just good luck that we got to be here for the Fourth."

"I hear that," he says. "Well, enjoy your stay."

And then he walks off to chat up another group.

Seems pretty harmless to me. But will Ryan's and my names go into some report he files with his superiors in Beijing? Will they start a dossier on us?

I've seen too many movies.

Rob finds us after a while. We report our interaction with the Chinese guy. He doesn't seem too concerned.

"Okay," he says. "Our work here is done. Let's get out of here."

Cool.

I assume we'll take a cab back to the hotel and change.

"Nope," says Rob. "We're going out just like this."

In chokers?

"Yup. I want to see what happens."

What happens?

Now, I am not a member of the intelligence community. But every bit of training I've ever received on how to conduct oneself in a foreign country has stressed the importance of blending in. Do *not* call attention to yourself. Three dudes in chokers in Zagreb will certainly call attention.

As it should, because we look damn good.

Still, I think it's a pretty terrible idea, and I tell Rob so. But Ryan's indifferent. He's up for anything. Ultimately, I lose the argument, and we find ourselves in a pub a few blocks from the embassy.

As expected, heads turn abruptly the moment we walk in.

We make our way to the bar and order drinks. The bartender is amused. He looks at us like we're in Halloween costumes.

Some random guy eventually walks up to us and asks in decent English, "What is *this*?"

He sounds just as skeptical as I am.

"Excuse me?" Rob replies.

"You know," the guy continues. "What's with the uniforms?"

Fair question.

"We were at an official event," Rob says, "and didn't have time to change."

The guy stands there for a few more seconds, staring at us. He doesn't seem the least bit threatening. Just curious. Finally, he shrugs and walks off.

We finish our drinks, and I suggest we move on. Whatever experiment Rob is conducting has presumably run its course. Rob decides to head home, and Ryan and I go back to the hotel to change. Finally.

"I didn't like that at all," I tell Ryan in the cab.

"Whatever," he replies. "Forget about it."

So we do. And we never learn what the point of it all was.

The next night, it's just Ryan and I. We'd kicked around the embassy and shot the shit with the Army guys most of the day. Upon returning to the hotel, we'd asked the concierge to recommend a restaurant for dinner.

"Make it nice," Ryan tells him. "And authentic. We're going back to the US tomorrow."

"Ah, yes," the concierge replies. "I know just the place." He calls and makes us a reservation. "I think you'll be most pleased," he says.

When we arrive, Ryan and I are escorted through the restaurant to the courtyard outside. A small number of tables are arranged in an area the size of a basketball court, flanked on all sides by centuries-old-looking stone walls overflowing with chrysanthemums. A string quartet plays in the corner, and the whole place smells like rose water.

The host guides us to our table near the center of the courtyard. The tables are spaced at exactly the right distance. Cozy, but not crowded.

As we take our seats, the host lights the candle in the middle of our table and hands us the wine list. The sun is setting. A slight breeze kicks up. The couples at the surrounding tables gaze lovingly at each other. Ryan orders us a bottle of chardonnay.

"How many times in your Navy experience have you found yourself in some incredible, romantic place, not with your wife, but with some other dude?" he asks.

Plenty, I tell him, appreciating the observation.

"Yup," he says, "just a couple of dudes out having a nice romantic dinner. Nothing wrong with that, right?"

Nope, I respond.

"Well," he continues, "for whatever it's worth, you make a great date."

Thanks, man. So do you.

"And by the way, what the hell was Rob thinking last night?" Ryan asks. "That was totally awkward."

Agreed. As awkward as two dudes sitting in a courtyard having a romantic dinner?

"But, hey! How about Zagreb? Glad you came, right?"

Sure.

I guess.

If you say so.

High-Performance Takeoff

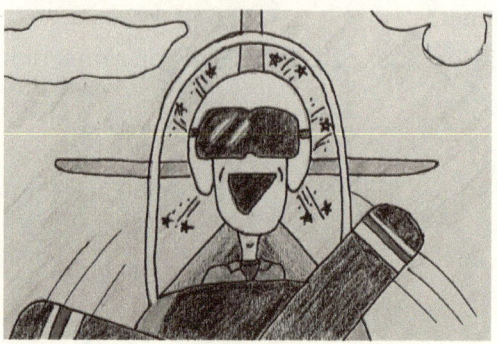

"SHOOTER TWO-THREE-SIX, YOU'RE cleared for takeoff, runway two-nine."

"Roger, cleared for takeoff, two-nine," I repeat to the guy in the tower.

St. Louis Regional Airport. I'm on my first cross country. There's an instructor in the back seat. Marine Corps captain. C-130 pilot. Things have been pretty chill since we left Pensacola three days ago.

Approaching St. Louis, the captain asks me, "Think you can find your girlfriend's house from here?"

I look down at my chart and find I-55. Looks like it's ten miles east of us.

"Yes, sir," I say. "No problem."

"Then let's go have a look," he says.

We find her house and proceed to buzz it at low altitude, causing quite a stir in small-town Illinois. And making me something of a legend.

Thanks, Captain.

The next day, we head to Chicago to do some approaches at O'Hare. You know, one of the busiest airports in the world.

"We're gonna mix it up with the big boys," the captain tells me.

Great.

I inch the throttle forward and maneuver us onto the runway. As I do, the guy in the tower speaks up again.

"Hey, two-three-six, you gonna impress me with this takeoff?"

Impress him?

He knows I'm a student. I'm flying a bright-orange aircraft, for Chrissake. It practically has training wheels.

Is he calling me out?

Son of a bitch.

Sure, I'll impress your ass . . .

"I have the controls," the captain says.

"Roger, you have the controls," I reply.

"We'll show this guy," the captain mutters.

He stands on the brakes and runs up the throttle. Then, he lets go, and we go screaming down the runway. After a couple hundred yards, he eases us up to about twenty feet and lifts the gear. We continue down the runway, still in ground effect, building airspeed. Then, approaching the departure end of the runway, the captain says, "Gs coming on."

Gs, as in g-force. Gravity.

Shit. He's not going to do something stupid like flip us inverted, is he?

He pulls the stick back into his crotch and pops the nose toward the sun. We start trading airspeed for altitude and climb—fast. The T-34 is rated for 4.5 Gs. We must be pulling 4.49999999.

We continue our climb to five thousand feet, then the captain pushes the nose over and we level off.

"Looked great from down here, two-three-six," the guy in the tower says. "Have a good flight."

Thanks. Jackass.

"You have the controls," the captain tells me.

I take the controls and make a turn north for Chicago.

"Do . . . not . . . *ever* . . . do that at home field," the captain says. "Understood?"

Yes, sir.

Cross-country rules in effect.

A few years later, I'm in an H-60, sitting on a taxiway at Naval Air Station North Island, waiting for my turn on the runway. Even though I can take off from anywhere in a helicopter, I like to do running takeoffs like a plane.

Because they're more fun, that's why.

There's an F/A-18 Hornet in front of me. The pilot begins his takeoff roll and quickly goes full throttle. He picks the jet up a few feet, lifts the gear, and continues down the runway. Approaching the numbers at the opposite end, still only a few feet off the ground, he pulls the nose vertical, standing the aircraft on its tail, flames shooting behind him.

In a matter of seconds, he's nearly out of sight—thirty thousand feet or higher.

"Easyrider six-three, you're cleared for takeoff," the controller tells me. "Caution, wake turbulence."

No shit.

You can practically feel the hot wind still blowing down the runway from the Hornet's afterburner.

I taxi onto the runway and catch a final glimpse of the Hornet.

And as I'm about to pull power to start my takeoff roll,

I think to myself,

Big deal.

I can do that.

Totally.

Minor in Possession

I WEAR MANY hats. Husband. Father. American. *Seinfeld*-rerun-watcher.

And criminal, according to the US government.

Yeah, it was stupid. The kind of stupid you can only achieve as a teenager. Which I was.

Friday afternoon. My buddy John and I are on the way to see his girlfriend. She's a freshman at Grand Valley State University. We're five minutes away from campus and figured that was a good time for our warm-up beers. I fish two Bud Lights out of the cooler in the back seat. John's driving. About eighty. We crack open our beers. Two pulls in, and we see the lights behind us.

A cop.

"Maybe he's after someone else," John says, hopefully.

He's not.

Instinctively—stupidly—I cram the beers under my seat. Maybe the cop won't find them. By the time he gets to my door, a beer puddle has formed around my feet. The whole car smells like a dive bar.

"Step out of the vehicle," the cop says.

Funny how they say *vehicle* instead of *car*.

John and I are standing next to the vehicle as the cop searches it. He finds the two beers under the passenger seat, the cooler in the back seat, and the extra case in the trunk. He tells me to get back into the car. The cop then walks John back to his squad car and makes him spread his hands across the hood as he frisks him.

I can see it all happening from the passenger-side rearview mirror.

Then, the cop cuffs John and puts him in the back of the squad car. He then walks around to my door, telling me to get back out and dump all the beers. A real shame, considering how hard it is to get that much beer when you're seventeen.

So I stand there, dumping the beers, as the rush hour traffic goes by. I keep my face down, on the off chance someone I know drives by. Like my parents.

Shit. My parents.

I'm going to be in *so* much trouble.

The cop eventually lets us go, but not before issuing us citations—Minor in Possession of Alcohol. A misdemeanor.

John's stepmom is a lawyer, and she works some deal with the judge. We're made to appear in court, enter our guilty pleas, and pay a fine. And I get grounded for a month. A month, in the middle of my *senior year*!

I do my time and reintegrate into society. I get on with my life. And I try to forget my criminal past, until it comes back to find me.

As it did recently, when I had to reapply for my security clearance.

"I dunno," says the petty officer. "Sounds to me like you have to put it down."

The security questionnaire is asking if I've ever been convicted of an alcohol-related offense. To me, that means a DUI or aggravated assault *a la* booze-fueled bar fight. I have neither on my record. But there's that Minor in Possession.

"I paid a fine," I tell the petty officer in charge of processing security clearances. "And I'm pretty sure my buddy's mom made the whole thing go away. Plus, I got grounded!" I tell him, still seething at the injustice. "My senior year."

"I get it," he says. "But the form doesn't ask about any of that. It just asks about an alcohol offense, which it sounds like you got."

Ah, the consummate bureaucrat. I'm doing nothing to bring this guy around to my point of view. But I know he's just doing his job.

The form asks for all the details of the offense—where, when, resolution, details of the court proceedings. All of it. After hours of internet searching and a few phone calls, I finally get the details.

Bozung, Daniel B. Guilty. Minor in Possession of Alcohol. Misdemeanor. Kent County Circuit Court, Michigan. September 1990.

It all goes into the security questionnaire, which I submit, chagrined, to the petty officer.

Weeks later, I receive notice that my clearance has been renewed. The government has apparently forgiven me, but not before ripping open that old wound. The getting grounded part, at least.

Yeah, maybe we shouldn't have had those beers. And maybe we shouldn't have been driving eighty. I understand that now.

But ask any seventeen-year-old.

A cold beer at eighty miles an hour on the way to see a girl?

Pure bliss.

Stupid? Yes.

Worth it? Totally.

Let that *not* be a lesson to you kids out there.

Ode to the G-1 Leather Flight Jacket

ASK MAVERICK WHICH he loves more, the jacket or the motorcycle.

He'll say the jacket. If he's being honest.

I'm being honest: It's the coolest thing I own.

It's iconic.

And I look fantastic wearing it.

And I *earned* it, dammit!

After your final exam in ground school, you received this slip of paper—a chit, in Navy speak—which you'd take to gear issue to get your leather jacket.

If you passed.

The Navy wouldn't give you that gorgeous G-1, the same one my grandfather had been issued in 1943, until you'd successfully completed Aviation Preflight Indoctrination, or API. *All* of API, including water survival, land survival, the obstacle course, the fitness test, the mile swim in a flight suit, the academic stuff, and the physical.

Shit! The physical. A full day's ass-prodding at the Naval Aerospace Medical Institute. If there was anything wrong with you, the docs would find it. I mean *anything*. This one guy, his heart was off by two zeptoseconds every nineteenth beat. He was disqualified. Just like that.

Pack up your shit, son, and head to Newport. You ain't flying. You're driving ships for a living.

It was the infamous NAMI Whammy. No leather flight jacket for him.

I didn't get whammied, thank God.

A few years after receiving my jacket, I'm in the Persian Gulf. It's ninety degrees at midnight. You step outside the skin of the ship, and you're immediately soaked. You can't *not* sweat.

Doesn't mean I'm not wearing my leather jacket, though. Everything's over air-conditioned on a ship, what with all the weapons and sensors. It was blazing outside, freezing inside. So I wore my jacket. Everyone did.

But I hadn't worn it flying. There was no practical reason to do so. I wasn't making bombing runs over 1940s Germany. But it bothered me that my flight jacket hadn't left the ground. A flight jacket should *fly*, dammit!

So, I wait for the next time I'm scheduled for the dawn patrol. It's the coolest part of the day, right before sunrise. And if you climb high enough and crank the air-conditioning, it gets a little chilly in the cockpit.

I put on my jacket and my flight gear over top of it. While I'm strapping in, the copilot's looking at me like I'm an idiot. Screw him. Has *his* jacket been flying? Yeah, didn't think so.

So we go tooling around the gulf for three hours, and there isn't much going on. At first, I'm comfortable in my jacket. But then the sun rises, and things start to warm up. And warm up. And warm up.

And pretty soon, no amount of air-conditioning keeps me from sweating.

We land, and I climb out of the aircraft. The back of my flight suit is completely soaked through, and I feel like I'm wearing a wet diaper. One of the ground crew asks me if I pissed myself.

Jackass.

The fur collar is soaked, but my jacket is otherwise fine. It seems happy to have gone flying. The G-1 was designed to serve a purpose, not just to be an ornament. To take the jacket flying is to pay it its proper respect.

Can't say the same of the office Halloween party.

Twenty years later, I'm a corporate guy. The email said to dress up.

Dress up for a party with Tom and Brenda from accounting? And no booze? I'd rather stick a sharp pencil in my eye. But the boss expects everyone to dress up. I give it zero effort and recycle the same *Top Gun* costume I'd been wearing to such events for a decade. Out of the closet comes the G-1.

I'm in the elevator on the way to the downstairs conference room for the chili cook-off. Dude dressed as Dracula (I think) turns to me and says, "Awesome! Where'd you get that? eBay?"

Pensacola, I tell him, knowing the reference to the Cradle of Naval Aviation will go right over his head. And it does.

Makes me think of my grandfather. Did members of the Greatest Generation have to haul their G-1s out of the closet for office Halloween parties? Doubtful. It would have been disrespectful, both to them and everything a military flight jacket stands for.

Or is supposed to stand for.

I shake it off. I'm just doing what I gotta do. But I'm not proud of it.

Still, I'll never stop being proud of having earned my leather flight jacket.

I love you, G-1.
And I'm sorry about the Halloween parties.
But I did take you flying that one time.
Remember?
I sure do.
And, for whatever it's worth,
I still look *fantastic* wearing you.

LIFE

Nineties Hair

THE NINETIES WAS a great hair decade. I think we can all agree on that.

Exhibit A: Jason Priestly, *Beverly Hills 90210*, circa 1995.

In a word, glorious. Just glorious.

Flowing, wavy on top. Close, but not too close, on the sides. And those sideburns! Neatly trimmed and squared off at the bottom of the ears.

That was the look of the nineties.

Even before Priestly had achieved iconic status as the nineties hair-standard bearer, I'd sported a similar look.

Around 1986, I moved my part from the middle of my head to the side. The middle part made it easier for you to feather your hair, *a la* Alex P. Keaton, which is what you did for much of that decade.

But, late in my seventh-grade year, I discovered I had this great cowlick on the right side of my forehead that, when I parted my hair on the same side, gave me the same wavy look as Priestly's.

It was a highly fortunate turn of events.

From then on, my hair became one of my distinguishing features. In a good way.

There was, however, an *un*fortunate period of about five years in which I also elected to keep my hair longish in the back while neatly trimmed on the sides. It was a look Brett Hull and other pro hockey players had made famous. You may know it by its more colloquial name:

The Mullet.

Even more unfortunate, my Mullet Phase peaked at the time of my high school senior pictures. There I was, smiling, in jacket and tie, standing in the photographer's studio in front of a shelf of fake books, poised to dash off to Harvard Yard . . .

Looking like Joe Dirt from the shoulders up.

I know, I know.

But you don't realize you've fallen victim to one of the most highly regrettable style trends of the late twentieth century while you're living it. Only after.

And now, strangely, The Mullet is back.

Anyway.

A couple of months after my senior pictures were taken, I had my hair cut short in back. But I kept it flowing and wavy on top. And thus began one of the greatest hairstyling runs of my life.

My nineties hair.

This, even as I entered military service. I enlisted right after high school, which could have ruined my look in its infancy. And that is exactly what would have happened had I joined the Army or Marine Corps.

Instead, I joined the Navy. And there, I found the most permissive of all military hair environments.

Sure, I had to get my head shaved in boot camp.

Which was certainly traumatic.

But my hair had mostly grown back by the time I graduated. It lacked the same flow, but that returned shortly after. And then I reported to my first duty station, an aviation squadron in Puerto Rico, where I found not only a highly supportive work environment, but also a hair culture in which I could unequivocally thrive.

"Navy Air Has The Hair," as General Charles Krulak, the former commandant of the Marine Corps, would later tell me.

The general was exactly right.

This one guy in my squadron perfectly embodied the Naval aviation hair ethos:

Lieutenant Maddox.

I was young—still a teenager. And highly impressionable. So it was critical that I have good hair role models, especially after The Mullet.

The lieutenant was exactly that role model.

He was an F-14 Tomcat pilot. That alone was qualification enough. But he was also tall, built like a D-1 tight end, and had a casual nonchalance that made him the coolest cat in any room.

And his hair . . .

It was blond, slightly unkempt, and long enough to skirt the edges of regulation. He looked like a pro surfer, but with Jason Priestly's sideburns. And when he was all geared up in a G suit, swinging a helmet bag, walking the flight line, I mean . . .

How did Jerry Bruckheimer *not* cast this guy in the original *Top Gun*?

I carried the image of Lieutenant Maddox with me to Annapolis and through my entire Naval Academy experience. It sustained me. Inspired me.

And my hair, in turn, inspired others.

When I was set to depart the Coast Guard Academy following a semester as an exchange student my junior year, I was presented with a gift. It was a hand-drawn, professional-quality cartoon, produced by one of the underclassmen in my company.

And it was all about my hair.

The caption read, *Dan is nice. He doesn't yell. He isn't snobby or self-centered. And he has really cool hair.*

(Emphasis in the original.)

It still hangs on my wall, and I've left instructions for its care in my will.

Yeah, I had a pretty damn good run. And then I went to flight school. There, I discovered my nineties hair to be highly impractical while wearing a helmet most days, so I cut it short and flat. I kept it that way into the early two thousands.

Low maintenance: That was my new hair mantra.

But when I departed the cockpit and the active-duty Navy for business school, I decided to let it flow again. Not in the same *90210* kind of way. Rather, I just let it get shaggy. I was a graduate student, after all.

Class pictures were taken late in the first semester. My classmates and I donned suits, and my shaggy hair seemed inappropriate to the occasion. So, I combed it, *Mad Men* style. Hard part on the left slide, slicked back in front. I thought it looked great.

But I was apparently the only one.

"You look like your mom combed your hair," said one of my more outspoken classmates.

What?

When I shared the comment with my wife, she lit up.

"Yes!" she said. "That's *exactly* what I was thinking."

To hell with both of them, I thought.

And, for the next decade, I returned to the Don Draper look from time to time, trying to figure out how to get it right. Barbers encouraged me along the way.

"I think this is a really good look for you," said one who'd been cutting my hair for three years.

I flourished under her care.

And then summer rolled around, and I got annoyed with my long hair.

Cut it, I instructed her. I wanted low maintenance again.

She didn't take it well. "No, no, no . . ." she pleaded. "I mean, yes, I can cut it. But then what?"

She started to get a little emotional.

"This is your gift," she continued. "And you'd be depriving the world of that gift."

True story.

Damn, I miss her. And I miss my nineties hair.

So, guess what?

I'm bringing it back, folks. That's right—I've decided to let it flow again. It doesn't move quite the same way it did when I was a teenager. And apparently that's normal, according to my current barber. He's all in favor of my growing it back out.

Because he, too, understands it's my gift. The truth is, *any* hair is a gift at this point, let alone a long, flowing mane, and things are looking great so far.

This is me.

The real, honest me.

With my nineties hair.

So, thank you, Jason Priestly.

Thank you, General Krulak.

Thank you, Lieutenant Maddox.

And thanks to all the barbers through the years who believed in and supported me.

Hair is a journey.

And I'm happy to be coming home.

And, no, dammit!

My mother did *not* comb it.

Three Things Unsaid

LEAVE THREE THINGS unsaid. Every day.

I read that somewhere. It was a pro tip on how not to piss off your spouse.

Have you ever tried it?

It works. Quite well, actually.

But that doesn't mean it's easy.

I can be a know-it-all jackass. And when a topic arises with my wife about which I know something—possibly everything, in my mind—I can't help myself.

Do you know how much sugar is in that granola bar? I'll ask her.

She'll be standing in the kitchen, minding her own business.

It's like you're having a Snickers for breakfast, I'll continue. Look it up. It's true.

Here, I'll expect her to drop the granola bar like a murder weapon and slowly back away from it with a look of mild horror on her face.

That's what I'll expect.

But actually, her countenance will just change from pleasant to annoyed, and she'll respond with a curt, sarcastic, "Thanks."

And then she'll walk out of the kitchen.

Still eating the granola bar.

Some version of this scene has played out countless times through the years. I know exactly how she'll respond to such comments. It's never good. And, frankly, I can't blame her. If someone pulled that shit with me, I'd come right back at him, knife-handing like a maniac. I wouldn't have the composure to simply walk away.

So why do I continue to do it?

Why do I have to be the know-it-all?

Why can't I leave such things unsaid?

I must have some deeply rooted insecurity, because that's what it usually comes down to. We all crave validation, even the highly accomplished. That, or you must be a total narcissist. Or maybe you're both insecure *and* a narcissist.

Like some of the clowns I sat in class with last week.

I was at the Naval Justice School in Newport, Rhode Island. The Navy had decided to send me to its Senior Leader Legal Course. Among other things pertaining to military justice, the course focuses heavily on ethics.

Which makes sense in the wake of the Fat Leonard scandal.

You may have heard about it.

"Fat" Leonard Francis was the CEO of Glenn Defense Marine Asia. His company provided services to ships in various ports throughout Asia. Francis orchestrated a yearslong scheme in which he corrupted numerous officers in the US Navy's Seventh Fleet to steer business to his company.

He was highly successful, but the scandal ultimately got him arrested, and numerous collaborating officers were made to face criminal charges. It ended careers. And it left a moral stain on the Navy that endures to present day.

The commanding officer of the Justice School, a Navy captain and career JAG officer, had worked on both sides of the scandal in previous roles. He'd been both a prosecutor and defense counsel, and so he personally taught our ethics class, drawing heavily from his experience.

It was inside baseball at its best, with useful, interesting details and anecdotes that had never made the news.

The captain was ideally suited to lead the discussion, but that didn't stop certain others in the class from interrupting him. Like, constantly.

It came in two forms:

The *So There I Was* and the *Totally Obscure, Run-On Hypothetical.*

The former describes a situation in which a person has had some practical experience with a concept the instructor is describing. And that person is wholly convinced the class *needs* to hear about it.

"So, let me tell you what this looks like out on the deckplates," this one guy started. "I had this situation on the ship where . . ."

The guy was sitting in the second row from the front. Rather than direct his comment to the instructor, he had instead turned around to address it to the rest of us. He was totally hijacking the class. Now, in fairness, this person was not without qualifications. He'd been the commanding officer of a destroyer.

In my mind, there is no more awesome responsibility in this business than command at sea. You're in charge of four hundred or so twenty-somethings who are highly skilled and eager to do a good job. But many of those twenty-somethings totally suck at adulting and do unfathomably stupid things.

That's one aspect of the job.

Another one is that, as the commanding officer, you're responsible for enough weaponry and firepower to start a world war. And the Navy doesn't give such responsibility to just anyone.

So, yes, I have the utmost respect for those who command at sea. Including this guy, who could not, for the life of him, keep his goddamn mouth shut.

But I have my limits.

This former commanding officer didn't interject just once. Or twice. Every other comment from the instructor elicited some kind of extended response from him. It was so, so tiresome.

The same was true of the Obscure, Run-On Hypothetical guy.

We had a couple of those in the class, and one of them was particularly annoying. His interruptions always began with, "So, what if..."

In one lesson, we discussed the legalities of receiving gifts, either personally or on behalf of the Navy. There are numerous rules surrounding such occasions. But there are also exceptions to those rules, further muddying the waters. So, as became a recurring theme in the course, the advice from the instructors was to simply ask a JAG for guidance.

But that wasn't good enough for this one dude. He insisted on taking the entire class down this ridiculous rabbit hole.

"So, what if," he began. "What if I'm on a ship and I pull into Sasebo and the local mayor wants to give me some samurai sword as a gift and it's during this public ceremony and I don't want to embarrass him or make the Navy look bad by not accepting it, and he gives me the sword and I see that it has my name engraved on the blade, which makes it personal, and I have no idea how much the sword is worth, and there's my name on it, and I think I saw one on eBay once that was, like, five hundred bucks, but I have no idea how much this one's worth, and there's the mayor standing there, all smiling, and it's a guy I'd actually met before when I was on a different ship, and maybe we're not exactly friends, but I do know him, and..."

Blah, blah, blah.

Everyone's eyes just glazed over.

And the instructor, trying to be polite, started unpacking this dude's hypothetical, making the experience all the more painful for the rest of us.

Of course, this didn't happen just once. It happened, like, every ten minutes.

Which raised some important questions.

How in the *hell* can such people lack the self-awareness to not realize how rude they're being to the rest of us? And why is the Navy promoting such people?

I wasn't the only one asking myself such questions.

One of the other captains in the class, the prospective commander of a submarine squadron, finally spoke up.

"Listen," he said to the Run-On Hypothetical guy, "the purpose here is to make you *aware* of the rules, so that you'll know what questions to ask. We're not here to become experts in this stuff."

God bless you, sir.

I walked over to him at the end of class and thanked him for his comment. And I hoped it would prompt both the So There I Was and the Obscure Hypothetical guys to change their behavior.

I hoped.

But it didn't. They couldn't help themselves.

"Let me tell you about a time on my ship when . . ."

And, "So, what if . . ."

My grandfather once shared a bit of wisdom with me. "The less you say, the smarter people will think you are," he'd said.

I have found that to be true.

The same goes for the converse.

The *more* you say . . .

Well, you're not doing yourself any favors.

So, yes:

Leave three things unsaid.

Every day.

Especially with your spouse.

And especially if you're sitting in a room full of accomplished professionals who,

Whether you realize it or not,

Really just wish

You'd shut the fuck up.

Keep Telling the Story

I'VE BEEN WRITING a commencement address.

In my head.

It's what I do when I drive. Or mow the lawn. Or sit in a meeting on a topic about which I can't give two shits.

Which is frequent.

So, I've been crafting my narrative for some time. Not because anyone has ever hinted that I might be invited to deliver such an address. My alma maters are out of the question.

I've been long forgotten in my hometown, so it's doubtful I'd ever give a speech to the graduating seniors of my former high school. The Naval Academy's out—the president or a cabinet member typically keynotes commencement exercises there. It ain't happening at Harvard. Because, well, it's Harvard. People like Bill Gates or Oprah take the podium there.

Still, I keep working on my address.

Part of it is vanity. I love the idea of being on a stage, spouting wisdom to a rapt audience. The thought of crafting a story that hooks and holds people from opening syllable to climactic end thrills me. A story that simmers in the minds of both young and old. One that delights and entertains in the moment, but ultimately informs and enlightens upon reflection.

Public address as performance art, that's how I see it. And somehow, despite being more introverted than extraverted, I crave such a performance.

I want to be on that stage.

Plus, life's kicked me in the stomach enough times to give me something interesting to say. Perhaps even useful, I think. It's mostly about my quest to make sense of it all. To connect the dots.

The dots that seemingly ran off the page some twenty years ago.

That was the point at which friends and colleagues stopped saying, "Wow . . . you make it look easy," and would instead console me with, "Tough break. That was hard." It was when people—bosses in particular—stopped talking about my amazing potential. And instead began wondering aloud why I was wasting it.

It was also when I discovered that some people—bosses in particular—are complete shit, and *fuck them.*

That's beside the point.

My commencement address opens with an observation. That those in attendance likely conform to a normal distribution. A very small number of graduates knows exactly what to do with their lives—they're outliers.

They've always known, in fact, and will go on to do precisely what they've intended. They will experience success, perhaps even happiness, never staring into the abyss, asking, "Who am I?"

They're the lucky ones.

And they disgust me.

In a polite way.

There is another small number—also outliers—that has no idea what to do, never has known, will never figure it out, and really doesn't give a shit.

They'll live in people's basements, play hours of *Fortnite*, and show up late to work. If they work at all. To those people, I say, so be it. Just pay your taxes, keep your online rants to a minimum, and stay out of the way.

Peace.

And then there are those graduates clustered around the mean, comprising the majority of the area beneath the bell curve. These are the people who may have vague notions of what to do, but aren't entirely sure, and feel a bit overwhelmed with the whole concept of Figuring It Out.

Their lives will unfold as a series of fits and starts, of minor successes and failures, that may or may not, over time, lead them to what it is they're *supposed* to do.

They will come to appreciate the Buddha's observation that the purpose of one's life is to find one's purpose.

Or was that Oprah's?

She spoke at Harvard, you know.

Such people will learn to put one foot in front of the other and make the best of it, come what may. And will likely find their way to mostly satisfying lives.

Or not.

And that's fine.

At this point in my remarks, I will concede that none of this is particularly novel or insightful. Nearly everything, and everyone, conforms to a normal distribution. But then I'll share what I didn't appreciate when I was a graduate:

That one could move between the different areas within the distribution at multiple points throughout one's life.

You can move from certainty to doubt and back again many times. The question is, how do you effectively manage those transitions? Because they can be quite unsettling.

I, for example, was certain in high school that I was going to be a lawyer. Of course, there was not a *scintilla* of evidence, to borrow a legal term, to suggest I was the least bit equipped for a career in jurisprudence. But I was certain nonetheless. Mostly, I liked the *idea* of being a lawyer.

Well, it never happened. I wound up in the Navy instead. And there, I fell in love with the *idea* of being a Navy pilot.

This time, I did make it happen.

Even after I nearly ran off a runway in flight school, at full throttle, because I had memorized the wrong rudder pedal to step on to counteract the propeller's torque and keep the nose straight.

I was not a Chuck Yeager or an Alan Shepard, despite having every expectation I would be. I assumed that one day I would wear a Top Gun patch on my sleeve and four stars on my shoulder. It was a foregone conclusion, at least it was in my mind.

Eventually, I came to understand how such a course failed to align with reality. Being a career Naval aviator just wasn't in the cards for me.

So, I pivoted to business, where I assumed I'd be the next Jack Welch. But then discovered, following years of pain and frustration, that I didn't give a shit about making or selling widgets.

And it's all widgets.

So then what?

By coincidence, I came across two pieces that spoke to the same predicament, but in different ways.

A friend forwarded me a link to Steve Jobs's 2005 commencement address to Stanford's graduating class. I'd seen parts of it before, but never the entire thing. In it, Jobs says that you can't connect the dots looking forward, only backward. Exactly how the events in one's life will unfold to support a certain outcome cannot be discerned by contemplating tomorrow. Only by looking to the past can a person appreciate how certain things *needed* to happen to provide the raw material for one's current success.

Jobs didn't understand it at the time, but by dropping out of college and later being fired at Apple, he was better equipped to do all the wonderful things he did when he returned to the company he'd cofounded.

Like create the iPhone.

The message is to persevere. And to trust that it will all add up to something one day.

But what if it doesn't?

That was the question posed by *Asteroid City*, Wes Anderson's 2023 weirdo-artsy movie. I saw it the day after I'd watched Steve Jobs's commencement address. Frankly, I'm not sure I got the movie.

But that may have been the point.

In one of the closing scenes, the main character steps off the stage and approaches someone—the producer or director, I don't know—and says, distraught, that he still doesn't understand the film.

He'd been acting as the main character for the entirety of the movie, but still didn't *get* it.

And it bothered him.

In response, the producer-director tells him that his fear is insignificant, so long as he keeps acting anyway.

Keep going.

One foot in front of the other.

Whether you're certain or in doubt, don't think too hard. Just keep on writing your life story. Life may indeed be a series of random, disconnected events that don't add up to anything. You may never get the chance to connect the dots.

I doubt I will. And I'm cool with that.

But that doesn't make my life, or anyone's else's, a failure. Hardly. I've had a rich life, filled with interesting experiences and unexpected plot twists. It's been a *fantastic* story. And so, to the graduates of Wherever State University, I would say,

Keep telling the story, whatever it may be.
Until your time runs out and there's no more story to tell.
That's the point.

So, there you have it. That's my speech. The commencement address I'll never give.

Except, maybe, in the shower.

What do you think?

That's some pretty great shit.

Right?

Mason-Dixon Mea Culpa

I DECIDED TO CALL the police dispatcher back and send a bunch of pizzas to the mechanics. Mostly to say thanks.

And also to assuage the mild case of guilt I'd developed for having written off the entire southeastern United States.

You know, NASCAR country.

More on that in a minute.

First, I received exactly the call I did *not* want.

"Uh, yeah," my daughter began. "The car quit running, and we're stuck on the side of the road."

Shit.

My wife and daughter were making the drive back to the University of Tennessee following Christmas break. A break that had lasted nearly six weeks.

Why in the hell would they give college kids that much time off? What purpose did it serve? I mean, I doubt many of them were returning to the family farm to help bring in the harvest.

Anyway, it was a long enough period of time that my daughter had lobbied my wife for permission to bring her car home for the holidays. Bad idea, I thought.

The car, a 2016 Nissan Versa, was purchased for my daughter's sixteenth birthday. It's a little Japanese job with go-cart wheels and a lawn mower engine. It was never intended for road trips. It was intended for knocking around town.

That's it.

But, of course, in the eyes of a teenager, any car is road-trip worthy. We've all been there.

Still.

Why does a kid need a car at college in the first place? A decent pair of shoes and a bus pass should work just fine, right? But, following my daughter's freshman year, both she and my wife decided the car was a necessity.

"You don't understand," my wife had said. "What if she wants to go to the gym at night? Do you really want her taking a bus?"

I mean...

Whatever.

Pick your battles, right?

If the car was going with my daughter to college, some seven hundred miles away, I wanted a mechanic to look it over and give it a clean bill of health. My wife took it to the local shop, and it was declared fit for travel. That was at the start of the semester.

Now, five months later, it was stuck on the shoulder off I-64, just outside Lexington, Kentucky, decidedly *un*fit.

Are you all way off the expressway? I asked.

Do you have your hazards on?

Can people see you?

Yes, yes, and yes, my daughter answered.

But the shoulder was narrow, and the car sat in the middle of a wide turn just before an exit. Not a great place to be.

"Every time a truck passes, it rocks the whole car sideways," my daughter added.

I called the insurance company's roadside assistance service and got a tow truck on the way. It was supposed to arrive in about an hour. That's a long time to sit on an expressway with semis screaming by.

Do you feel *safe*? I asked my wife.

She "supposed" so.

I decided I was uncomfortable enough with the situation to call the cops. Get a cruiser out there with its lights on to alert drivers coming around the turn, I figured. Rather than call 911, I found the number for the Lexington Police Department. The dispatcher answered on the first ring.

Nobody answers on the first ring anymore, I thought. Not a human, at least.

Nice touch.

I explained the situation as best I could, trying to minimize the sound of agitation in my voice. I'm calling from Kansas City, I said. But my wife and daughter are stuck outside Lexington.

Once the dispatcher got the details she needed, she said an officer would be on his way. I relayed that to my wife and asked her to let me know when the cop and tow truck arrived. Both did so at about the same time, and the officer and tow truck driver could not have been friendlier or more professional.

The tow truck driver attempted to deliver my daughter's car to a Nissan dealership whose service department had already closed. No dice. He then pressed on to a nearby Firestone, where manager Donnie Baker was willing to take a look.

Being in the South, of course he went by Donnie. Not Don or Donald.

Things must have been slow at the Firestone, because Donnie and his guys immediately went to work on diagnosing the problem. In short order, they got the car running and were doing test laps around the parking lot. My wife put Donnie on speakerphone as he shared his findings.

"Probably the modules," he said. "We're getting some codes we can't read. But, more than likely, the modules aren't talking to each other the way they're supposed to."

Not having an ounce of mechanical knowledge or capability, I politely asked Donnie to explain what modules were.

In essence, he said, the car's three brains weren't communicating with each other via electrical signals the way they were supposed to.

"Could be a loose connection somewhere," he said.

When the car was jolted onto the back of the tow truck, it must have reestablished whatever lost connection had caused the car to fail on my wife and daughter.

"I think you're good to keep going," he said. "Just get it to the dealership as soon as you get to Knoxville."

Okay, I thought. End of story.

Donnie and his guys had spent nearly an hour looking over the car but wouldn't accept any kind of payment.

"No, no," he said. "We didn't fix anything."

Still, time is money, right?

When he continued to refuse, I asked if I could send over some pizzas.

Would that be all right?

He said sure.

Who doesn't like pizza?

So, I got that figured out. And then I wanted to do something nice for the police, who had also impressed me with their professionalism and kindness.

Maybe I'll just call back and say thanks, I thought. They probably don't get thanked very often.

So, I did, and the dispatcher seemed to appreciate the gesture.

I started to feel relieved.

Especially considering that, incredibly, the parents of one of my daughter's friends, who lived in Knoxville, decided to take off driving to Lexington the moment they heard of the car troubles. My wife had been in touch with them because they'd all planned to get together that evening when my wife and daughter got to town. She'd been sending them updates from the Firestone.

We hadn't asked them to do so, but these incredibly kind people had decided to caravan with my wife and daughter through the mountains from Lexington to Knoxville.

They had backup.

Turns out, they needed it. The car quit again an hour short of its destination, and the second tow truck didn't arrive until nearly midnight. Then, Monday morning, I got the news from the Nissan dealer in Knoxville that the car's transmission would need to be replaced.

Fantastic.

But so be it.

I was just happy to have my wife and daughter safe, thanks in no small part to the kindness of the good people of Lexington, Kentucky, and our friends in Knoxville.

And that's a lesson. For me, at least.

My daughter remarked upon returning to Kansas City following her second semester at the University of Tennessee that, "This place sure isn't the South."

Of course not. But how so?

"People aren't nearly as nice," she said. "No one says hello to you when you're walking down the street."

Interesting. The Midwest has a reputation for being nice. Was she saying the South was nicer?

"Totally," she said. "Not even close."

Following the whole car fiasco, I'm beginning to understand. See, I've spent time in the South and have known plenty of people from the region through the years. I can't say I've ever had a bad experience there or found any of its inhabitants disagreeable.

But I have harbored a growing sense that the place, and its people, aren't for me. It's likely a sense borne of the various stories I've read and the region's general portrayal in the press over the past decade.

All of which is biased, at the very least, and, quite possibly, completely inaccurate. I know that. And I also know there are kind, generous people south of the Mason-Dixon line. Probably lots of them.

And assholes like me would do well to remember that.

Particularly when their wives and daughters are stuck on the side of an expressway outside Lexington, Kentucky, in a go-cart with a lawn mower engine.

I still don't love the idea of my daughter having a car at college that was never intended to leave our town.

But, if she must,

I suppose I'm glad

It's in the South.

Go Vols!

Getting Old, Part 1

I'LL JUST COME right out and say it.

I don't want to get old.

And by old, I don't mean the inevitable state of physical and mental decline that awaits all of us. I'm enough of a realist to accept that. There are no Botox treatments or hyperbaric oxygen chambers in my future.

At least, I don't think there are.

No, what I'm talking about here is the old-age mindset.

The attitude.

And the curious phenomenon by which people of such mind relish the opportunity to complain to anyone about their array of ailments. They positively delight in sharing the gory details of every failing body part, abnormal growth, and creaking joint, as well as the various medical procedures intended to correct them.

It's the damnedest thing. And it happens everywhere.

"Yup, there I was, sitting on that goddamn table with my ass hanging out of that gown," explained the guy in the waiting area at the local Walgreens pharmacy. He was probably eighty, sitting next to another octogenarian.

We were all there to get shots. I'd just had another milestone birthday and was eligible for the shingles vaccine. Which had me a little freaked out, to be honest. They don't give those things to kids, you know. If you're in line for a shingles shot, I have bad news for you. Even if you don't consider yourself old, you can't exactly call yourself young.

I would have been fine to skip the whole thing.

But I'd had chicken pox as a kid, which is apparently borne of the same virus that causes shingles and remains dormant in your system for the remainder of your life.

When I was a kid, if someone in your house came down with chicken pox, all your siblings were kept close by, so the virus would spread. That way, everyone got chicken pox at the same time, and your parents could get the damn thing over with. By today's standards, this seems about as good an idea as bloodletting was to treat a cold a couple centuries ago.

But what do I know?

So, I was hanging out at Walgreens on a Friday afternoon with the other seniors, listening to these two guys go on and on about their various ailments. It was like a sport for them. And the more they talked, the more excited they got.

The one guy continued. "And I'm not lying! I went in there for a checkup, and I came out with an appointment to get my hip replaced. My hip! Of course, I'd already had one knee done..."

The other gentleman nodded along, approvingly. "Yup, yup," he said. "That's how they get you."

And then he offered one of his own experiences.

"I went in to get a funny-looking spot on my back checked. Looks fine to me, I said, but okay. The doctor, she says she wants to get a sample. So, she cuts off this little piece with some wire cutters and sends it off somewhere."

But, of course, that wasn't the end of the story.

"Few days later, I get a call from the doc's office, and the lady says the whole thing has to come off. But instead of going back to the same office, I have to go to this other place," he explained.

And the other place was not a doctor's office, but some kind of surgical center.

"I get in there, and there are these bright lights and all kinds of beeping machines. I mean, are they taking a freckle off my back or removing a goddamn kidney?" he asked rhetorically.

It was a little disconcerting for the gentleman, but it gave him a story to tell, and that's all that mattered. He probably would have preferred they'd taken out his kidney, if only to give him something better to bitch about.

Sure, I understand. The truth is, everyone loves a little sympathy.

When I was a freshman in high school, I broke my arm snowboarding. I had to get a cast that ran from my knuckles to my armpit. And it was the best damn thing that happened to me that year.

"What the hell happened to you?" people would ask me.

Well, you know, I was carving this mean frontside turn, and I hit a patch of ice. Went down pretty hard, I'd tell them. And the doctor had told me I'd nearly fractured a growth plate in my elbow.

At least, I thought that's what he'd said.

It didn't really matter. I used that detail to embellish my story, explaining to people there was a chance my broken right arm might grow to be a few inches shorter than my left.

I'm sure this was complete bullshit, but it made for a better story.

And that was the whole point of having a broken arm in the first place.

It was a great thing then, but life accelerates as you exit childhood, and sickness and injury become huge inconveniences. Working, living, functioning adults don't have time for that stuff.

I've largely avoided the medical establishment for years, except for routine physicals. The human body is a marvel in its ability to heal itself. And that's why the first, and usually only, thing I do when I experience any ailment is ignore it.

It'll work itself out, I figure.

And it usually does.

I'd like to continue in this vein indefinitely. Why? Because I don't ever want to seek attention or amusement again by regaling people with stories of my physical ailments.

I don't want to get *that* kind of old—I want to get Tony Bennett old. I want to belt out duets with Lady Gaga when I'm ninety. Yeah, baby!

I want to get Queen Elizabeth old, and give audiences to heads of state well into my ninth decade. Right-oh!

I want to get Charlie Munger old. Be the billionaire right hand to a titan, able to move markets with my witticisms as I approach the century mark.

That's how you do it.

So, for now, I'll do what I can to keep myself healthy and maintain a life of maximum vigor.

I'll try to get more sleep, but probably won't.

I'll tell myself to drink more water, even while I'm pouring myself another cup of coffee.

I'll keep working out and skip rest days, even when I probably shouldn't.

And I'll continue to adhere to a strict, Paleo-Keto-Vegan-Carnivore diet.

Or whatever's currently in fashion.

Yeah, I'll do what I can.

And *please* . . .

If you ever encounter me at Walgreens waiting in line for a shot,
And, unprompted, without even knowing you, I launch into some dissertation on hemorrhoids, incontinence, or bad breath,
Do us both a favor,
And tell me to shut the hell up.
Like, immediately.
Thank you.

Getting Old, Part II

I'LL GET RIGHT to the central question.

Is it okay to watch squirrels chase each other around your backyard on a Sunday morning rather than sleep off a hangover?

Because that's what happens in my house. And I'm not sure I'm cool with it.

I recently decided to confront the issue.

What are we doing here? I asked my wife.

She gave me a confused look. I get that a lot from her.

I mean, *really*, I continued. What is going on?

"What could you possibly be talking about now?" she asked me.

Look at us! I said. What is wrong with us?

It was about eight thirty on a Sunday morning. We were sitting downstairs in our robes and slippers, having coffee, looking out across our back porch and into the woods.

It was our standard weekend-morning ritual.

Our house backs up to a wooded area, beyond which is a golf course. It's nice and quiet back there, and we get a variety of wildlife that passes through. The woods, our porch, and our yard seem to attract all kinds of animals, and it can be highly entertaining.

One Saturday afternoon, a deer walked right up to our living room window, pushed its nose onto the glass, and started watching a football game with us.

And it stood there, watching, for, like, five minutes.

And it's not just the deer.

My wife has this great picture of a fat groundhog doing exactly the same thing in exactly the same window.

Sports are big in our town. Big enough, apparently, that even the animals like to get in on the action. I find this amusing, maybe even delightful. I've always been an animal lover.

No, I don't want one living, shedding, and shitting in my house. But, I have to admit, I thoroughly enjoy watching animals of any kind run around outside. Especially the squirrels.

This particular morning, my wife and I had been watching about six of them fly across the treetops, moving deftly from branch to branch. It's incredible how they do that. Two of them stopped not far from each other and began adding leaves and branches to separate nests that occupied the same tree.

Are they together? we wondered.

You know, like a couple.

If they were, then why the separate nests?

"Maybe that's the guesthouse," my wife offered. "They need a place for when friends visit from out of town."

Out-of-town squirrels?

"That's right," she said.

And we went back and forth like this for a while.

Which is what we do most weekends.

And then it hit me right in the face.

Holy shit! I told my wife. We're a couple of old people.

"What are you talking about?" she asked.

I'm talking about this, I said. This is what old people do. They watch animals in their backyards. And they do stupid shit like give them names and create backstories for them. Exactly as we did for the squirrels. How did it come to this?

As a thought experiment, I asked what the twenty-five-year-old version of myself would have thought about this ridiculous weekend-morning routine. It wasn't much of an experiment, because the answer was immediately clear.

Twenty-five-year-old Dan would not have approved.

That guy would have rolled in from the bars at about two in the morning, having hit several with friends the night before. He'd have dragged his ass out of bed around nine or ten, forced down some coffee, then gone out for a run to sweat out some of the booze.

He would have been miserable and bitched the entire way. But he would have done it, without fail.

Then, he would have showered and gone right back out to meet the same friends for brunch, immediately downing a Bloody Mary on arrival to reignite the previous night's buzz. Several more Bloodies would have followed until someone suggested going to the beach.

Dan would have then gone to the beach, passed out on a towel for an hour, then gotten up to play football with his buddies or bodysurf. The beach trip would have then turned into an impromptu barbecue or dinner party at someone's house, followed by a semireasonable bedtime to be back in a cockpit or simulator the following day.

That was how you spent a Sunday.

The very thought of squirrel watching would have sent twenty-five-year-old Dan running back to the bar for a round of tequila shots.

I suddenly felt judged.

And a little ashamed.

We gotta do something about this, I told my wife.

"Relax," she said. "It's not like we're some of those crazy people who put out bird feeders."

That was a fair point.

It was one thing to be looking out over your backyard on a Sunday morning and to observe a bunch of squirrels that *happened* to be running around. But it was entirely another to *bait* said squirrels—or birds or rabbits or whatever—into one's yard.

That was crossing a line. The line that separates young from old.

The same was true of binoculars.

Watching the animals run around with the naked eye says nothing of one's age or station in life. But adding any form of magnification, like binoculars or a telescope, to make such observations, again, crosses the line. Especially if the binoculars are accompanied by a guidebook that enables you to identify specific species.

"That's odd," you may say. "You don't usually see the American goldfinch in these parts for at least another three weeks. They should still be in Mexico."

Yeah, I've got news for you if you're that guy.

You're old.

Or an ornithologist.

But, come on. How many ornithologists do you know?

So, is the solution simply to return to the bars every Saturday night?

Maybe. But I couldn't make a habit out of it.

First, I like to sleep. A lot.

As I've learned, quality matters, perhaps even more than quantity. And everyone knows that drunk sleep is shit. I've had plenty of that in my life, and I don't need any more.

Second, I have stuff to do.

Mornings are my most productive time, and I'd hate to waste them. That includes weekends. And let's be honest. If I were to go out booming next Saturday night the same way I did when I was in my twenties, I wouldn't be able to get out of bed until Tuesday. I just can't rebound the way I used to.

So, returning to our central question, is it okay to watch squirrels on a Sunday morning?

I say yes.

But with caveats.

No baiting of squirrels, birds, or any other animals via feeders. If they show up in your yard, great. But that's their call, not yours.

Also, no binoculars. And no guidebooks.

Making up ridiculous stories and anecdotes to explain squirrel behavior is okay. But it cannot be done with any serious intent. It is *not* okay to name the squirrels or to make any claim they have any awareness of you or connection to your yard.

"Oh, there's Rudy again! Yes, that's him! He loves it here. Shows up every morning. Funny he's not with Sheila anymore . . ."

Wrong.

So now it's settled.

And I can return to my Sunday-morning routine guilt free, provided I follow the rules.

Which I will.

Even as part of me wishes

That I could be passed out on a towel

On a beach

Somewhere.

Don't Touch My Stuff

SOME PEOPLE ARE GENEROUS. They'd give you the shirts off their backs.

I am not such a person.

I would not give you the shirt off my back. Not because I'm not generous, but because it's my fucking shirt. And I like it.

So, no, you're not getting my shirt. But maybe I could help you find one of your own. I'm sure there are charities that specialize in procuring and distributing shirts to those in need. I could point you to one of those. Perhaps I'd even make a donation. That would, in a small way, increase the likelihood that you'd get your shirt.

But you're still not getting my shirt.

So just forget about that.

Bottom line, you're not touching my stuff. Any of it. Why?

Because it's *my* stuff.

"What's the big deal?" my wife asks. "It's just a stupid charging cord."

I'd come home to find her earbuds occupying the charging station I'd created in my little corner of the kitchen counter.

My corner. My turf. My cord.

I tried to be casual about it.

I see you helped yourself to my charging cord, I said to her. There was not a hint of confrontation in my voice. It was just a simple observation.

Intended to shame her.

For violating my space. My sovereignty. And for touching my stuff.

Which she knows is a huge no-no.

But, sometimes, she likes to stick it to me. I'll catch her walking out of my office, a room she knows is off-limits. I have a shredder in there, which I use to dispose of documents containing financial or other personal information. My wife should do the same with her own documents, for sure. And get her own damn shredder. Or, simply ask me to shred her documents for her.

She instead prefers to take the lazier, more expedient path, and goes into my office to use my shredder. She knows I find this infuriating, but she makes a habit of doing it anyway.

When I protest, she's dismissive. Or patronizing. Or both.

"Yup. Mmm-hmm. Sure," she says. "No, you're right. I definitely shouldn't go in there."

And then she pulls up a cat video to watch on her phone, as I'm standing there, just to emphasize how seriously she *isn't* taking me.

Can you believe that?

And don't even get me started about my shelf in the refrigerator. All I ask is for my own uncluttered space to put my stuff. A space I use, like, every day. It's one of the little shelves in the refrigerator door.

See, I like to have a kale smoothie every morning after my

workout. The ingredient list is pretty extensive, containing a dozen or so items that I've worked to refine over the years. Given the prep time required, I like to put it all together the night before.

I load up the blender and place it on a shelf—the same shelf, every day—in the door of the refrigerator.

Where I'll often find water bottles or jars of condiments my wife has placed there.

Again, just to stick it to me.

I mean, she has the entire refrigerator. Why use that shelf?

My shelf.

She's doing you a favor, you might say. She's teaching you an important lesson. When you live with others, you have to share. Even the simplest of primates understands that. If, for some reason, I am unable to do so, then *I* am the problem, not the other primates.

My wife should be free to use my charging cord.

And my shredder.

And my shelf in the refrigerator.

Provided those things exist in the home we share.

Which they do.

Got it.

Here's the problem:

I grew up in a large family where sharing was encouraged, if not required. And this had the perverse effect of *dis*couraging sharing.

Take, for example, a simple box of cereal. The sugary type was strictly forbidden in my house. You know, the good stuff.

Cap'n Crunch. Count Chocula. Froot Loops. Lucky Charms.

If a brand of cereal had a commercial playing during Saturday morning cartoons, there was zero chance it would find its way into our pantry. My mother was convinced we were all hyperactive, so all we ever got were Cheerios, Grape Nuts, and Raisin Bran.

Old man cereal.

Which kept us regular, but hardly satisfied.

To get a decent bowl of cereal, you had to spend the night

at a friend's house, where the friend's parents would look at you quizzically as you got abnormally excited over a goddamn bowl of Frosted Flakes.

Anyway.

Every once in a while, my mother would spring for the name-brand Raisin Bran. The real deal. It was way better than the generic stuff we usually got. Real Raisin Bran had sugarcoated raisins, which typically settled to the bottom of the box.

So, as my siblings and I knew, the best bowl came at the very end. Whenever there was a decent box of cereal in the house, we all knew precisely, down to the ounce, how much was left in the box. And, when it got near the end, you'd have to wake up earlier and earlier to ensure you got the last bowl. That last serving of delicious, sugarcoated raisins.

Scarcity encourages competition. And fights. Which often took place in the early-morning hours in the kitchen.

Over cereal.

And it wasn't just cereal—it was everything else. Sometimes, a well-intentioned relative would get us kids something nice for Christmas.

"Danny, you open it," the relative would say, smiling.

As soon as I did, the relative would spring the trap.

"I thought you kids could share it," she'd say.

Share it?

Fucking *share* it?

Are you kidding me?

That's a terrible idea. The last thing any kid wants to do is share a Christmas present. Doesn't everyone know that?

Early childhood traumas involving cereal, Christmas presents, *Star Wars* figures, baseball cards, and numerous other things shaped my adult views on property and the sanctity of one's space. That much is clear.

What's also clear is my wife does not share these views, because she grew up with one much younger sibling, her own room, an in-ground pool, and all the Cocoa Krispies she could eat.

That Barbie Corvette was hers and hers alone. No sharing required.

It was kid nirvana in her house.

Still, I recognize that a mature, rational-thinking grown-up should be able to set such differences aside and peacefully coexist with one's spouse. Which we mostly do.

Except when it comes to my stuff.

I'd like to say I'm working on myself. That I'm making a conscious effort to keep my selfish impulses in check.

But the truth is I'm not. And I really don't care.

So, please.

Come on in.

Make yourself at home.

Let me pour you a drink.

Stay a while.

But this?

This shirt?

No, I'm afraid you can't have it.

Because it's my fucking shirt.

So just get your own.

Okay?

The Story That Wasn't

"**MY NAME'S RUSS,**" he began. "This is my bus, and that's no fuss."

Great, I thought.

A friggin' comedian.

"But if you cuss, you gotta get off my bus."

By that standard, I assumed I'd be getting off soon.

"But seriously, folks, I'm your driver. I should have you to Union Station in about an hour and a half."

Russ was trying. I'd give him that. And he had a full, glorious head of vintage, circa-1983 Kenny Rogers hair. It was fantastic.

But I had no desire to be on his bus.

It was half past midnight. Day after Christmas. Well, it *had* been the day after Christmas. That was when the ordeal had started.

We were in the parking lot of the Amtrak station in Sedalia,

Missouri. I had started out from Alton, Illinois, some ten hours before on Amtrak's Missouri River Runner, destined for Kansas City's Union Station. It had become an annual trek, taking the train between my in-laws' in Illinois and my home in Kansas City the day after Christmas.

The week between the holidays is a particularly productive one for me. I like to tie off loose ends from the closing year and get things organized for the coming one. I get my finances in order for tax season, make the outlines of a budget, and get my calendar arranged. Then, after a productive week, I make the return trip to Illinois to celebrate New Year's with the family.

I look forward to that time, particularly the portion spent on the train. It's my Xanadu. To me, it's the perfect mode of travel. Cars just make my ass hurt after a while. Buses are often crowded, uncomfortable, and filled with weirdos. Planes and airports can offer an enjoyable experience, but they can also be complete disasters during the holidays, with impatient people and unpredictable weather threatening to turn your plans sideways at any given moment.

And then, after cars, and somewhere between buses and planes, is the train.

It moves gracefully through small towns and the countryside at a steady, leisurely pace. Staring out the window, sipping coffee from the dining car, you get a throwback experience. You travel in much the same manner as members of your grandparents' generation did. It reminds you of simpler times.

Or, more accurately, it makes you idealize what you assume to have been simpler times.

Because no time is really that simple.

Moving on.

I like to daydream on the train. My mind wanders where it pleases, and I'm happy to let it do so. I don't try to force it into productive use, although it often finds its way there on its own. I do some really great thinking. I figure stuff out. And then I take a nap.

Such is the train.

For all these reasons, I did *not* want a story to emerge from my train experience. I wanted it to proceed exactly as planned, without any strange or noteworthy events or people emerging from it.

Since committing myself to writing weekly essays on life as I observe it, I've actively looked for stories in the petty, mundane, and otherwise unremarkable. Mostly, I've taught myself to become highly attuned to those things that annoy the shit out of me.

Aha! I tell myself as some random person does something stupid to piss me off. *There* is a story. And then I totally reframe the experience in a way that's far more interesting.

I'm certainly not the first to do this.

I've read authors' accounts in which they describe how they become keen observers of their of own lives the moment they decide to write about them. It keeps things far more lively when you can detach yourself from certain circumstances and take a third-person view of your own experience.

Precisely what I did not want to do when the Missouri River Runner rolled into the station in Sedalia, Missouri.

After we'd sat there ten minutes longer than scheduled, I began to wonder if something was up. Twenty minutes later, a conductor came by and said a freight train had broken down on the tracks ahead of us. We'd have to sit there until the track could be cleared, and no one knew how long that would take.

Twenty minutes became an hour.

Then two.

Then four.

I tried to make the most of the time and check in with a few friends.

Upon describing the delay to one friend, she replied, "Oh, good! Now you'll have something to write about next week."

Yeah, I know, but . . .

A handful of people had already arranged rides and gotten off the train. Most of us just sat there, leaving our fates in the hands of the Amtrak gods. And when the gods finally spoke, their answer was: buses. Two were apparently on their way to Sedalia from Kansas City.

At that point, I decided to take my friend's point of view and started looking around for a story. I expected some of those passengers still on the train to become irate at the thought of riding a bus and start doing stupid things.

Given the opportunity to be stupid, many people will. I've learned that.

They'll start harassing the conductor at least, I assumed. They'll make the delay out to be his fault and demand he *do* something.

"I'm not getting on some damn bus at midnight!" I thought I'd hear from someone.

But I didn't.

People were strangely calm about the whole thing. Most just went to sleep in their seats or scrolled around on their phones. By the time Russ showed up with the first bus, a wet snow had begun to fall. A small crowd of us stood waiting to board the bus, getting cold and wet.

Now begins the bitching, I assumed.

I was among the last to board the first bus, and nearly every seat was taken. We were packed in, with many people holding their bags on their laps. I took one of the last open seats near the middle of the bus next to a tall dude wearing headphones.

After I'd sat down, he politely informed me, "Excuse me, you're sitting on my coat."

Sorry, I said. And I assumed it would be awkward after that.

"No problem," he said, casually.

And not a bit of awkwardness ensued.

Nor did a single person on the bus start bitching.

Things were quiet for the entire trip to Union Station in downtown Kansas City, where we arrived around two thirty in the morning.

Fifteen minutes later, I was in an Uber headed for my house.

The entire train-delay experience had failed to yield a single story.

Remarkable.

I was disappointed. And thankful.

When I got in the Uber, the first thing I noticed was the music. It was a recording of a person chanting in Arabic and reminded me of the Muslim call to prayer I'd heard blaring from speakers atop mosques in the Middle East. Sitting somewhere in the desert, I'd always found such music to be equal parts enchanting and spooky.

Where are you from? I asked the driver.

"Somalia," he said. "Have you ever been?" he asked me.

No, I said. But I've spent time in the Navy and know the US military has a presence in Djibouti. You know. Just trying to make conversation.

Big mistake.

The driver became irritated. "Why? Why?" he asked me. "Why does the US not fight in Somalia? Why!"

Uh...

He then told me about members of his extended family still in Somalia being extorted by Al-Shabaab militants. Why wasn't the US doing something to stop them?

I'm sorry to hear that, I told him.

But, as memory serves, the US had a pretty bad experience in Somalia back in the nineties, I explained. Remember? That whole *Black Hawk Down* thing?

He wasn't satisfied, so I quickly changed the subject. And then we sat in awkward silence for the remainder of the drive to my house. I'd made it all the way from Sedalia, Missouri, without any notable incident.

And I sure as shit didn't intend to have one with this Somali Uber driver at three o'clock in the morning.

No, thanks.

I was quite happy to have the story end
Without there having been
Any story to tell
In the first place.

In Trouble on Christmas (Again)

I GET CHEWED out the first time around Thanksgiving.

"Why did you buy that?" my wife asks me. "You should have put that on your Christmas list."

I'm not supposed to buy myself anything within eight weeks of December 25th.

"That is *soooo* inconsiderate," she says. "Someone could have gotten that for you."

At issue was a package of V-neck T-shirts I'd ordered from Amazon. I'd been struggling for the past year to find exactly the right brand of T-shirt, and that bothered me, because I'd reached a point in my life at which I should have already committed to a certain brand—*my* brand.

I'd cycled between Calvin Klein, Jockey, and a couple of other labels I'd read about in *The Wall Street Journal*.

Yes, *The Journal* occasionally has articles on high-end underwear.

Because people like me are interested in that stuff.

Anyway.

Not even the more expensive brands fit me just right. So, while in Annapolis for a football game, I paid a visit to the Naval Academy's Midshipmen Store and picked up a package of old-school Hanes T-shirts.

They were the same I'd worn under my summer working blues when I was a midshipman. And, it turned out, some thirty years later, they fit perfectly.

They were exactly what I'd been looking for.

So, when I got home, I ordered another package. And now I'm a Hanes T-shirt guy. Which should have been cause for celebration—I'd come full circle in my choice of undershirts!

Aren't you happy for me? I ask my wife. Why can't you just be happy for me? Finding those Hanes T-shirts in the MidStore had been a triumph, I tell her.

"You're a jackass," she says.

But this is underwear, I argue. Do you really expect people to buy me underwear for Christmas?

"You just need to think about someone other than yourself," she scolds me.

And so, I'm in trouble. Like I am every year.

Now, I'm not a child of the Great Depression or anything like that. I didn't grow up wondering where my next meal was coming from. And I recognize how lucky I am not to have had such worries. I am eternally grateful to my parents for having provided for my siblings and me. We always wanted for something, like most kids, but needed for nothing. And that was no small thing during the recession of the early eighties.

Still, there were plenty of things I was sure I desperately needed but had to do without. Air Jordans. Levi's jean jacket. Vuarnet sunglasses. Mongoose BMX bike. And, as a result, I looked forward to the day when I could buy myself whatever I wanted, whenever I wanted it.

Which, for the most part, is now.

I don't buy lake houses, boats, or motorcycles on a whim. But if I want a nice bottle of aftershave, a new sweater, or a watch, I don't wait. I buy it.

Because I want it, like, *right the fuck now.*

And I'm not going to wait until Christmas to get it, though this violates both the spirit and letter of the holiday protocols to which my wife's extended family has abided for years. In her family, everyone, young and old, must have a stack of no fewer than nineteen presents at his or her feet on Christmas day. Anything less would suggest a breakdown of the Christmas order and potentially lead to hurt feelings.

This, despite the fact I have told my wife, repeatedly, that the ideal Christmas for me would be the one in which I receive no presents at all.

I mean, seriously. I don't need anything. And I'm happy to just sit and drink coffee and watch other people open their presents.

"Yeah, that's a nonstarter," she says. "Ain't happening. So you better get to work on that Christmas list."

Even if I don't dutifully submit my list in late October, as I'm instructed to do every year, it won't stop the presents from piling up on Christmas morning. I know this because I've tried.

One year, I refused to make my list in protest.

Tell your mom I'm sitting this one out, I told my wife.

I should have known better. When Christmas rolled around, the presents piled up in front of me, just as they had in previous years.

I opened the first: deodorant.

Then the second: soap.

Then the third: shaving cream.

Turns out, my wife had gone through my drawers in the bathroom, taken note of the various brands of toiletries I favored, and put them all on my Christmas list.

Why in the *hell* would anyone want to buy a person toiletries for Christmas? I asked my wife.

"Because that way, you'll have something to open like everyone else," she explained. "You *have* to have something to open."

Have to?

Does anyone really *need* to open a present on Christmas?

Why should I have to wait on Saint Nick for my Hanes T-shirts?

"You don't get it," she says. "You take all the joy out of gift giving."

Okay.

"You suck at Christmas," she continues. "And Father's Day. And your birthday." Some people genuinely enjoy giving gifts, she explains. Like her entire family.

And I, apparently, suck all the happiness from the occasion with my obstinate determination to forego gifts.

That's unfortunate.

But I can explain. Two forces that reside within me collide during the holidays.

First, I hate clutter.

Too much stuff stresses me out. I'm a huge fan of the one-in, one-out policy that prevents objects from accumulating in one's house. If you get something new, then you have to get rid of one corresponding item, so the net gain is zero. All those presents at Christmas require that I get rid of a bunch of stuff to make room.

Which is a chore.

Second, I am *very* picky.

I have highly specific tastes, which I've worked to refine over the course of decades. And the odds that someone will get me anything that agrees with my tastes are low. So, I'd much rather people save their hard-earned money and just let me sip my coffee, present-less, on Christmas morning.

Of course, my dear wife knows all this about me. But that doesn't stop her from rendering the same verdict every year at Christmas. And on Father's Day. And on my birthday.

"You're an asshole," she says.

Okay, I'm an asshole.

And this is supported by my total inability to feign delight in anything that does not suit my tastes. I completely lack that talent.

The best I can usually manage is, "That's interesting. How thoughtful."

My wife, on the other hand, is a gift-opening virtuoso. Even if she hates something, she can still produce a very convincing, "Wow! Look at that! I *love* that color. This is totally me."

It's brilliant.

Now, I know how this all sounds.

I must have it pretty damn good if receiving gifts on holidays causes me stress.

And it's true. I have it quite good. Probably better than I deserve.

So, I guess I'll suck it up.

And when I open that stick of deodorant,

I'll smile.

And be grateful.

And I'll say,

Wow!

Look at that!

I *love* that color.

This is *totally* me.

Six-Hundred-Dollar Oil Change

MY GRANDFATHER DID his own oil changes in his garage.

He'd drive his car up on these little ramps that fit under the front wheels, then he'd slide underneath it, lying on this board with swiveling office-chair wheels attached to it.

He'd empty the oil into a pan. And then he'd dump the oil in a patch of dirt behind the garage reserved for that purpose, likely contaminating the groundwater underneath.

But, hey . . . you didn't worry about such things back then.

My grandfather always kept a bag of kitty litter in his garage. Not because he ever had a cat. But because that's what you put on the floor to sop up any of the oil that may have spilled. All the piles of oil-soaked kitty litter made it hard to ride your skateboard in the garage on rainy days. But, looking back, I see the logic in my grandfather's methods.

Unfortunately, I'm not sure he'd see the same in mine.

I take my car to the dealership for oil changes, which, everyone knows, is exactly what you're *not* supposed to do. Maybe you don't have to change your own oil like my grandfather did. But, rather than take your car to the dealer, where you're likely to get screwed, you're supposed to take it to the local independent guy.

I've done this from time to time. The shop in town does good work.

I think.

How the hell would I know?

The trouble is, it can be a very frustrating experience. Whereas I can schedule everything online with the dealer, the local guy just tells you to park your car in his lot, and then he'll get to it when he gets to it. He doesn't use some fancy website and a bunch of "service consultants" to run his business.

He just does the work.

I called the shop once to try to schedule something. My car's owner's manual said it was due for its whatever-thousand-mile service.

"Sure," the mechanic said, "we can do that. Just drop it off next Friday morning."

So, I did. Even though the lot seemed strangely empty that day.

I parked my car and walked the two miles back to my house in twenty-degree weather. Later that afternoon, after I hadn't heard from the mechanic all day, I gave the shop a call. And I got a recording that said the shop was closed for some random holiday.

I walked back to the shop, retrieved my car, and promptly scheduled an appointment online with the dealer. And I haven't been back to the local guy since.

But that still doesn't make me feel good about going to the dealer, like I did the other day. I pulled into the service bay behind the clear-glass garage doors that opened automatically when you drove up to them. Inside, the place was sparkling, with the service lanes flanked by a row of small offices housing the service consultants.

The moment I stepped out of my car, I was met by someone, maybe a mechanic. It was hard to tell. They all dressed the same.

"Who'd you schedule your service with?" the guy asked me.

Who? That's an odd question, I thought. I hadn't scheduled anything with any person. I just needed a stupid oil change. I didn't care who did it.

When he saw my quizzical look, he asked, "Who do you usually work with?"

Again, an odd question. I didn't *usually* work with anyone.

"I'll set you up with Tom," the guy finally said.

And then he asked me the first logical question of the day.

"Can I get you a cup of coffee?" he asked.

Yes. I'd enjoy a cup of coffee. Thank you.

Inside Tom's office, I was invited to sit down.

"Okay, Daniel, let's see what we got here . . ." he started.

I hate it when they call me Daniel.

Dan's fine, I told him.

"Well, Dan, it looks like you're due for your sixty-thousand-mile checkup," Tom said, looking over my file in his computer.

Sure enough, I wasn't getting out of there with just a simple oil change.

Fucking dealership.

"The good news," Tom continued, "is we can knock that out today. Should only take a couple hours."

And what might that cost? I asked Tom.

"Let's see," he said. "Brake fluid . . . cabin air filter . . . tire rotation . . . labor . . ."

I had an ominous feeling.

"We should get you out of here for six hundred and eighty-five dollars," he concluded.

Are you kidding me?

"Oh! I forgot to mention, we'll also replace the battery in your key fob and the service-reminder sticker in your windshield," Tom added quickly.

As if those things somehow justified the ridiculous price.

Guys like Tom love it when guys like me walk through the door. That's because they know that guys like me know their six-hundred-dollar oil change is the least bad of three options. Those include, one, skip the dealer and go back to the flakey local mechanic; two, roll the dice and forego the "extended service package" altogether; or, three, pay the six hundred bucks.

I'm a big believer in preventative maintenance, and I have no patience for flakes of any variety. So, as Tom and his brethren know, I'll pay. Dejected, I told Tom to go ahead with the full checkup.

He smiled approvingly . . . knowingly.

I grabbed my briefcase and walked to the waiting room.

At least they have snacks, I told myself.

I grabbed a bag of peanuts and another cup of coffee and headed for the "quiet lounge." It's a separate room, adjacent to the main waiting area where HGTV blares in unison from four televisions. I opened my laptop and started in on some emails. A moment later, I was interrupted by pounding coming from the wall across from where I sat.

What the hell? I wondered.

The pounding continued for several minutes.

Curious, and annoyed, I walked out of the quiet room and back into the main waiting area to investigate. The children's play area sat right next to the quiet room and shared a common wall. The wall from which I'd heard the pounding. And the source of the pounding, I discovered, was a little kid with a toy Thor hammer wailing away on the wall.

Which the kid was still doing, uninterrupted, while the woman, whom I assumed to be his mother, blabbed away on her phone.

That's some fine parenting, I thought. I hope the kid puts a goddamn hole in the wall, and you have to deal with it, Mom.

Unbelievable.

As I stood there, judging, Tom found me. "So, the mechanic completed your inspection, and you should have gotten a text," he said.

They liked to send you a video clip of the mechanic describing the underside of your car while it was up on the lift. It's supposed to give you peace of mind, I guess. Or to make you pay for even more unnecessary service. I'd watched the video once before. It was all gibberish to me.

Thanks, I told Tom. I received it.

"Looks like those are new tires," Tom observed.

Yes. They were new. And I sure as shit didn't buy them at the dealership.

"Did you get an alignment when they were installed?" Tom asked.

Why? Are they not aligned?

"Well, it's just a good idea to have an alignment done to prevent uneven wear and tear on the tires," he explained.

Thanks for the tip there, Tom. But I think the $685 you're taking from me today is plenty, don't you?

"Okay," he conceded. "But if you change your mind..."

I drove out of there a short time later.

It was the drive of shame.

The same shameful drive I make every five to ten thousand miles.

I don't think my grandfather would have approved.

And I wouldn't have blamed him.

But, maybe, at least the dealer doesn't dump used oil in the dirt behind the garage.

That's a good thing, right?

Right?

Early Riser

"HE'S A MILITARY GUY. Of course he wakes up early."

So said a friend with whom I recently caught up, answering a question on my behalf. He did so, in part, to defend his own practice of waking up ridiculously early.

He was right, of course. I do wake up early. *Stupid* early, by most people's standards.

But that has little to do with my military affiliation. I'd be a morning person even if I'd never marched a step or snapped a salute in my life. My buddy's comment flowed from a commonly held stereotype. It was the old Army commercial:

"We do more before nine a.m. than most people do all day."

Fair enough.

But it struck me the same way as the comment people make about my assumed tolerance for cold weather.

"He's from Michigan. He doesn't mind the cold."

Actually, I do. I fucking hate the cold. And I always have. But, again, I understand why people think that. It's the stereotype.

Sometimes they're accurate, sometimes not.

The whole wake-up-early-in-the-military thing is somewhat flawed. If you're up and functioning at four in the morning, as many military people are, it's either because you got out of bed before that time, *or* you never went to bed in the first place. Like when you're deployed.

Even in the twenty-first century, there are tactical advantages to operating at night. Nearly all my flight hours in operational theaters took place between ten at night and six in the morning.

"Vampire hours," as one friend described them.

Some guys loved working all night and sleeping all day. Others did not.

Like me.

Not long after my second deployment, a three-star admiral, a former F-14 Tomcat guy, asked me what my favorite mission was in the Persian Gulf. He assumed I'd say something about sneaking around with the SEALs or chasing patrol boats with Hellfire missiles all night, but it was neither.

My favorite mission, I told him, was going to the carrier to pick up the mail.

He looked at me funny.

I then explained it was one of the few times you could fly in broad daylight, without a heavy pair of night vision goggles snapped to the front of your helmet, and just cruise around and enjoy the day. Plus, the air wing wasn't usually flying, and you could get on and off the aircraft carrier with minimal hassle. It was pretty ideal.

I thought I was making sense, but the admiral didn't seem to think so.

"The only *real* flying is *night* flying," he said, dismissively.

And never bothered talking to me again. That was fine—I didn't particularly care for the admiral.

But his comment did support the idea that, at least in an operational setting, the military is better suited for night owls than early birds.

And I am firmly in the latter camp, a useful way to be when I transitioned from sea to shore duty and traded the cockpit for an office.

Still, it was a little bumpy at first.

I was working for the Naval Academy commandant, a future four-star general. While I was learning the ropes from the officer I'd eventually succeed as executive assistant, I noticed the boss walked into the office at exactly eight o'clock every morning. I mean, *exactly*. Not a minute before or after.

That was by design.

He would later explain the importance of a leader's being predictable and establishing a steady operating rhythm. It was one of a thousand lessons he taught that I still carry with me.

I walked into the office the morning of my first official day on the job, having completed turnover with my predecessor. Eager to make a good impression and get my tour off to a positive start, I rolled in at seven thirty to be a step ahead of the commandant.

I opened my email inbox and discovered it was completely full, with messages having poured in from the boss nearly continually since four o'clock that morning. I couldn't possibly get through them all before he arrived. When I walked into his office for our daily morning meeting, the first thing he asked for was an update on the various things with which he'd tasked me in those emails.

Shit.

I fessed up immediately, explaining that I'd seen them for the first time only thirty minutes prior.

The commandant smiled and explained in a fatherly tone, "Just because I walk into this office at zero-eight hundred doesn't mean my workday starts then."

That was suddenly obvious.

"My workday starts the minute I wake up and doesn't end until the moment I shut my eyes at night," he continued. "And that can be late."

In other words, this job was going to consume every waking minute of my day. And that was going to be a very long day. I was fine with this—I'd signed up for exactly that.

I quickly learned to arrange my day to mirror the commandant's. If he was up before four o'clock to work, I would be too. We got in the habit of exchanging emails in real time for the first ninety minutes of every day. Then, around five thirty, the boss would head out for his daily run and pull-ups, and I'd take off for the gym.

I'd roll into the office at quarter to eight for another quick email check and to print out a copy of the calendar for the eight o'clock meeting. Having already been at work since four, it usually lasted no more than fifteen minutes.

Then, we were off and running, in and out of a continuous procession of meetings and events stretching to dinner and beyond. It was exhausting, but I loved it. And the experience firmly established the zero-four-hundred wake-up, sometimes earlier, as my normal routine.

Even to present day.

The big difference now is that I have no desire to have any interaction whatsoever with *anyone* during the early-morning hours. It's *my* time, far and away the most productive, creative, and enjoyable period of the day.

The silence, the stillness, the newness—not to mention a few cups of the strongest, blackest coffee I can make—all combine to set the conditions in which I do my clearest thinking and best work.

There's an optimism to the early morning that you don't get at any other time.

As Colin Powell famously observed, "It ain't as bad as you think. It will look better in the morning."

So true.

This same idea established Ronald Reagan's 1984 "Morning in America" ad campaign as the greatest in political history. "It's morning again in America . . . our country is prouder and stronger and better," said narrator Hal Riney.

No way would "Evening in America" have had the same effect. Because evening sucks, by comparison. No one ever says, "It will look better at night."

Think about it.

So, yes, I'm a military guy. And, yes, I wake up early.

But one doesn't necessarily have anything to do with the other.

I'm naturally inclined to morning.

Just as some people are to the evening.

And that's great.

Hey, do your own thing.

Just don't do it anywhere near me after eight p.m.

Because I'll be waking up early.

In the morning.

Pentwater, Revisited

"**YOU'RE ALL OVER** the place, man." Pete swung his arm in a circular motion to emphasize the point.

I'd asked him to critique his namesake essay collection, *Pete's Garage*.

"I mean, one week you're complaining about being stuck in traffic, and then the next, you're sitting in some five-star general's office."

It was true. There's no rhyme or reason to the subject matter of *Pete's Garage*. I just write whatever the hell I feel like.

"You've had all this crazy stuff happen," he continued. "You're like . . . I don't know . . . Forrest Gump."

I liked the comparison.

I've never been shot in the ass or awarded the Medal of Honor, but I have had a rich and varied life. The place where I'd caught up with Pete was evidence of that. Pentwater, a Lake Michigan beach town.

If you do the hand thing to make a map of Michigan, Pentwater sits at about your second pinkie knuckle. It was the summer playground of my middle and high school years.

From the eighth grade onward, I'd been invited to tag along with my buddy, Kevin, and his family on vacations there. When I'd moved from Indiana to Michigan, Kevin was among the first kids I'd met at Northview Middle School. He was an immediate friend.

And tormentor.

Kevin was fond of sneaking up on me while I was chatting up the latest duo of girls we'd met at Pentwater's Charles Mears State Park. Like Jenny and Jody from nearby Rockford. He'd crouch behind me, then jerk my shorts down as I was mid-sentence, much to the girls' delight.

And my horror.

I was a tighty-whitey guy back then. Not a good look for a fourteen-year-old.

Or anyone.

And how did one later face the Jennies and Jodies of West Michigan out on the sand volleyball court, having been so exposed? Awkwardly, to say the least. And that was all Kevin ever wanted.

Thanks, jackass.

But, sometimes, when he wasn't busy humiliating me, he could be helpful. Even friendly. Like the morning not long after we'd graduated from high school when I woke up in our tent, fully clothed, with sand in my mouth, and a melted Dairy Queen Dilly Bar in my pocket.

"Don't say a fucking word," he said when he saw I was awake. "Just get in the car."

And then we drove to our usual breakfast spot in downtown Pentwater, where he debriefed me on all that had happened the night before—*after* I'd single-handedly downed half a fifth of Bacardi in less than an hour.

That was a poor choice.

At one point, we'd apparently encountered Kevin's mother outside Rinaldi's Mini Golf. He'd somehow convinced her that I wasn't drunk, but the girls on either side of me, propping me up, were.

"You're welcome," he said. "Just try to act normal when we get back, okay? Just be *fucking* normal for a change."

Okay. Sure. I could do that.

And then, later that day, he yanked my shorts down while I was talking to two girls.

Fucking Kevin.

Anyway.

Pete and I had never spent any time together in Pentwater. This, despite the fact he'd been going there since he was a little kid. Just like his parents and his grandparents before them.

That probably had something to do with the fact Pete's dad wouldn't let us take vacations at the same time during the summer. Someone had to stay behind at Petersen Oil to cut the grass and paint the curbs at all the stations.

It was the best damn summer job a kid could have. We were completely unsupervised, entrusted with riding mowers, Weedwackers, and our own pickup truck. One of us *almost* lost a finger, toe, or limb only once. Per week.

It was fantastic.

Then there was that time Pete caught his face on fire, but that's a whole different story.

One day Pete and I walked through the little neighborhood connecting the beach and downtown, headed for an early dinner at Antler Bar. Many of the houses, still quaint looking, had clearly undergone extensive renovations. Money had found its way to Pentwater, but it had been thoughtfully and tastefully deployed throughout the town.

Even Sandra Bullock's place, with commanding views of the channel and the Pentwater South Pierhead, lacked ostentation. I appreciated that. Had our paths crossed at Pentwater Beach when I was last there in 1993, perhaps Sandra could have seen me with my shorts down, thanks to my friend Kevin.

That was before *Speed* and *Miss Congeniality*. Who knows? Maybe we would have hit it off.

After we'd placed our orders at Antler Bar, I asked Pete if he thought I should keep the *Garage* going. I'd committed to doing it for a year, and I'd kept that commitment. So now what?

"Well, do you enjoy doing it?" he asked.

An important question. And the answer was yes.

"Then you have to figure out how to monetize it," he said.

Ah, Pete. Ever the businessman.

Now, don't misunderstand. With Pete, it's not all about money—the object. It's about *making* money, with productive assets. Perhaps he thought *Pete's Garage* could be such an asset. I took it as a compliment.

After dinner, as we walked back to the state park and Pete's camper, I asked if he'd ever thought about buying a place in Pentwater. I mean, why bother with a campsite when you could have your own house?

And why stop there? Hell, Pete would buy most of downtown if he thought it a worthwhile investment.

"Yeah, I thought about getting a place," he said. "But can you really improve on this?"

By *this*, he meant the site's proximity to both the beach and downtown.

The views from Old Baldy, the highest point in Charles Mears State Park, with its steep, sand-covered face running directly into the campground.

The pervasive smell of campfire at dusk and frying bacon at sunrise.

The packs of roaming, spying teenagers, of which we'd been a part a generation ago.

The sense of continuity one enjoys from seeing the same people every year.

And the fact that none of it had changed, substantively, in our lifetime.

Pete had a point.

The state park had qualities, even a permanence, a house couldn't offer. Like a good friend.

I need to get back here more often, I told Pete, which was unexpected. Truthfully, I thought I'd be disappointed with Pentwater. As it turns out, the title of that Thomas Wolfe novel is typically pretty accurate—you can't go home again. Such places become idealized in one's memory, caged in nostalgia. They rarely measure up in later years and are probably best just left alone.

But I didn't find that to be true. Not this time. Not in this place.

I bade Pete farewell in the beach parking lot, just as the park's first campfires were being lit.

It was good to catch up.

And good to get reacquainted with Pentwater,

Among the most significant places,

Holding some of the happiest memories,

Of what has indeed been

A very rich

And varied

Life.

Speed Limit Epiphany

IT'S HEALTHY TO make yourself uncomfortable from time to time. Like I did the other day. I hadn't attempted this particular feat since high school, or maybe ever.

I drove the speed limit.

Not just around town, but for the entire drive from St. Louis to Kansas City. It's about 250 miles, and usually takes around four and a half hours. That's a long time to be uncomfortable. But I've done worse.

As a military guy, I was trained to Embrace The Suck. Seek pain, and make it your friend. Pretty stupid, if you think about it. And something I've largely rejected as I've gotten older. But I do make exceptions. Especially when I feel like I'm getting soft. Or if I believe a temporary period of discomfort will yield new insights or long-term benefit.

That was the idea behind the drive to Kansas City.

For starters, I hate road trips. More precisely, my *ass* hates road trips. After about thirty minutes in a car, I get stabbing pains in my backside. I run a fair amount, and runners have chronically tight hamstrings. Hence the pain when I sit.

That's what I tell myself, at least.

I'd much rather attribute a physical ailment to a sports-related activity than to weakness or a feeble constitution. Sore shoulder? Must have hit it too hard in the pool the other day, I tell myself. Aching knees? Had to be the deadlifts.

It's easier that way.

In the car, I get a pain that starts right where my hamstring meets my glutes and then wraps around the outside of my leg down to my knee. It's excruciating. I've heard this condition called *sciatica*, which I'm pretty sure is bullshit. I'm no doctor, but I think sciatica was invented by some marketer to sell more of those copper sleeve things. Which are also bullshit, by the way. But, hey, you're free to spend your money however you want.

Regardless.

The day before the Kansas City drive, my wife and I had driven from Knoxville, Tennessee, to her parents' place outside St. Louis. We'd delivered our daughter back to college, and the drive from Knoxville started out well enough. The weather was nice, and the mountain vistas on the road to Nashville were quite pleasing.

But then we discovered the second Tuesday of the month is apparently Asshole Trucker Appreciation Day in Tennessee. They were everywhere. If there wasn't one riding your ass, there was one parked in the left lane, backing up traffic all the way to North Carolina.

I mean, who do these dipshits think they are trying to pass each other *in the mountains*?

They'd start out around seventy miles per hour, then slow to, like, forty-five as soon as they hit an incline. And there were *only* inclines. For miles.

As a result, I was constantly on the brakes, decelerating, then on the gas, gunning it, as soon as I spotted an opening to get around one of these assholes. It was impossible to set the cruise control for more than a couple minutes at a time. Not only was it infuriating, but it also forced me into an increasingly uncomfortable sitting position as I continually worked the pedals.

By the time I stepped out of the car some seven hours later at the Mexican restaurant where we met my in-laws, I resembled a large portion of the mostly elderly clientele—stooped, stuttering, and shuffle stepping.

You'd have thought I was ninety.

The whole experience sucked, for sure. But, up to that point in my life, I just accepted such things. The point of a road trip, after all, is to get it the hell over with. That means you only stop when you're down to your last gallon of gas and your eyes are watering because you have to piss so badly.

Any sooner, and you're doing it wrong.

Or are you?

My wife's parents have been driving to Florida three or four times a year for nearly two decades. They're road-tripping machines.

"We stop every two hours, no matter what," my mother-in-law told me. "Who wants to sit there and be miserable?"

Okay. Maybe that's a fair point.

"Of course," she added, "we aren't in any hurry."

Ah . . . there it is. They aren't in a hurry.

But I, along with two hundred million other drivers on the road, am in a big hurry. To get it over with.

Still, I went to bed that night, spears of pain shooting through my hamstrings, thinking there had to be a better way. The next morning, as I was loading the car, I had an epiphany. What if I drove the speed limit? Only a small fraction of cars do so. I could set the cruise control, sit comfortably in whatever position I wanted, and plod along undisturbed in the right lane.

But wait, I thought. You'd have to be some kind of loser to

voluntarily drive the speed limit, right? Or a senior citizen. Did I really want to subject myself to the judgment of every driver that passed me? I have my pride, after all.

But, as I thought about it, I realized I had exactly the asset I needed to escape judgment:

A white minivan.

I'd rented it to haul my daughter's shit back to school. Anyone who saw me taking my time in the right lane would have to think, "Oh, right. Minivan. He must have a bunch of kids in there. Better to take it easy and be safe."

It's like when you drink too much at a costume party. You can always blame it on your alter ego.

I am absolutely not a minivan guy. But, for the drive to Kansas City, I decided I would be. We took off driving, and I maneuvered my way into the right lane. I couldn't really put my plan into effect until we got to the point outside the city at which the speed limit turned to seventy. Once there, I set the cruise control for sixty-nine, sat back, and waited to see what would happen.

My first observation was of the awkward discomfort I felt. It just didn't feel right to be sitting there, lollygagging along at anything less than seventy-five. I had to fight the feeling.

Stick with the plan, I told myself. Just give it a chance.

The next thing I noticed was how many cars were passing me. And it wasn't just cars. The semis were passing me, too. I was watching the same scene play out as the one I'd experienced during the drive through Tennessee the day before. Stressed-out drivers were dueling with asshole truckers. It was an interesting phenomenon to observe. From the perspective of the right lane, the left lane is *The Jerry Springer Show*.

Who wants to deal with that?

And as I was watching this all play out, I noticed how much pain I *wasn't* experiencing in my backside. With the cruise control set and my feet comfortably off the pedals, I could shift my weight around, stretch out, and avoid the various pressure points that gave rise to the pain I typically endured.

It was fantastic.

Then, to make matters even better, I stopped for coffee. Real coffee. At a Starbucks. Not gas station coffee. And then, exactly two hours later, I stopped at a rest stop. A rest stop! When's the last time you visited one of those? It then dawned on me that, if you stop regularly, you can drink as much coffee as you want when you drive. That's huge.

As we pulled into our driveway in Kansas City, I noted the drive had taken only thirty minutes longer than usual.

Thirty minutes: That's it.

A very worthwhile investment, I thought. And while I still felt like I'd been sitting in a car for five hours, I did not feel like the ninety-year-old man of the day before.

My conclusion: All road trips will henceforth be driven at or below the speed limit.

Feel free to judge me as you pass by in the left lane.

Call me an old man, I don't care.

There will be plenty of spaces available at the next rest stop,

Where you'll find me unloading another cup of coffee,

Of which I enjoyed every sip,

At exactly sixty-nine miles per hour.

The Balanced TV Diet

WAIT A MINUTE, wait a minute... what day is today?

I'm asking my wife, even though I already know what day it is. But I want her to tell me.

We're having dinner. *PBS NewsHour* is on in the background.

Come on, I say. What day is it?

She knows exactly what I'm doing. And she's not amused.

"Are you really going to make me say it?" she asks.

Come *onnnnn*, I say. Tell me. What day is it?

Finally, she relents. "It's Monday," she says, flatly.

Monday! I say. Do you know what that means?

Again, I know exactly what it means. But I want her to tell me. And, again, she relents, knowing I'll continue to nag her until she says it.

"*Antiques Roadshow*," she says.

Yes! That's right, I say.

Monday means *Antiques Roadshow*.

"Are we finished now?" she asks.

Yes, I tell her. Until next Monday.

See, my wife hates *Antiques Roadshow*. Absolutely loathes it. She considers it Old Man TV. I, on the other hand, think it's one of the finest shows on television.

Have you seen it?

These appraisers travel around to different cities, and people bring them their old junk, hoping to learn it's worth something. And the appraisers specialize in everything from art to sports memorabilia to sampuru.

That's the Japanese Art of Fake Food. It's the lifelike pieces of plastic sushi you see displayed in the window of every restaurant from Sapporo to Fukuoka.

I'm not kidding—about the appraisers' varied specialties or the ubiquitous plastic sushi.

The typical *Roadshow* episode is comprised of scenes that go something like this:

> *A frumpy, sixty-ish woman in Des Moines stands next to a table with a flowered porcelain vase at its center.*
>
> "I remember that it sat on my grandma's mantle forever. She kept pennies and clothespins in it. When she passed away, it went to my mother, and then my mother gave it to me. I don't know where it came from or how old it is. My husband thinks it's ugly and wants me to get rid of it."
>
> *The appraiser, having flown in from New York, looks dapper, yet awkwardly out of place in his peak-lapel suit as he stands on the opposite side of the table.*
>
> "Perhaps your husband would be interested to

> learn that it's a thousand-year-old plum vase that dates to the Song dynasty. At auction, I would expect it to go for between forty and fifty *thousand* dollars."
>
> *The lady, stunned, stammers . . .*
>
> "Well . . . I guess Earl's just gonna have to live with it then."

That's classic *Roadshow*.

But such scenes are not why I most enjoy it. I tune in for the Rolexes. I'm a watch guy, always have been, and nearly every episode features at least one watch appraisal. Rolexes are my favorite.

Perhaps the most well-known piece came from a Vietnam vet who'd bought a Rolex Daytona in Thailand in 1974 for, like, three hundred dollars. Upon returning from Southeast Asia, he'd put the watch in a safe deposit box and forgotten about it. It was pristine, and he had all the original packaging and paperwork—the receipt from the base exchange, the warranty, the instruction manual . . . everything.

The guy tells the appraiser his story. And then the appraiser explains to the guy how rare and desirable such a watch is, telling him it's the finest version he's ever seen. Of course, the kicker comes at the end when he reveals the auction estimate.

Five to seven hundred thousand dollars.

The owner literally falls over upon hearing the news.

That's why I love *Antiques Roadshow*. The big reveal! You always learn something, and you get to see people in some of the happiest, most nostalgic moments of their lives. Then you go walking through your house, thinking, *Hmmm . . . I wonder what Grandpa's old pipe collection might be worth.*

Different people want different things from their TV shows. For me, it's pretty simple. I want balance in my viewing diet. At one end of the spectrum, I want my news as dull, dry, and factual as possible.

I want meat-and-potatoes brain food. That means *BBC World News* and *PBS NewsHour*.

This likely stems from the summers I spent in Washington, DC, as a Naval Academy midshipman. I stayed with a retired Navy captain while interning on Capitol Hill. Every night, he'd make me sit and watch the *MacNeil/Lehrer Report*, the precursor to *PBS NewsHour*. And he'd make me drink dry gin martinis and smoke cigars while doing so. My palate then was more calibrated to *USA Today*–type news and Bud Lite, making the whole exercise rather excruciating.

And, he would repeatedly ask me what I thought about a particular news story, then make me defend my views, all while choking down pine-needle-tasting booze and a Dutch Masters.

I mean, who wants to actually *think* about anything?

Suffice it to say I didn't enjoy it then. But I'll be damned if I didn't subsequently develop a taste, bordering on obsession, for dry martinis, dry news, and working-man cigars.

The news, then, forms the base of my TV food pyramid. In the center, one finds shows that feed my sense of nostalgia. I'd put *Antiques Roadshow* there. And the original *Magnum, P.I.*, of which I will never tire. It's like *Ferris Bueller's Day Off* or any *Seinfeld* episode. I don't care how many times I've seen it. I'll never get sick of it.

At the tip of the pyramid, opposite *PBS NewsHour* on the TV-viewing spectrum, resides my brain's candy aisle. Mindlessly stupid. High-fructose corn syrup.

Juvenile? Good.

Fart humor? Even better.

Gimme some *Beavis and Butt-Head*, baby!

Have you seen it lately? Whereas in the nineties the boys had only music videos to ridicule, now they have the entire internet. It's given them an entirely new medium with which to work. And the results are genius.

Do you know how much stupid shit is on the internet? Of course you do.

I discovered some new episodes recently while on a plane. I was flipping through the television selections on the screen in front of me, thinking I'd find something useful, like a TED talk. I often feel the need to be productive on planes. Then I saw it: four episodes of *Beavis and Butt-Head*.

So much for being productive.

I assumed they were originals, which would have been a terrific find. But imagine my delight to learn they were entirely new. I dove right in. And laughed my ass off for two straight hours. What a pleasure. And kudos to Mike Judge for preserving everything that was great about the original nineties version.

Of course, it's best to consume *Beavis and Butt-Head* only *after* you've eaten your vegetables. Read *The Economist*. Checked out some BBC. Saw where the markets closed on your *Wall Street Journal* app.

Then watch the boys eviscerate some TikTok idiot. You'll feel far more satisfied.

So, there you have it, folks.

The balanced TV diet.

NewsHour at the base.

Roadshow and *Magnum* in the center.

And *Beavis and Butt-Head*—to be enjoyed infrequently and only in small servings—at the top.

Bon appétit!

An Idiot Wears Contacts

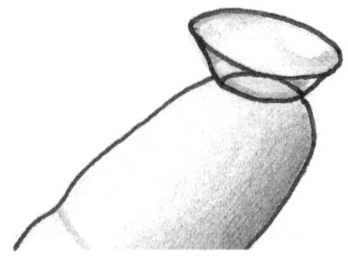

FOR STARTERS, I'M AN IDIOT. But let's set that aside for the moment.

My eyes started going bad on my fortieth birthday. Not *around* my fortieth birthday. *On* my fortieth birthday. The day of. Literally.

I'm sitting in my office, trying to read a book. All of a sudden, the page is blurry.

What the hell? I'm thinking as I push it farther and farther away from my face.

"Your eyes are changing," the optometrist would later say. That was a polite way of saying they were going to shit, which was a huge problem for me. I'd always taken pride in my better-than-perfect vision.

Back at the Academy, good eyes were what separated front-seaters from back-seaters among prospective Naval aviators. You needed perfect vision to be Maverick. Glasses? You got to be Goose. Nothing wrong with being Goose, of course. But everyone wanted to be Maverick.

Including me.

And I had a good run for those forty years leading up to my birthday. My vision held strong. Looking back, I probably took that for granted.

I remember going to the eye doctor once with my wife. Her eyes had been crap her entire life. She'd worn contacts all day and *thick* glasses at night. We were at the doc's office for a consultation on corrective surgery.

Yes, she was a candidate for the procedure, the doc concluded. After doing so, she asked if I'd like to see what the world looked like through my wife's eyes. She directed me to a chair and swung these binocular-looking things attached to a long swiveling arm in front of my face.

After turning a few dials on the binoculars, the doc said, "There. How's that look?"

How's what look? I asked. I can't see a damn thing. It's all blurry.

It was like being underwater with your eyes open. I could see color and light and random shapes but couldn't make sense of any of it.

"That's how the world looks to your wife," the doc replied.

No frickin' way, I thought. No one's eyes are *this* bad.

My wife underwent surgery a few weeks later. And emerged with perfect vision.

Welcome to the club, I told her.

Yeah, I was pretty flippant about it back then, but not anymore. I started with reading glasses. The ones from the drugstore were a little awkward but worked fine. I'll only need them occasionally, I thought. No need to spend a bunch of money on real glasses.

And, for a while, that was true. Until I started needing them at work. And in restaurants. And on planes. And then everywhere.

The worst part was having to remember to take the damn things with me. So, I started staging pairs in various places. In my briefcase. In my car. In my desk drawer.

Still, I'd occasionally forget them and have to borrow someone else's. I was out with a few guys from work. We'd all forgotten our "cheaters." We had to ask the waitress for hers. We passed them around the table until everyone had ordered.

The waitress was amused. We were embarrassed.

Eventually, I had to concede that glasses would be a permanent fixture in my life. I sprung for a pair of trifocals. None of those half glasses balanced on the end of my nose like Chuck Schumer, I decided.

And, I have to say, it was a pretty good look for me. Glasses made me appear smarter than I was. Like a guy to be taken seriously. I'd stare through them at people during meetings. And I could tell they were impressed. Still, I didn't wear glasses all the time. I only needed them for reading.

And then my distance vision started to go. It took a few years, but, slowly, it did. I couldn't read street signs. I couldn't tell who people were from a distance. So then I was wearing glasses most of the time.

A huge pain in the ass.

Glasses fog up. And get dirty. And slide off your nose when you sweat. They're not practical for any form of strenuous physical activity. I got lost during a run through a centuries-old Portuguese city because I didn't have a map. The map was on my phone, which I didn't bother taking, because I couldn't read it, because I refused to wear glasses on a run.

I was gone for more than two hours.

Stupid frickin' glasses.

So then I decided maybe I should give contacts a try. I'd initially been opposed to them, because I was afraid to touch my eyeball. It's unnatural. Then I was reminded that my daughter had been doing it since middle school. If a twelve-year-old could do it, I suppose I could too, I thought.

The girl at the optometrist's office with the happy-sounding name—Chloe or Kelsey or some bullshit like that—made it look easy. She, too, had worn contacts since middle school and was able to whip them in and out effortlessly.

"See, you get them balanced on the tip of your finger, and then *pop!* In they go," she said. And, to take them out, you just swipe your finger across your eye and pull the lens from the corner. "Could anything be easier?" she asked.

Okay. That did seem pretty simple.

Until, of course, I got home and had to do it on my own. And then it was a disaster.

The contact would invariably snag an eyelash on the way in and get deflected from my face to the sink or bathroom floor. Then I'd be down on all fours with a flashlight trying to find the damn thing. And is it okay to wear a contact that's been on the floor? Is there, like, a five-second rule as with food?

Trying to get the lenses out was even worse.

This whole swipe-your-finger-across-your-eye thing was complete garbage. All I managed to do was swipe my finger everywhere the lens *wasn't* and thoroughly irritate my eyeball in the process. It took a week of watching YouTube videos to finally discover the pinch technique that enabled me to get the lenses out reliably.

When I could find them, that is.

About once a week, the right lens would slide off my pupil and get stuck in the side of my eye. I have no idea why. The first time it happened, I assumed it had somehow fallen out of my eye and gotten lost. Then, three days later, I'm standing in the kitchen pouring a cup of coffee, when suddenly my eye becomes itchy. I start scratching and rubbing. And then out comes this deformed blob of silicone.

The missing contact: It had been in my eye all along.

I alerted the doc to my various misfortunes, who politely informed me it was all likely attributable to operator error. So, I soldiered on. For almost a year.

Then, recently, the same thing happens. The lens in my right eye goes MIA.

Shit. Here we go again.

I sit through an entire day's worth of meetings unable to see anything that's projected on the screen in the conference room. Later that night, I pry my right eye open and ask my wife to shine a flashlight around.

See anything? I ask her.

She doesn't.

So, knowing the stupid lens will probably work its way out in the next few days, I take the lens out of my left eye and start brushing my teeth.

And then my left eye starts getting itchy.

What the hell . . . ?

And out of the corner of my eye comes another deformed silicone blob—the same eye from which I had just removed a contact. Turns out, I had put *both* lenses in the *same* eye.

I apparently hadn't been paying attention that morning.

So, yup. I'm an idiot.

I do miss my better-than-perfect vision.

But it's gone forever.

And I do favor contacts over glasses, so I'll keep wearing them.

But I'll always remember that quote from the John Wayne billboard.

"Life is hard. It's even harder when you're stupid."

So true, Duke.

So true.

Jury Duty

"**I JUST WANT OUT**, man . . . I just want *out*." This behemoth, linebacker of a man was sobbing to the detective. "I don't want any of this," he continued. "I don't want this kind of life."

It was a recording of a police interrogation, played in the courtroom while the detective was on the witness stand. The defendant sat expressionless at the defense table. It was an interesting twist to an already fascinating experience.

Jury duty.

Of course, nobody *wants* to do jury duty. Liz Lemon, Tina Fey's character on *30 Rock*, would dress up as Princess Leia and fake a mental illness to get out of it. I wasn't prepared to go that far, but I certainly had no desire to be seated on a jury. I mean, who wants to spend days, even weeks, listening to some lowlife's sob story?

Not I.

But, alas, I'd been summoned. And I intended to do my civic duty.

It all happened pretty fast. I showed up at the courthouse, checked in with the clerk, and was directed to a large silver urn of free coffee sitting in the corner. So far, so good, I thought. And I'd brought a book. The book, plus the coffee, plus the bountiful people watching was plenty to keep me entertained.

Eventually, a group of us was directed into an adjoining courtroom and told to sit in the back. There, the defense and prosecuting attorneys were busy reviewing our prospective juror questionnaires. If there was any way to get out of being selected for the jury by answering the questions a particular way, it hadn't been obvious to me. Once complete, the page resembled a watered-down version of my resume.

The benches in the courtroom were like church pews. Not built for comfort.

The lawyers eventually got around to my questionnaire. The judge asked me to stand, making me feel like I was the one in trouble. Instinctively, I stood at semi-attention. It's what you do after thirty years in the military.

The defense attorney, a woman I immediately disliked, noticed. "Hey, military man . . . look at you," she said.

"The military's got nothing to do with it," I shot back. "I've been sitting on this bench for an hour, and my back hurts."

No way am I taking shit from a lawyer, I thought.

The judge, sensing this, gave me a look that said, *Easy, there, tiger . . .*

The attorney asked me two softball questions about my background and then let me sit down. I judged my chances of being selected for the jury were low, for no particular reason. And then, of course, I was.

Ten minutes later, I was sitting in the jury room with a dozen other people being read instructions by a clerk.

Then something funny happened.

The clerk asked us if we'd selected a jury foreman. We hadn't.

We didn't know we were supposed to. But that didn't stop everyone in the room from pointing at me in response to the clerk's question.

"That guy," one lady said. "The guy in the yellow shirt."

That stupid yellow shirt.

See, nobody'd told me jury duty was a come-as-you-are affair. Most people showed up in shorts and flip-flops. Me? I went with business casual. Khaki pants, pale-yellow oxford, and a blue blazer.

Apparently, this marked me as foreman material.

Even though I hadn't said a single word to anyone.

Whatever.

We were then led out to the courtroom, and the trial began. The defendant was charged with possession and distribution of illicit drugs and the illegal possession of firearms. The story went like this:

Dude with a criminal record leaves his hometown looking for a fresh start. He moves to the city and rents a room from a guy named Frog, paying through a combination of cash and handiwork. Eventually, the handiwork includes running drugs for Frog, whom the defendant believes will kill him if he refuses. Then, reimmersed in the drug culture, he starts using again. The defendant's downward spiral begins anew, and he eventually sells dope to an undercover cop. The police then raid Frog's house and, having obtained the necessary warrants, gain access to the defendant's safe. There, they find drugs, drug paraphernalia, guns, ammo, and, sadly, handwritten letters from his kindergarten-aged daughter.

What a story.

Witness testimony went on for three days. Most memorable was the showdown between the detective who'd conducted the interrogation and the defense attorney. The attorney—evil woman she was—tried to paint the detective as a bully.

She wanted us jurors to discount any information gained through the interrogation, because, she argued, her client had been coerced. She repeatedly attempted to bait the detective. She antagonized him. *She* bullied *him*.

And the detective, in turn, was the very picture of composure. He spoke evenly, without emotion, and stuck to the facts. He didn't seem the least bit bothered by the attorney, which only seemed to make her angrier and more antagonistic.

It was beautiful.

But that's not to say the attorney hadn't scored a few points with certain jurors. Throughout the trial, the defense attorney had repeatedly taken various facts of the case, rearranged and packaged them a certain way, and then presented them to advance a certain argument. Of course, the same facts could have been rearranged a thousand different ways to advance a thousand different arguments. It was obvious, I thought.

Not so for one guy.

He completely bought the defense attorney's version of events, and we remained deadlocked in our deliberations as a result.

"She's trying to manipulate you," I told the guy. "Yes, that's her job. But it doesn't mean you have to believe any of it."

The more I argued, the more the guy dug in.

"I don't care how many different ways you try to explain it," he said. "You're not changing my mind."

Wow. Of course, the very last thing someone who's been manipulated is going to admit is that he's been manipulated.

We deliberated for two full days, and we weren't getting anywhere. It was looking like a hung jury. And this reflected poorly on my foremanship, I thought.

Then, out of nowhere, the clerk informed us the trial was over. The attorneys had struck a deal. The defendant had pleaded guilty to the lesser charges, and the prosecutor dropped the others.

I felt . . . cheated.

By the outcome. But certainly not by the experience. It had truly been fascinating.

There are indeed bad people in the world who need to be locked up. For a long time.

Like Frog.

And then, there are otherwise good people who repeatedly put themselves in bad situations, from which they cannot escape.

Like the defendant.

And I think that's sad.

As I was leaving the courtroom, I heard someone calling after me.

"Excuse me... Mr. Bozung?" It was the defense attorney. "Could I have a word with you?" she asked.

What the hell is this all about? I wondered.

"I'd really appreciate any feedback you'd be willing to give me about the trial," she said, "and anything you think I could have done better."

What? Are you kidding me? This was not the same person I'd observed in the courtroom. This person was nice. And humble. And considerate. I was floored, and, I must admit, impressed.

The detective totally outclassed her, I said. The more she antagonized him, the more she turned me against her and her client.

"Fair enough," she said. She'd actually known the detective for years, and they were apparently friendly outside the courtroom.

I did *not* share with her how successfully she'd manipulated certain jurors with her tactics. That was a behavior I did not want to encourage. I ended on a positive note by telling her how much I admired that she'd sought my feedback.

"Thanks for that," she said. "I just want to get better."

So maybe she wasn't evil. Maybe she was just a professional.

She had a job to do and intended to do it to the very best of her ability.

Or...

Wait a minute...

Had she just manipulated *me*?

Dammit!

Evil woman!

Well, whatever the case,

If ever I'm summoned again,
I hope I get chosen.
Because jury duty, it turns out,
Is a pretty damn cool experience.

My Freakishly Hairy Forearms

"**I DON'T THINK** you want to do that," my wife said.

I'd just informed her that I intended to have all the hair burned off my forearms with a laser.

"That would be . . . weird, right?" she continued. "I mean, you'd look like some kind of creepy, wannabe bodybuilder. Or a woman." She held out her bare right arm to demonstrate.

I disagreed. I didn't think there was anything the least bit strange about it. My freakishly hairy arms had tormented me my entire life.

And there had long been a technological solution available to rid me of it.

Lasers.

But I had never considered it. Until now.

"I think it's handsome," my mother had once lied to me. "It's masculine to have hair on your forearms."

I was probably in the third grade. And I had come home from school, crying, for having been ridiculed for my apelike hairy arms. Even then, it was thick and curly and extended from above my elbows down to my knuckles.

My mother did her best to console me, even saying my arms made me resemble Tom Selleck in *Magnum, P.I.* I knew the comparison was a stretch, but I certainly didn't mind the idea of bearing even the slightest resemblance to Thomas Magnum. With or without the Ferrari.

Still, it didn't stop me from taking action. The next day, during art period, I snuck a pair of scissors into the bathroom. I held them in my right hand as I gave my left arm a close trim. The result was exactly what I'd hoped for.

Finally! I said to myself. I looked like a normal kid.

And then I ran into trouble.

I switched the scissors to my left hand, whereupon I discovered that I lacked the dexterity to cut any hair off my right arm. I tried for as long as I could, but I didn't want to get in trouble for being in the bathroom for too long. I gave up, defeated, and returned to my classroom with one smooth, hairless arm, and one still-hairy, chimpanzee-looking arm.

The kid who sat next to me recognized it immediately.

"Look!" he practically shouted. "Look what Danny did! He cut the hair off his arm!"

The other kids were merciless. And continued to be the remainder of the school year. Because that's how long it took the hair on my left arm to grow back and even things out.

It's a helluva thing.

I'm sure I possess numerous beneficial qualities that distant family members bequeathed to me through the genes I now carry. None of them come to mind. But I am daily reminded of the not-so-beneficial qualities I inherited:

A genetically defective liver that prevents me from enjoying my martinis.

And these ridiculous, furry, afro-wearing forearms.

The hairy-arm problem is most pronounced in spring. Warm weather brings short sleeves. And short sleeves reveal a contrasting palette of pasty-white skin and thick, near-black hair, neither of which have seen the sun in months. It's not a good look.

When I was a kid, it took a few trips to the city pool and a couple of sunburns for my skin to tan and arm hair to lighten to the point where the contrast between the two was sufficiently reduced. The mostly blond hair remained nearly invisible throughout the summer and into the fall. And then the cycle would repeat itself the following spring.

It's been that way my entire life.

Even as a graduate student, I couldn't escape the cycle. I wore a polo to class one day in early spring. Upon completion of the lecture, the girl who sat in front of me turned around and caught sight of my forearms.

"What the . . . ?" she asked out loud. "Is that for real?"

I knew immediately what *that* meant.

"Wow, Dan," she continued. "You have some seriously hairy forearms."

No kidding, sweetheart. Thanks.

And, of course, everyone who'd heard the comment had to come have a look. It was the third grade all over again. I accepted my fate and extended my arms out in front of me for all to see. And it was thereby confirmed that, yes, I indeed had abnormally hairy forearms—quite a discovery for my classmates. Others in the class were quickly called over to have a look, and I got to imagine what the bearded lady at the circus must have felt like.

Now, maybe I was better equipped emotionally to manage the situation than I had been in the third grade. But the thirty-year-old me hated it just as much as the eight-year-old.

And I still hated it fifteen years later.

I was on a Navy ship in Japan. I'd shared with my buddy, Kyle, my practice of gifting myself a new watch at the end of every deployment. He thought it was a terrific idea, and we'd spent considerable time presenting each other with various post-deployment watch ideas.

Kyle settled on a Hamilton Khaki Aviation. He bought it at a mall outside Yokohama.

Me, I was undecided. And I remained so well after Kyle had left the ship for his next duty station. Finally, with only a couple weeks remaining, I sprang for a Breitling Superocean. I shared the news with Kyle by sending him a picture of the watch sitting on my wrist.

"That's awesome!" he replied. "But where's the watch? I can't see anything through that jungle of hair on your arm."

Kyle, Kyle, Kyle . . .

I thought we were friends.

"Just kidding," he said. "Great choice on the Breitling."

See? This is the shit I deal with. It never ends.

Returning to the topic of arm hair removal with my wife, she offered up an alternative to lasers.

"Why don't you just trim it?" she asked. "You know, just tame it a little."

I'd already shared with her the story of my third-grade bathroom-scissors debacle. She knew how sensitive I was to the idea of trimming. Plus, wouldn't that just make the problem worse? It would grow back longer, thicker, and darker, right?

"Maybe," she said. "But if it bothers you that much . . ."

I thought it over.

What the hell? I decided.

I ordered a beard trimmer with various attachments from Amazon, and it arrived the next day. I stood in the kitchen and examined the different blade guards to decide upon the proper length. Even the guard that cut the least would reduce my arm hair by more than half. It was that long.

So, the risk: I would be irrevocably committed to an arm-hair-trimming regimen the rest of my life.

And the benefit: I might look like a normal human fucking being for a change.

The benefit outweighed the cost.

Okay, I said to my wife, holding the buzzing trimmer above my left arm. Here we go.

We both stood around the trash can as I made the first pass with the trimmers. The hair piled up in dense balls, like tumbleweeds, atop the blade guard before falling into the trash can. I wasn't following any set course at first and just ran the trimmer anywhere I saw hair. My wife disapproved of the haphazard approach.

"No, no, no," she said. "You have to do it in rows."

Okay, I said. I was open to suggestions.

I made successive passes in parallel rows, causing the hair to peel off my arm like wool from a sheep. I continued in the same manner to finish my left arm before switching to my right. When both were finished, I held them out in front of me.

What do you think? I asked my wife.

"Better," she said. "Much better."

I agreed. This was what normal looked like. And it felt fantastic. I felt . . . lighter.

Now, I wait.

How quickly will it grow back?

And what color? How thick?

Have I indeed made matters worse?

Will I ultimately need to resort to lasers?

Questions for another day.

In the meantime, I'm putting on a polo.
Spring is in the air.
And I do look forward to short-sleeve weather.
Especially this year.

To Hell with Mulch

IT'S SPRINGTIME, and that means mulch. I fucking hate mulch.

Is there anything more worthless? I mean, you go to the trouble to spread this stuff all over your yard, and then it looks nice for, like, ten minutes.

Ten minutes!

Mulch makes me hate living in a house. Maybe I should live on a boat. Or in an apartment. I think I'd like an apartment. Funny, when I had an apartment, all I wanted was a house. Now, I have a house, but the house has mulch, so I hate it.

The problem isn't the mulch itself. My neighbor, who knows about this stuff, tells me it helps regulate soil temperature and prevent weeds. Plants like that. So, okay, maybe it serves a useful purpose. And it smells good when it's new. Like warm weather. And, for the ten minutes it looks nice, it looks *really* nice. Makes the yard look tidy. And if you're an uptight prick like me, you appreciate tidy.

The problem with mulch is the torment it inflicts upon me every year regarding where to get it and how much to pay. And, if I go the DIY route, how much pain I'm willing to endure, and for how long, to get the mulch installed. You don't spread mulch. You *install* it.

But whatever.

There are two schools of thought when it comes to mulch.

One, never pay someone to do what you can do yourself. This is the old-school, Great Depression approach. Yes, I am physically capable of installing my own mulch. I've had a company dump a huge pile of it in my driveway, which I then wheelbarrowed all over my yard. I've also had Home Depot deliver a pallet of packaged mulch to my house, then carried the bags all over the yard, ripped them open, and spread it around.

Both methods suck. Especially for my yard.

My house was built into the side of a ravine. Okay, maybe not a ravine, but I have a ridiculously steep-ass yard. On three occasions, I've had dudes lose control of their stand-behind, wide-deck lawn mowers and go careening into the woods behind my house. It's that steep.

And, thanks to my ridiculous yard, I get to enjoy having the occasional needle stuck behind my kneecap. Like a couple years ago, when I was maneuvering a load of dirt through my backyard. I felt gravity start to take hold of the wheelbarrow and pull it from my hands.

Screw you, gravity! I said and started to put the brakes on with both feet.

And then I felt something pop in my right knee. Torn meniscus.

Luckily, it didn't require surgery. But it did require that I get some sort of lubricating fluid injected into my knee, right behind my patella. Which is exactly as much fun as it sounds.

So, you see, my yard doesn't just suck. It's straight-up dangerous.

The second school of thought on mulch, and a variety of other things, is to pay people to do the shit you don't want to do. All the productivity books suggest that what's drudgery for you is pleasurable for someone else. So, in the market-based economy in which we're fortunate to live, one can outsource one's drudgery to someone who actually enjoys, and perhaps even makes a living, doing precisely that which one hates.

Like installing mulch.

It was easy when I lived in Houston. About the first week of March, dudes with trailers full of mulch would start circling the neighborhood. You'd get a knock on your door, and one of them would ask if you'd like some. And they had the good stuff: thick, black, and fragrant. And because there were competing packs of trailer-hauling mulch dudes roaming the Houston suburbs, it was cheap.

So, you'd say yes, give the guy a couple hundred bucks, and then an entire crew would descend upon your yard and have the mulch installed, to professional standards, in less than an hour.

Easy. That was Houston.

Here, in Kansas City, you have to call a professional landscaping service. And that service—having overhead, payroll, and taxes with which to contend—charges you through the frickin' nose to deliver and install mulch.

I mean, it's ridiculous . . . like, *five times* what I paid the dudes in Houston.

And, rather than offer same-day installation, it takes the landscapers a month to get to your yard. That's a problem if, because you hate mulch so much, you procrastinate like I do. By the time they show up, all the flower beds are already overgrown with weeds, which means the landscapers charge you even more to get them cleaned up.

Total scam.

The long-term solution, of course, is to get rid of the mulch. I looked into replacing every splinter of the stuff in my yard with Missouri river rock. The guy from the landscaping company walked me through the entire process. His crew would re-edge all the flower beds and, in some places, install permanent brick borders to act as mini retaining walls. He showed me photos of several projects he'd done.

The river rock looked nice. Really nice.

And cost twice as much as my kid's car.

Twice.

So, no, I won't be getting any river rock this year. Or ever.

But I will be paying the landscapers to install more mulch.

Which will look nice for ten minutes.

And then go back to looking like shit.

I don't intend to stay in this house forever,

And if I don't get my boat or apartment and have to live in another house,

I won't give a damn about bedrooms or square footage or hardwood floors.

Nope.

My criteria is simple.

Mulch, or no mulch?

That is the question.

The Best Damn Day-After-Christmas

"**WHAT THE HELL** is this?" asks my brother-in-law Zeb as he fishes another bottle from the back of the refrigerator. "*No* idea where that came from."

Famous words from an epic day-after-Christmas.

But I'm getting ahead of myself.

December 26, about five years ago. We go over to my wife's sister's around eleven in the morning. The family's there, as well as a few longtime friends. We're doing a day-after-Christmas brunch. I'm down with that.

Zeb's just finished the bar in his basement. And it's a far cry from your typical DIY job. See, Zeb's one of those annoying guys that knows how to build and fix stuff. The centerpiece is the high-polish, sturdy-as-a-tank, chest-high bar he's constructed out of reclaimed mahogany. Or cherry. Or oak. I have no frickin' idea.

Anyway, the thing is absolutely gorgeous. Looks like it came straight from the Raffles Hotel in Singapore.

"What do you think?" he asks.

I think it's the most incredible thing I've ever seen.

Zeb's behind the bar, and I'm on one of the stools. The Poulan Weed-Eater Independence Bowl, or some shit like that, is playing on the TV mounted to the adjacent wall.

"Look what I got," Zeb says as he puts a brand-new bottle of Bombay Sapphire in front of me.

He knows I'm a martini guy, and he's very generously stocked the bar accordingly. He sets a jar of olives, a bottle of dry vermouth, and a shaker full of ice next to the gin.

"I know you're picky," he says. "So I thought you could make your own."

Good man.

It's about 11:30 a.m. now. Which is a terrific time for a martini. And why stop at one? Or two? You can see where this is going. Pretty soon it's night, and we've been drinking all day. The girls join in at some point.

Beneath the mahogany-cherry-oak bar, Zeb's installed one of those beneath-the-counter, commercial refrigerators. It's exactly what you'd find at a proper club or restaurant. Zeb gets the idea to go rooting around inside the refrigerator. He's recently transferred the contents of his old basement refrigerator into this one.

That includes all the random booze people have brought over in the previous decade.

"What the . . . ? Look at *this*," he says, holding a bottle of pineapple-citrus Zima.

Just the sight of it gives me the dry heaves.

"You know what we have to do, right?" Zeb continues.

Uh-oh.

"Drink it," he says. "*All* of it."

And he's not just talking about the Zima.

He pours shots of Zima into four glasses he's pulled from the shelf behind the bar and hands them out to the girls and me.

"Mazel tov!" he says.

The Zima is awful. The girls barely let it touch their lips. But I power through the entire thing. After a full day of drinking, I somehow love this idea of cleaning everything out of Zeb's fridge. And, in doing so, I break every drinking rule I've learned since high school.

"What's next?" I ask.

He pulls out a bottle of pumpkin apple cider. It's even worse than the Zima.

And it goes on like this for another two hours, until there's nothing left in the fridge. I'm definitely feeling it at this point.

Now, my memory of what happens next is a little blurry. All I know is, we're getting ready to walk upstairs to leave, and I lose my balance. My wife reaches out to grab me. She *claims* she tried to catch me. But I'm pretty sure she shoved me—right onto some giant plastic toy, which I then broke into a thousand pieces. Everyone was pissed. Except Zeb. He was in as bad of shape as I was. Somehow, I have the wits to pull out my phone and order a new one from Amazon right on the spot.

The next morning is about as pleasant as you'd expect. It's one of my top five hangovers of all time. Easily. I'm so hungover, I can barely sit up.

It's nearly dinnertime before I manage to get a shower.

And, of course, the Zima and pumpkin cider don't seem nearly as good an idea as they'd been the night before.

But, looking back, you know what?

That Christmas Zeb and I cleaned out his refrigerator?

One of the best I've ever had.

So, next holiday, consider cleaning out that basement refrigerator.

You'll remember it for years to come.

Well, some of it.

Toilet Seat Scam

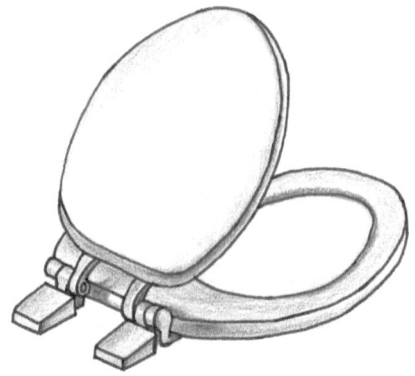

TOILET SEATS ARE a total scam.

That's right.

The hinges on two toilet seats in my house broke at the same time. Coincidence? I think not.

I am well familiar with the razor blade business model. Gillette charges you ten bucks for the Mach3 Turbo, then three times that for a pack of blades. And they do so in perpetuity. It's pretty genius, actually.

But toilet seats?

"Just get new ones," my wife says.

Why? The seats are fine. It's just the hinges.

I go online. Let's see . . . *Bemis toilet seat hardware and accessories . . .*

(Who the hell names a company "Bemis," by the way?)

Amazon has replacement hardware, of course. *Fits all Bemis models*, it says. Sweet. I order two sets. Costs me nineteen bucks. Five days later, they're on my doorstep.

I go to the bathroom and hold up one of the packages to the toilet seat. I want to make sure everything lines up before I open it. Nothing lines up. Not even close. Now I want to write an Amazon review that calls bullshit on the whole Fits-all-Bemis-models statement.

Of course, I don't. Who actually takes the time to do that?

So besides two broken toilet seats, now I have to figure out what to do with this toilet seat hardware I don't need. Return it? That takes effort. Shove it under my workbench with all the other hardware I've bought and don't need? Probably.

So, my next move is to actually go to a hardware store. Before I do, I take a bunch of pictures and measurements. I'm getting it right this time, dammit.

I drive to the Ace Hardware down the street.

"Can I help you find anything?" asks the friendly dude in the plumbing section.

I show him the pictures of the toilet seat on my phone. And hope he doesn't think it's weird that I walk around with toilet seat pictures.

"Uh-huh . . . okay . . ." he says after looking at the pictures for a few seconds.

He walks me over to the toilet aisle and starts looking around.

"Yeah," he eventually says. "Didn't think so. Sorry."

They don't have toilet seat hinges.

So now I drive to the Lowe's twenty minutes away. I find the toilet guy there and show him my pictures.

"How old's that toilet?" he asks me.

I don't know. It's probably original to the house. Almost twenty years, maybe.

"Oh, well . . . there you go," he says, getting all uppity. "Just buy a new seat," he says.

Because he makes a better commission on the seats, I assume. I know what's up.

Screw him.

I drive to The Home Depot another five minutes away. This time, I find the toilet aisle by myself. No way am I getting upsold by another toilet-seat-pushing clown.

They have toilet seat hardware, but do they have the *right* toilet seat hardware? I consult my photos and measurements. And I find what appears to be exactly the right set of hardware. Two packages set me back thirteen bucks. That brings my total sunk costs to thirty-two dollars. Plus time and mileage.

I go home and walk straight to the bathroom. I unscrew the seat from the toilet and remove the broken hardware. Then I rip open one of the packages, certain I got the right stuff. I lay the new hinges on top of the toilet seat, and discover the screw holes don't line up.

Shit. I did it again.

So, I get in my car and drive back to The Home Depot. I return the hinges and go back to the toilet aisle. I find exactly the same stupid Bemis toilet seat I already have and grab two of them. That costs me another forty-two dollars for the pair. My grand total for this toilet seat adventure climbs to seventy-four bucks. Plus time and mileage.

I go home, bolt the two new seats in place, and toss the old ones in the trash.

Now, I don't love the idea that those perfectly good toilet seats are going to sit in a landfill for the next thousand years.

But I'm done.

And I've learned my lesson.

The next time I have a broken toilet seat

I'm moving.

Antidote to the Life of Quiet Desperation

SUNDAY MORNING. PLAZA Art Fair. An absolutely gorgeous late-summer day.

My wife orders a sangria from a food truck. Lady asks if she wants a glass or the half-bottle carafe.

"Carafe? How am I supposed to drink that?" she asks.

The lady hands her a straw the length of her forearm.

Perfect.

We walk toward the sound of jazz coming from the fair's main stage. It's flanked on either side by booths exhibiting various artists. A light breeze kicks up. The sun shines. My wife sips her sangria. I realize I wore exactly the right shoes. It's pretty damn ideal.

Then . . .

"And here you are, out walking around on the Sabbath, having a good time. Meanwhile, you have no idea where your soul's gonna spend eternity. Not a clue! Well, I got bad news for you, friends . . ." It was one of those sidewalk preachers, bellowing into a megaphone.

"You might think you have all the answers," he says ominously, "but I'm here to tell you . . . you don't."

My wife and I exchange a look and cross to the other side of the street. We continue on in the direction of the jazz, smiling, unbothered. And that's that.

Now, there was a time when sidewalk preachers made me uncomfortable. And people who sing in subways. And those guys who cover themselves in metallic paint and stand frozen on boardwalks.

Anyone willing to put it all out there for public ridicule used to creep me out. I mean, do they *want* people to think they're freaks?

I think differently now.

After a year in the corporate cubicle, I realized I was dead wrong to have judged such people—those willing to step, unafraid, onto whatever their stage and do their thing. See, it takes guts to do your thing. And I admire guts. The cubicle doesn't require guts. It requires a pulse. Barely.

Things were pretty bad there for a while. I went off the existential deep end after I reread *Walden*. You know the story. Thoreau goes to live in solitude in the Massachusetts woods and pens the line, "The mass of men lead lives of quiet desperation."

I was among that mass of men. And the realization terrified me.

Then there was that line from Oliver Wendell Holmes about people dying with the music still in them—about going to their graves with unrealized potential.

I had plenty of unrealized potential. And it made me wonder, had I really thrown away my Navy career to do . . . *this*? What a waste. I didn't wanna die with my music still in me.

I know, I know. You have to make a living somehow, right? That Lisa Loeb wannabe you see on the street doesn't strum her guitar every hour of every day. She has some crappy job to go to like the rest of us.

But that guitar sustains her. And she doesn't give a shit what you think about it. I understand that now.

In the movie *Yes Man*, Zooey Deschanel plays opposite Jim Carrey as Allison, the lead singer of "Munchausen By Proxy," a fictional band with a dedicated, but limited following—of five people. She opens a set by greeting each of the five audience members by name, as an amused Carrey watches on.

I'm sure she'd rather play to a packed Wembley Stadium. But she seems content with these five. She's doing her thing, and that's totally cool. Even if it's fictional.

Adam Wainwright, the St. Louis Cardinals' former pitcher and all but certain Hall-of-Famer, likes to write and sing his own country music songs. And they're bad. *Really* bad. The broadcasters once played one during *Sunday Night Baseball*. It was so hard to stomach, I had to mute the television.

But he should keep right on singing those horrible songs, loudly and often. Right on, Adam Wainwright!

And that sidewalk preacher? Keep on preaching, bro! Not my cup of tea, but I admire your conviction.

Me? I do a little writing. And I dabble in watercolors. Neither is likely to land me in the White House or an exhibition at The Met, but so what? They make me happy.

I do think Thoreau and Holmes were right. And that's sad. But to hell with them.

That whole life-of-quiet-desperation thing?

Not on my watch.

How does one avoid going to his grave with the song still in him?

Simple.

Start singing, baby!

Just start singing.

Whatever that means for you.

Pete's Garage

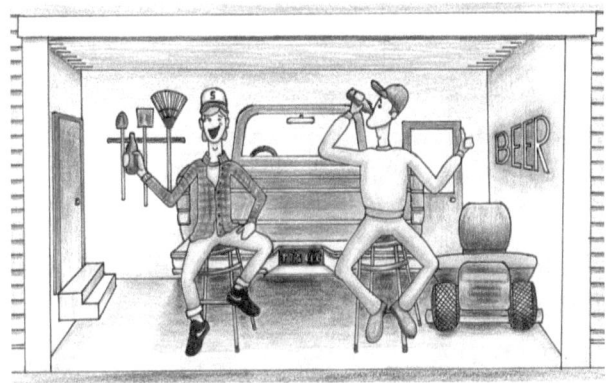

LIKE ALL GREAT TRADITIONS, it just happened.

Beer. Workbench. Black-and-white TV. Propane heater. Riding mower parked next to the pickup.

Pete's Garage.

Pretty ideal setup for a couple of sixteen-year-olds slogging through a Michigan winter. It was Mike Petersen's dad's house. We called Mike "Pete." Except Kemp and Arntz—they called him Peter North, a tribute to the porn legend. Kemp and Arntz were authorities on the genre.

Pete's dad was pretty casual about beer, as long as we weren't drinking it right in front of him. What's the harm, he figured? Pete had drunk his body weight in beer during that summer trip to Germany. Didn't seem to slow him down one bit scrubbing the floors or painting the curbs at Petersen Oil when he got home.

All Pete ever wanted was to work in the family business. He never talked about anything else. His grandfather had started it and his dad and uncle had taken it over. Eventually, Pete would take it over from them. Simple. Me? I was going to be a lawyer. Figured I'd do that for a while before being elected governor of Michigan.

We'd talk it over while drinking our Winter Lagers. Pete would get the Samuel Adams holiday sampler pack for Christmas. (Yes, he got beer for Christmas.) Then he'd call me up, I'd come over, and we'd sit in his garage and drink it.

We knew we had it pretty good, so we kept our mouths shut. If we called up Sloke or Weadley or Truesdell and had them come over, pretty soon, it'd be a party. And then someone would go blabbing about it. Probably Truesdell. And then Pete's dad would shut it down, and maybe Pete wouldn't get beer for Christmas anymore.

Yup, we had it good. So we kept it quiet, and that's what kept it going.

Pete went to college after graduation. For one semester. An economics professor told him there wasn't anything he'd learn in college that he couldn't learn at Petersen Oil. That was all Pete needed to hear.

I joined the Navy. My parents had told my siblings and me repeatedly that there were too many of us kids, and they weren't paying for college. We were on our own. I didn't realize they were serious until six weeks before graduation. So, I went to see the recruiter.

I made it home only a handful of times after that, and the Pete's Garage tradition faded.

Until recently.

Thirty years later, Pete and I are having dinner at the Clifford Lake Inn. I hadn't been there since the 1990 Petersen Oil Christmas party. Pete asks me if I remember. Of course I remember.

In high school, I was the naive idealist. Pete was the practical realist. The last time I'd looked out on that lake, I was certain I was on my way to Michigan State to be a Sigma Chi. Then a lawyer. Then governor.

Mike was certain he'd take over the family business, which he did. Then he grew it. And grew it. Then sold it and semi-retired. In his forties. And the only reason he didn't completely retire was that he decided to buy the old Klackle apple orchard and totally reinvent it.

But that's a whole other story.

Me? I didn't do any of the things I intended. But I've still had a rich life. Not even close to what I'd imagined, but rich.

So, there we are, looking out on Clifford Lake, and I'm reminded of Pete's Garage. I wonder what the grown-up version of me would say to the sixteen-year-old sitting on the stool at the workbench.

Hope you enjoy getting kicked in the nuts, kid.

And Pete?

I don't know. He'd probably just tell himself to stay the course.

Stay the course.

It was good to see my old friend, and to consider where we'd been. And how far we'd come. I think of Pete's Garage as any place good friends meet to reconnect and contemplate life. Or business. Or beer.

It's a metaphor. Or a simile. Whatever.

That's some pretty deep shit, I know.

I look over at Pete, and I wonder if the profundity of the moment—of all that's come and gone in the three decades since we last sat in that spot—is as striking to him as it is to me.

He stands up and nods in the direction of the waitress.

"Tell her I need another IPA," he says. "I'm taking a piss."

Yup.

He gets it.

That's some pretty deep shit.

Pathetically Weak Hips

"**I DON'T CARE** about your back."

The physical therapist cut me off mid-sentence, which was a little surprising since I was there to discuss . . . you know, my back.

At least I thought I was.

Sensing my surprise at her retort, she explained, "Listen, I understand what the doc said about your back, and I know what the X-rays suggest, but you haven't said one word about having any pain back there."

That was true. When she'd asked me what issue I was trying to resolve, I only spoke of the knife in the ass I felt whenever I sat for more than thirty minutes or ran for more than five miles. The doc had said it was all likely associated with the scoliosis, vertebrae compression, and general deterioration he'd discovered when he'd reviewed my back X-rays.

It turns out, flying and marathon running aren't conducive to good lower back health. I'd done a fair share of both, and now I had the spine of a ninety-year-old woman to prove it. Which, the doc explained, was likely the source of all my ass and hamstring pain.

Armed with this knowledge, I'd made an appointment to consult the physical therapist. About my back.

But not right away. It took me some time to decide to go the therapy route. Two reasons.

First, the doc hadn't given physical therapy a ringing endorsement. Not in my case, at least. He knew I worked out regularly and surmised I was likely already doing everything that could reasonably be done to strengthen my back and prevent further deterioration.

"Make an appointment if you want," he said, "but it might not be worth your time."

The second reason was that I had based my concept of physical therapists on what I'd seen in movies and on television. I'd pictured therapists as quasi healthcare professionals who specialized in getting people like Lieutenant Dan to walk again after he'd gotten his prosthetic legs. They said stuff like, "Dammit, we're gonna get you up out of that chair! Now, come on . . ." And then you'd see Lieutenant Dan get up, fall down, and get back up again. Until, one day, he would triumphantly take that first step.

That's what physical therapists did. In my mind.

They weren't people who cured ass pain for skinny middle-aged dudes like me.

But what's the harm? I thought. Maybe they could teach me some stretches or something. Might as well give it a try. Of course, none of this was of any interest to the therapist.

"Lie down on your stomach," she instructed me.

Okay.

And then she started pressing around on my butt. "What about here?" she asked as she dug her thumb into the spot where my glute met my hamstring.

I nearly jumped off the table.

Yes! I said. That's the place.

"So, I think we've isolated your problem," she concluded.

Then she had me lie on my left side with my right leg extended up at a forty-five-degree angle, scissors-style. She started pressing down on my foot and told me to resist.

I was completely incapable. My right foot collapsed onto my left with minimal force.

The therapist continued to be direct. "Your problem is that you have *pathetically* weak hips," she said.

Oh, really? Pathetically weak? Screw you, I thought. My hips are just fine. And what the hell do my hips have to do with anything, anyway?

Quite a lot, it turns out.

The therapist went on to explain that my weak hips were causing my body to compensate in unnatural ways whenever I ran or worked out. And that compensation, in turn, contributed to the tightening and knotting in my hamstrings and glutes. And my monkey's-fist hamstring, when pressed against the underlying nerves, was the likely cause of the pain I experienced when sitting for extended periods.

So, it all began with my hips. Not my back.

She prescribed exercises. "We'll start with resistance bands," she said. "You can work your way up from there." She gave me two bands of different resistances and copied pages of old-lady hip exercises from a therapy manual. Clamshells. Side planks. Fire hydrants. I'd be on the floor, waving my hips around like Richard Simmons, for at least half an hour.

The therapist also gave me a hard-rubber lacrosse ball. "Put this where it hurts the most, and sit on it with all your weight," she instructed. I'd be giving myself a deep-tissue massage, which should help alleviate some of the tightness.

And hurt like a motherfucker in the process.

"That's how you know you're doing it right," she said.

Fantastic.

I left the therapist's office, questioning: Were my hips really *that* weak? And were they, in fact, the cause of all the pain in my backside?

I tried the exercises the following day. Just to ensure I maintained proper form, I started with the lower-resistance band. Even while I assumed it wouldn't provide sufficient resistance to give me much of a workout.

I mean, come on. I'm no amateur here, right?

So, I started with some clamshells, doing the minimum recommended number of reps and sets. Then the side planks. Then the fire hydrants. And about five other exercises, each performed precisely as described. As expected, it took about thirty minutes. And when I stood up at the end, I was shocked.

I could barely support my own weight. My entire core was in spasms.

What the hell is? I wondered. Was it true?

There was no escaping it—my hips were indeed pathetically weak. And this caused me a minor existential crisis. Where else was I weak but didn't know it? How many other problems in my life had I attributed to the incorrect root cause? What other pain in my life was I either ignoring or addressing in the wrong manner?

The upperclassmen at the Naval Academy were fond of reminding us plebes that, "Pain is weakness leaving the body."

Is that so? Or is it your body telling you that you're an idiot?

For years, I'd trained myself to ignore pain. I refused to see doctors. And when I did, I acted like a POW, unwilling to volunteer any information. Name, rank, and serial number. That's it. If there's anything wrong with me, it's on you to find it, doc. Because I'm not about to tell you there's anything wrong. That was my way of thinking.

You can get away with that when you're young, but then you eventually grow up and realize that living with pain is stupid. As I recently had. But even after I'd chosen to confront the stabbing pain in my ass, I'd been misled.

Well . . . misguided.

The doctor hadn't been wrong in his assessment—X-rays don't

lie. My back is totally screwed up. But to focus on my back as the correct path to alleviating issues with my glutes was the wrong approach. It took the physical therapist to teach me that. Someone I had previously ignored.

And the result?

My hips are getting a little stronger every day, thanks to those medieval old-lady exercises. And stretching. Lots and lots of stretching. The stabbing pain in my backside isn't entirely gone, but I'm getting far less of it. How about that?

So, the moral of the story:

Don't be stupid. Don't ignore pain. Don't discount possible solutions.

Challenge assumptions, including those made by experts.

And don't be offended to learn that you're weak.

Even pathetically so.

Perhaps this was best summarized by my Harvard finance professor when I asked him to describe his entire philosophy in one sentence.

"Be skeptical," he said.

Especially of yourself.

And your back. And your ass. And, of course,

Your hips.

Don't forget the hips.

On the Yard

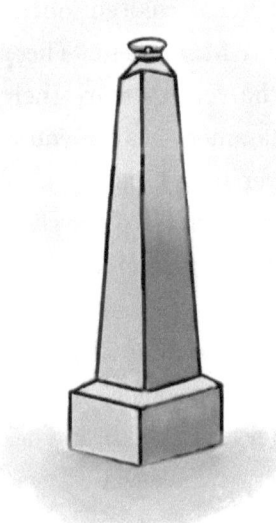

I WAS BACK on the Yard the other day. That's what we call the US Naval Academy campus in Annapolis, Maryland.

It was a Saturday, less than a week before graduation. I expected the place to be crowded with the families of graduating midshipmen. But it wasn't. It was quiet.

The cool temperatures and passing rain showers may have had something to do with that. Or maybe it was because, on a Saturday afternoon, midshipmen would rather be anywhere else on the planet than on the Yard. I get that. I used to be one of those midshipmen.

Things are different now.

Today, I wouldn't consider *not* visiting the Yard if I were within a hundred miles of the place. Plus, if you still hold a military ID card, it's a convenient place to park and then walk into town. Parking in Annapolis is awful, especially in summer and on weekends. I parked my car across from Alumni Hall. Then I walked in the direction of the main gate, past the chapel and the Herndon Monument.

Herndon is the charcoal-colored obelisk that resembles a miniaturized Washington Monument. The plebes, or freshmen, climb it at the end of the year to mark their ceremonial passage from under- to upperclassmen. Maybe you've seen pictures of it. The upperclassmen cover it in Crisco and place a plebe's "Dixie Cup" hat on top. Someone from the plebe class must then retrieve it and replace it with an upperclassmen's hat. Thus marks the official end of plebe year.

Sometimes it takes minutes. Usually, it takes hours.

The ceremony had taken place only a few days before. A longtime friend's daughter was a plebe, and he'd been there to see it. He'd sent me pictures.

The place still smells like lard, I texted him.

He informed me that his daughter was on the Yard that day.

You should say hello, he texted back.

I told him I would. Right after lunch.

I continued to the main gate, out into downtown Annapolis, then over the drawbridge into Eastport. The route took me past the Annapolis Yacht Club, where the sound of halyards clanking on masts rose from the basin. I love that sound. It's so . . . old money. Right out of *The Official Preppy Handbook*.

I stopped at the Boatyard Bar and Grill, where you're immediately hit with the smell of Old Bay Seasoning when you walk in. They put it on just about everything there. During lunch, I made arrangements to meet my buddy's daughter. She's a varsity sailor, so we agreed to meet at the Academy's sailing center. I hadn't been there in decades.

We linked up a short time later, and one of her teammates was with her.

So, what's the plan for the summer? I asked them.

Sailing, of course, they said. And also PROTRAMID, or Professional Training of Midshipmen. It's a month in which you get to experience every major warfare specialty—aviation, surface, submarines, and Marine Corps.

It was exactly the same itinerary I'd had thirty years earlier. It had been a great summer.

I sailed to Bermuda, did barrel rolls in a T-34 in the skies over Pensacola, and dove off the dive planes of a fast-attack submarine during a swim call off the coast of King's Bay, Georgia. And I'd gone yut-yutting with the Marines through the woods of Quantico, Virginia. I didn't care for the yut-yutting, but everything else was awesome.

We chatted a while longer before walking in the direction of Bancroft Hall, the Academy's lone dormitory. I said goodbye to my buddy's daughter and her friend there, amused by how much the midshipman experience hadn't changed through the years.

And then I went to the MidStore. You *have* to go to the MidStore (short for Midshipmen Store). It's like a Nordstrom, with all things Naval Academy. You can get damn near anything there with the Academy crest emblazoned on it, from cocktail napkins to ski parkas. And, as a grad, you have to have it. All of it.

Do I really need another set of Naval Academy luggage tags?

Yes. I do.

Anyway.

I returned to my car after the MidStore, walking through Tecumseh Court, then down Stribling Walk. Stribling is the Academy's main drag, connecting Bancroft Hall with the school's original academic buildings. There's a certain spot on Stribling to which I always return when I'm on the Yard. It was the place where it all clicked for me.

I'd just finished the last final exam of my senior year and was walking back to Bancroft Hall to pack. Provided I could avoid being arrested and imprisoned in the two weeks that followed, it appeared

I would be allowed to graduate. That was significant, because I'd spent much of my time at the Academy certain I'd get kicked out. This may have been irrational.

I didn't get in trouble, and I did okay academically, but I never understood how the hell I ever got in. Surely it must have been a mistake. So, when I finished that last final and graduation became imminent, I finally felt part of the place. And, for the first time, I began to think of my Academy experience in the past tense. As an alumnus.

I remember exactly where I was when it all hit me, and I always go back to that spot.

The same is true of another place on the Yard. It's a stretch of road on Hospital Point that borders the Naval Academy Cemetery. It curves up and to the left until it runs in front of a row of red-brick apartment buildings.

My wife and I lived in one of those apartments when I worked on the commandant's staff. I'd returned to the Academy after my first flying tour, and our daughter was born not long after. It was idyllic.

I'd walk to my office every morning in Bancroft Hall, and before I departed in the evening, I'd call my wife to let her know I was on my way home. One day, when our daughter was still only a few months old, I spotted my wife walking with her down the road in front of our apartment to meet me as I came up the hill. My wife had her in one of those BabyBjorn things, strapped forward-facing.

As soon as I came into view, she said to our daughter, "There he is! There's daddy!" And then our daughter locked eyes on me and started giggling excitedly, flailing her little arms and legs around. She continued to do so until we came together on the hill, where I gave her a kiss on her little cheek. This became our routine.

And we always met in the same spot on the sidewalk in front of the cemetery.

It was directly in front of where Lieutenant Commander Erik Kristensen's headstone now stands. Kristensen, a SEAL, class of 1995, was killed in action in Afghanistan in June 2005 during

Operation Red Wings. He was on the Chinook helicopter that was dispatched to rescue the SEALs of *Lone Survivor* fame and was brought down by an RPG. All on board were killed.

I always return to that place when I'm on the Yard. And, in my mind's eye, I can see my wife and baby daughter, her little legs kicking, as though they were still standing there.

Later that evening, I met my old boss for dinner. He had been the commandant of midshipmen when I worked on the staff and went on to become a three-star admiral. He's retired now and has a house in Annapolis. I told him about my conversation with my buddy's daughter and her friend earlier that day.

"It's funny," he said, "I saw a couple of plebes in a coffee shop with their parents earlier this week. They must have been in town for Herndon." He continued. "I felt compelled to introduce myself and congratulate them on finishing plebe year."

That sounded exactly like something the boss would do.

Then he said, "I did the math in my head. If someone as old as I am now had done the same thing to me at the end of my plebe year, he would have been from the class of 1929."

Nineteen Twenty-Nine.

"Can you believe that?" he asked me.

Actually, I could. Because that's how it is with the Academy. In the course of one day, I had touched a segment of The Long Blue Line that straddled two different centuries and spanned five decades. And there I was, right in the middle of it.

It's humbling. And a privilege.

Such an incredible privilege.

The Naval Academy is a special place.

Which may help you understand

Why I *need*

More Naval Academy cocktail napkins

And luggage tags.

Of course, luggage tags.

A Run Around Capitol Hill

YOU RUN, but you're not a runner. That's what I told a friend who complained about how much he hated running.

But he ran anyway. He was trying to keep in shape, after all, a commendable goal. Predictably, though, he didn't stick with it. It's hard to do something consistently that you dislike.

That's why I don't play golf. Yes, I've occasionally golfed, but I'm not a golfer. Not even close.

I have stuck with running for a while, though, which I suppose makes me a runner. That makes sense. I'm skinny, with a decent set of lungs, so I don't have to work too hard at it. And it gets me outside. I don't spend nearly enough time outside. Plus, there's no better way to get the lay of the land in a new place than to go for a run. Or to indulge one's sense of nostalgia than to retrace one's steps through meaningful places of the past.

I love doing that.

Take Washington, DC, which I ran recently. I was in town for some meetings and took the opportunity to revisit some of the more prominent landmarks from a way-back-when summer.

I was all into politics then. Not anymore—I'm over that. Even though every Myers-Briggs-type temperament assessment I've ever taken has suggested I'm ideally suited for it. I have the optimum combination of ego and great hair. Yes, I might indeed make a good politician, but don't look for my name on a ballot anytime soon.

I thought differently when I was younger, though.

DC was the place to be, as far as I was concerned. And so I talked my way into an internship with my congressman, the Honorable Dave Camp of Michigan's Fourth District. He would eventually serve as the chairman of the powerful Ways and Means Committee.

"Sorry," his chief of staff had said, "but we've already hired all our paid interns for the summer."

Who said anything about getting paid? I asked. I was a Naval Academy midshipman drawing a stipend from the government. That was all I needed.

"Oh. Okay," the chief of staff replied.

And that was that.

The congressman and his staff worked in the Cannon House Office Building, across the street from the Capitol. I passed it on my recent jog, having run up New Jersey Avenue from my hotel, and it brought back a surge of memories.

I always enjoyed walking into the Cannon building, having emerged from the Capitol South metro stop. It made me feel all grown up. And I'd usually encounter one of Sonny Bono's staffers on the walk in.

The late variety-show host and California congressman had an office next to Congressman Camp's. Members of Bono's staff were remarkably similar. They were young. And female. And they all looked like they'd just stepped out of a Beach Boys album cover. I didn't mind that, and a friendly hello from one of them first thing in the morning was always a day brightener.

Always.

Congressman Camp took an interest in me. Maybe it was because I was a midshipman. Or that I worked for free. Whatever the case, he went out of his way to provide me with a good experience.

He taught me his tour route of the Capitol Building and then had me give tours to groups of visiting constituents. That was cool.

He took me to the House Chamber and had me sit in the gallery while he made a speech on the floor.

He took me to the Members' Dining Room and insisted I have the bean soup. That was apparently a big thing in Congress. The soup.

Then, one day, he came to me and said there was someone he'd like me to meet. A couple days later, I was ushered into Senator Bob Dole's office. The senator reached out his left hand to shake mine, his right hand gripping a pen. He had been seriously wounded in Italy during World War II and had lost nearly all the function in that hand. A photographer emerged from out of nowhere and snapped our picture.

"What's your boss up to?" he asked me.

The congressman was back in Michigan for a few days, I told him.

"Making money, I hope," Dole said.

Uhhh . . . yes, sir, I replied.

Fundraising was everything, even then.

A few days later, I received a signed picture of Senator Dole and me. To this day, it remains a favorite keepsake.

My run continued across Independence Avenue to First Street, past the Library of Congress and the Supreme Court. Then I looped around the Capitol and merged onto the sidewalk that paralleled Constitution Avenue and the Mall. I continued on the sidewalk, running in the direction of the Washington Monument. About halfway down the Mall, I came upon the spot where I had joined fellow members of Congressman Camp's staff for softball games on Tuesday nights.

We played against the members of other congressional staffs. I could hold my own, having had a respectable Little League career.

But that was hardly the point. Looking back, the very act of hitting a softball on a makeshift diamond situated between Capitol Hill and the Smithsonian's various museums seems surreal.

What an extraordinarily unique, American experience. And I sincerely hope today's congressional staffers still play softball on the Mall. It's good for them. And us.

As my time in DC that summer was winding down, I got a call from Senator John McCain's office. I'd been put in touch with his chief of staff through a mutual connection and was hoping to meet the senator. He was a Naval Academy grad, class of 1958, and a former aviator and prisoner of war in North Vietnam. I just wanted to shake his hand.

"Come on over," his chief of staff told me. "I'll get you in to see the senator."

And so I arrived at McCain's office at the appointed time and took a seat in the waiting area. There, I met a very nice lady about my grandmother's age. We struck up a conversation.

"Why are you here to see the senator?" she asked me.

I explained that I was a student at the Naval Academy, interning on Capitol Hill, and just really wanted to meet him.

"Is that right?" she replied. "My son went to the Naval Academy!"

And we chatted for a while longer before McCain's chief of staff came to escort me in to meet the senator.

Such a nice lady, I thought.

When I walked into the senator's office, the first thing I noticed was the flight helmet on the shelf behind his desk. He'd been an A-4 Skyhawk pilot and was shot down over North Vietnam during Operation Rolling Thunder in October 1967.

I was hesitant to ask him about his POW experience, concerned it might be impolite to do so. So, instead, I asked him about politics and life as a senator.

He brushed that aside. "Forget about all that," he said. "You need to focus on being a warfighter first."

And then we talked about his flying days and life at the Academy. The senator had made his point. And I appreciated that.

After about fifteen minutes, the chief of staff came into the office to usher me out. Again, a photographer appeared, seemingly out of nowhere, and snapped a picture of Senator McCain and me. A signed copy of that photo still hangs on my wall today.

When the chief of staff and I got to the senator's outer office, I noticed the lady with whom I'd been speaking was gone.

"Mrs. McCain told me to take care of you while you were in town," the chief of staff said. "You apparently made quite an impression on her."

Mrs. McCain? When had I ever met the senator's wife?

Then I figured it out.

"Mrs. McCain" was Roberta McCain, the senator's *mother*. She was the wife of the late Admiral John S. McCain Jr. and daughter-in-law to Admiral "Slew" McCain of World War II fame. She was the nice lady with whom I'd been speaking before meeting the senator.

I had no idea.

About a week later, McCain's chief of staff called me.

"Do you like tennis?" he asked me. The senator had tickets to a match and wondered if I might like them.

Of course! I said.

And that Friday night, I sat courtside while Andre Agassi, then in his prime, totally destroyed some other guy. It was incredible. I had no idea the pros hit the ball *that* hard.

Thank you, Mrs. McCain!

Yeah, that was a hell of a summer. And it all came back to me as I completed my lap around the Mall and Capitol Hill.

Camp. Dole. McCain.

Maybe if Congress were populated entirely with such people, I'd reconsider politics.

Maybe.

In the meantime,

I'll just keep running.
Because while I may not be a politician,
Or a golfer,
I do consider myself
One *hell*
Of a runner.

Funny Car Fountain of Youth

I'M SITTING AT the bar at the local sushi restaurant watching drag racing. What else am I going to do on a Sunday night?

The current heat features dueling Funny Cars. They resemble the stock cars driven in NASCAR races, but longer.

You may be more familiar with the Funny Car's sleeker cousin, the Top Fuel Dragster.

That's the car with the huge tires in back and awkwardly small wheels in front. Like Tyrannosaurus rex arms. It runs about ten percent faster than a Funny Car, but both versions clock speeds north of three hundred miles per hour, approaching Mach 0.5. And drivers experience forces of nearly five Gs through the course of a quarter-mile, four-second race. That's more than what an F/A-18 Hornet pilot experiences during a catapult shot off an aircraft carrier.

Not that I give a shit about any of this.

But that's what's on the TV behind the bar, muted, while two Japanese guys turn out spicy salmon rolls.

My wife and daughter are out with friends, so I'm flying solo for dinner. Not wanting to look like a loser sitting at a mostly empty table, I opted for the bar. The guys making sushi pay no attention to what's on TV. It's always tuned to the same channel: ESPN2. Usually, it's golf. Occasionally, it's cornhole. Today, it's drag racing.

The featured race, at Seattle's Pacific Raceways, is the latest stop on the Summer 2023 NHRA Western Swing. The NHRA is the National Hot Rod Association.

But you already knew that, of course.

I continue watching the TV as the light on the post between the two Funny Cars flashes green. The cars take off screaming down the track, smoke trailing behind them. Seconds later, they both pop parachutes and begin decelerating. I have no idea who won until I see members of the pit crew for one of the cars start jumping around and high-fiving.

Yay, team.

Whatever.

Eventually, the winning car winds its way back to the pits, and the driver emerges from the "cockpit," as they call it. He takes off his helmet while champagne goes spraying over his head. The driver looks . . . old. Okay, maybe that's unfair. Let's say he looks *older* than I was expecting. Not that I should have any expectation, given my complete ignorance of, and lack of interest in, drag racing.

Still, I pull out my phone to look up the driver. I learn that Tim Wilkerson of Springfield, Illinois, is sixty-two years old.

Sixty-two. Hm.

Even if sixty is the new fifty in drag racing, I can't help but think Wilkerson is past his prime. I decide to investigate further as I wait for my seaweed salad. That's when I discover "Big Daddy" Don Garlits. He drove his last qualifying race at 320 miles per hour. When he was *seventy-one* years old.

Wow.

But Big Daddy has nothing on "The Golden Greek," Chris

Karamesines. He clocked speeds in excess of three hundred miles per hour right up until his retirement. At age eighty-six.

Eighty-six, for Chrissake!

So then I'm thinking maybe this drag racing stuff isn't nearly as impressive as it looks. Maybe you just strap in and hang on. I mean, how else does an octogenarian do *anything* at half the speed of sound?

Turns out, there's a lot going on in the cockpit during a race. The driver must continually tweak the engine's fuel mixture to achieve optimum performance, taking numerous variables into account. He must also shift gears—five, in total—through the course of a four-second race. And he must steer. Well, for the last couple of seconds, at least. The front wheels typically leave the ground during the car's initial acceleration, making steering impossible.

So, yeah. The driver's workload is pretty damn high.

To be capable of doing all this with a Medicare card in one's back pocket would seem to contradict Arthur Brooks's premise in *From Strength to Strength: Finding Success, Happiness, and Deep Purpose in the Second Half of Life*.

According to Brooks, most people have already entered a state of cognitive decline by the time they turn forty. We get slower on the uptake and begin to experience a deficit of what psychologists call *fluid intelligence*, or that which gives us the ability to learn new things and gain new skills. So, be it from muscles or neurons, a person's fast-twitch capabilities decline much sooner than they perhaps realize.

There are exceptions, of course. The remedy, as explained by Brooks, is to find ways to employ one's *crystallized intelligence*, or knowledge gained through experience, to add value in the latter half of one's career. I suppose that makes sense. For most people.

But I have two issues with this.

First, I've never done the same thing twice in my career. I'm an inch deep and a mile wide. That means I have no repository of accumulated knowledge in any industry, function, or geography.

Second, the only thing at which I've proven adept in my career is finding new and creative ways to get kicked in the nuts. Mine is not an experience to be emulated. By anyone.

Therefore, I see no opportunity to leverage whatever wisdom I've gained to transition to a slow-twitch, crystallized-intelligence kind of existence. Sorry, Arthur Brooks. I'll need to continue to move-shoot-communicate my way through whatever series of bizarro situations I face for the foreseeable future. Perhaps indefinitely.

For that, I'll need every ounce of fast-twitch, fluid-intelligence capability I can muster.

That's why I love the stories of Big Daddy and The Golden Greek.

Yes, things slow down as you gain experience. You begin to feel the wind in the helm . . . the slip of the plane in the rudder pedals. I'm sure there's plenty of that going on with seasoned drag racers. But there's also a lot of split-second, in-the-moment, hair-trigger reacting and decision-making going on. And for guys to be doing it effectively in their eighth and ninth decades of life is nothing less than extraordinary.

Most studies on longevity feature Okinawans skilled in gardening and tai chi, not American Funny Car racers who routinely strap their asses to flame-spitting rockets.

Who knew drag racing could be so enlightening . . . and inspiring?

Thanks, Big Daddy. Thanks, Golden Greek.

And rest assured, Tim Wilkerson of Springfield, Illinois,

At sixty-two years young, you still have a long way to go.

And me?

I don't know.

What's the corporate equivalent of Funny Cars?

Maybe that's the business I should be in.

I'll have to catch the NHRA Midwestern Swing.

If there is such a thing.

In the meantime, I'm signing off.

My nigiri platter just arrived.
Your friend,
Dan
"Big Daddy"
Bozung.

www.ingramcontent.com/pod-product-compliance
Lightning Source LLC
LaVergne TN
LVHW091541070526
838199LV00002B/153